The Miners of Llay Main
first published in Wales in 2011
by
BRIDGE BOOKS
61 Park Avenue
WREXHAM
LL12 7AW

A CIP entry for this book is available from the British Library

ISBN: 978-1-84494-079-0

Printed and bound by
Gutenberg Press Ltd
Malta

Contents

Dedicated to
those men who lost their lives at Llay Main Colliery

Llay Main Colliery Memorial, Miner's Welfare Institute. This mine car was used to bring coal up N°. 2 Shaft at Llay Main and the memorial was originally sited on Rackery Lane in 1971.

Glossary of Mining Terms

Airway	Underground roadway, tunnel or shaft along which air passes.
Back over turn	Rail siding or set of points where normal direction of travel has to be reversed to enter. It is probable that the empty tubs had to pass over rail points so that they could return to N°. 6 district.
Back ripping	Road repairs where parts of the top and sides were removed and either new rings were to be installed or the old rings were lifted.
Banksman/ Browman	Man employed to load and unload the cage at the pit head.
Batty	Fissured (as in 'batty roof').
Bench	When a high wall becomes too high for safety a bench is used to act as a buffer for falling rocks.
Bind-coal	Mudstone.
Brakesman	Man controlling the haulage rope on self acting incline.
Brassey	Used in association with the occurrence of iron pyrites. At Llay Main the Brassey seam was later renamed Quaker.
Brattice	Ventilation construction used in an airway to redirect or regulate the airflow. Generally made from timber and fire resistant material.
Browett Lindley set	High speed inverted vertical compound steam engine coupled to an alternator for the production of AC electricity.
Burster	Hydraulic tool formed from a tube in which telescopic cylinders are inserted at right angles to the main tube. This is inserted into a drill hole, coupled to a hydraulic pump and the pressure forces out the telescopic cylinders thereby splitting the rock or coal. The operator is called a Burster man.
Bye-man	Underground labourer.
Cench	Place of work (term may be local to Llay).
Checkweighman	(1) Man employed by a group of miners paid piecework (by the ton mined) to check coal weight recorded by the mine management. (2) One who weighs the tubs of coal when they reach the surface.
Corporal	Man in charge of a certain district under the deputy.
Creep	(1) Upward movement of a relatively soft floor of a seam under pressure from adjacent coal pillars – can be called floor heave. (2) Sometimes used for widespread movement of the upper strata as pillars left for roof support were too few over a relative large area.
Cross measure drift	Inclined passage between two coal faces.
Dataller	Man employed to do service work underground and paid by the day.
Deputy	Supervisor in charge of a section or district of a mine, and all employees working therein.
Dinting	Removal of parts of the floor which lift due to floor heave.

Dirt	Valueless rock broken from the bottom or top of the seam.
District	Underground area of the mine, normally indicating separate coal faces.
Doggy	Charge man (foreman) for the haulage hands.
Downcast	Shaft down which fresh air passes from the surface.
Drift	An inclined access from the surface to the coal seam or from one coal seam to another coal seam.
Drift mine	A mine that opens into a near horizontal seam of coal. This type of mine is the easiest to operate as the mine opening enters into the coal outcrop.
Driving	Advancing a heading, drift or coal face.
Fireclay	Clay found in coal measures, resistant to high temperatures. Used for making fire bricks to line kilns.
Firedamp	Explosive mixture of methane and air.
Fulling mill	Place where woollen cloth was finished. Water mills would have large water driven hammers for beating the cloth.
Gate conveyor	Conveyor in a roadway leading to a working place in long-wall mining.
Gateway	Passage through the goaf secured by a pack-wall on each side, for the purpose of bringing out the coals worked on the long-wall system.
Goaf, gob or waste	Space behind the coal face into which the roof is allowed to collapse. The collapse is required to assist with roof control by relieving the 'weight' on the coal face working area.
Haulage	The transportation of men or materials from one point to another generally in a near horizontal direction.
Headgear	Construction at the top of the shaft including winding gear.
Heading	Roadways being made to extend the district.
Hewer	Coal miner using hand tools (pick/shovel) to dig coal
Hoppit/hoppet /kibble	Bucket used in shaft sinking to hoist men, materials and rock.
Inbye	Going towards the working face, away from pit bottom.
Insets	Entrances to underground roadways at the bottom or part way down the shaft where the cages are loaded and there is access for men and materials. Also called a 'porch'.
Ironstone	Sedimentary rock containing iron carbonate or iron oxide.
Lasher (or hooker) on	Man who attached or detached tubs to or from haulage rope at the face.
Loader	Man filling tubs, trams or mine cars at the underground loading point.
Long-wall method	A system of working coal in which the seam is extracted on a broad front or long face. All the coal between two development headings is removed. Can be carried out away from pit bottom (long-wall advance), or back towards the pit bottom (long-wall retreat).
Metal	Shale above the bind coal. In mining, rock is called metal to distinguish it from coal.
Metalman	(1) A man employed to service the tunnels and rails in the haulage system. (2) Person who takes the roof down to give more height.
Mottey	It was important to identify the amounts of coal got by each coalface team as they were paid by piecework. A mottey was a tin label with a distinctive number which was attached to a short nail inside the tub to identify a particular getter. The coal was weighed in front of a representative of the miners' union as well as the colliery weighman, and the banksman shouted the number on the mottey to both parties. With the advent of long-wall faces this process was dispensed with and the tubs from a district or coal face were identified by chalking the number of the face on the side of the tubs or mine cars.

Onsetter	Man in charge of loading tubs and men into the cage at the pit bottom or intermediate landings.
Outbye	(1) The direction along a roadway away from the face. (2) Locations between the face and surface.
Output per man shift	Measure of productivity. Notional amount of coal mined by one man in a single shift.
Overman	Underground shift supervisor subordinate to the manager. The duties of the overman consisted of visiting the workings every morning, receiving the reports from the deputies, making observations on the air currents, and general management of the underground work.
Piechers	Full coal tubs/mine cars. This term may have only been used at Llay.
Pit-brow lasses	Lancashire term for young girls who worked on the pit surface.
Refuge hole	Man-holes required by law for retreat during the passing of the trains.
Rings	Curved girders acting as roof supports. Had to be one yard apart.
Ripper	Miner engaged in enlarging roadways by removing the rock above the coal seam and setting rings (arches) as the face advances.
Road or roadway	A passage underground.
Roadside pack	A construction alongside the roadways which was formed by building stone walls from the ripping or goaf collapse and then filling between the walls with finer rock material. It was used to help support the roadways. Usually 4 to 6 yards wide depending on the height of the seam and the size of the roadway. It was also used to dispose of the rock from the ripping or roadway enlargement without having to send it out on the conveyor belts.
Ropeman	Man installing and maintaining haulage ropes.
Set	Team of colliers, usually five or six, working on a stretch of the coal face e.g. '110s set' would indicate the section allocated to this group of miners.
Shunter	Man in charge of marshalling trains on the colliery surface in readiness for despatch.
Stopping	Wall built to seal off abandoned or dangerous areas of workings.
Strip packs	Same as roadside packs construction except that all the material came from the collapsed roof in the goaf and the packs were used to control the roof collapse behind the coal face.
Taker-off	Man detailed to unhook full coal tubs from the inclined-plane winding rope and attaching empty tubs to the rope.
Tippler	Rotating frame used for automatically discharging coal from tubs.
Tubbing	Rings of cast-iron or steel to support shaft walls.
Turnover	In the long-wall system of mining, before full mechanisation, the coal was undercut and then blasted (fired). The coal was loaded by the colliers onto the face conveyor belt and roof supports set. The conveyor was then dismantled and rebuilt nearer the coal face by a distance equal to the depth of the cut. The wastemen then withdrew a line of supports from the waste and built the strip packs and stored the supports alongside the conveyor ready for use by the colliers for the next cut. This process was called a 'turnover'.
Upcast	Shaft through which air returns to the surface after ventilating the mine workings.
Under manager	The person in charge of underground mining operations (often of a coal seam) and was next in authority to a manager or deputy manager.

Preface

Although I was born in Ludlow, I spent all of my childhood years in the village of Llay, near Wrexham in north Wales, and went to Bangor Normal Teacher Training College. As a consequence, I feel more Welsh than English and consider myself lucky to have lived in a mining village and to have experienced the benefits of growing up in a close-knit society. There was the added bonus of being in a loving, happy family which extended to aunts, uncles and cousins. This book tells the story of how the Llay Main colliery and the village of Llay were formed and of how a community, with its own distinctive character, grew during the time that the colliery was operational. The number of people with first-hand experience of working at Llay Main is inevitably dwindling and there are none still alive who raised the first coal in 1922. There are, however, still enough former mineworkers and residents with memories of the colliery to illustrate special events and the life of the village.

The model village of Llay was built during the early part of the twentieth century on agricultural land four miles north of Wrexham. A community of mineworkers and their families was established on what had been farm and park land, a situation far removed from fellow colliers living in the grimy terraces of the south Wales valleys. The colliery became the largest in Wales and the deepest in Europe and miners and their families were housed in cottages, fitted with indoor toilets and bathrooms, which had the benefit of direct-current electricity, facilities only dreamt of by most working-class people in the 1920s. The colliery, called Llay Main, had a relatively short productive life of around forty-three years from its first year of production in 1923. Ironically, although the last major colliery to be built in north Wales, it was the first to close down. As a result, in March 1966, a thriving village community was dealt a bitter blow to its social and economic future.

In the 1920s, mineworkers and their families came from all over the country to live and work in the new village and colliery. They came from south Wales, Lancashire, Yorkshire and Kent and some from Ireland. However, the mine owners' policy was to give priority to men from the local area. Colliers came in their hundreds from the old coal-mining villages around Wrexham – Brymbo, Coedpoeth and Rhos, and from the Flintshire mining villages of Leeswood, Treuddyn and Buckley. In parallel with the construction of the colliery, the village of Llay was built to house this influx of workers and their families. Both village and colliery were given state-of-the-art facilities and equipment and had a reputation for being friendly places to live and work. The following pages tell the story of how ordinary men and women managed to make a home and community for themselves in a rural backwater.

The story starts with early evidence of coal mining in the Llay area and with the Clark family who made the first moves towards the development of a colliery in Llay. I then look at how the colliery company was formed in 1913 and at why it took so long for the colliery to be built. The story continues with a period of frantic activity during the early 1920s when both pit and village were completed. Then follows a time of disasters, strikes and much poverty but, in spite of this, it was also a time of increasing coal production. After dealing with events at the colliery and village during the Second World War, I look at the legacy of nationalisation during the 1950s. My story ends with the last coal being raised in March 1966.

My initial approach in writing this book was to deal firstly with the colliery events and then with those of the village, but this did not work well. I finally decided to write about both aspects in the chronological order in which events occurred. This approach has occasionally resulted in the dislocation of the subject matter. Between 1923 and 1966, the life of this colliery was inextricably linked with progress in the village as I hope the following pages will show.

My thanks are due to the people of Llay, both current and former residents, and and those from other mining communities who have given their photographs, told their stories and shown keen support for this work. Particular thanks go to Greville Williams, for help with identifying the people on the photographs, and to Michael Adams, for improving many of the images in the book. Unless otherwise indicated, photographs are from the author's own collection.

For technical help on colliery equipment and mining operations, I am indebted to Stefan Thatcher of Pleasley Colliery and to Keith Folwell, former colliery manager at Llay Main. For their assistance with details of railway operations, I am grateful to Richard Prestidge and Bob Darvill, of the Industrial Railway Society, and to railway engineer, Paul Dally.

The roots of the Llay Main Colliery Company lie not in Wales but in the collieries of south Yorkshire and north Derbyshire and I am indebted to David Fordham for information on the Carlton Main Colliery Company and for researching Llay-related material in back issues of the *Colliery Guardian*. My thanks are also extended to Barry Hayes for information on Brodsworth Colliery and its village of Woodlands, in many ways a pre-cursor of the mine and village of Llay Main.

The kind attention of the professional staff at the Flintshire Record Office and at Wrexham Archives and Museum is also acknowledged. The following people have given information on their own family members: Amanda Clark, Rodney Gardner, Nick Humble, John Parry, Graham Hughes, Tony Partington, Sue Force, Rod Challenor, Michael Adams and Joan Hutton which has been an invaluable help in writing this book.

Finally, I am indebted to my wife, Sue, for proof-reading this document and for striving to make sense of my cavalier treatment of the English language.

Vic Tyler Jones
2011

1: The Great Enterprise (1906–17)

Mining for coal and the associated products of ironstone and fireclay has been carried out in the Llay area since the Middle Ages. At Hope, as early as 1353, lead and coal mines were rented for £3 a year and in 1414, the Earl of Arundel granted the burgesses of Holt permission to dig coal for their own consumption in the 'wastes' of Coedpoeth and Brymbo.[1]

The oldest surviving building associated with the north-east Wales coalfield is the Penrhos Engine House in Brymbo, four miles west of Llay. John Wilkinson, the Brymbo ironmaster, built it in the late eighteenth century in order to house an engine to pump water from his coal mine. It is thought to be the earliest surviving colliery engine house in Wales and was used as a cottage during the nineteenth century.[2]

The first recorded miner with connections to Llay was one 'Samuel Jones of Llay, collier' who appeared before the Denbighshire magistrates on 4 July 1720 to answer charges of assaulting John Ellis, labourer of Gresford, who went to remonstrate with him for allowing his beasts to wander into a neighbour's oat field. John Ellis was so badly beaten that one witness 'believed he was a dying man'.[3] Samuel was ordered to be of good behaviour and to appear at the next court session. At this time, there were no deep collieries in the area and we must assume that Samuel was working in drifts in the Alyn valley such as those at Gwastad.

The nineteenth century saw a great expansion of British industry and commerce stretching far beyond our shores and into an empire covering one quarter of the globe. The manufactured products of Britain were in great demand and steam locomotives and ships needed vast supplies of high quality 'steam' coal – the type of coal that lay deep under the ground at Llay.

By 1881, a number of collieries were operating within a three-mile radius of the present village of Llay, near enough for any local miners to walk to their place of work. A list of

Penrhos Engine House Brymbo, 2010

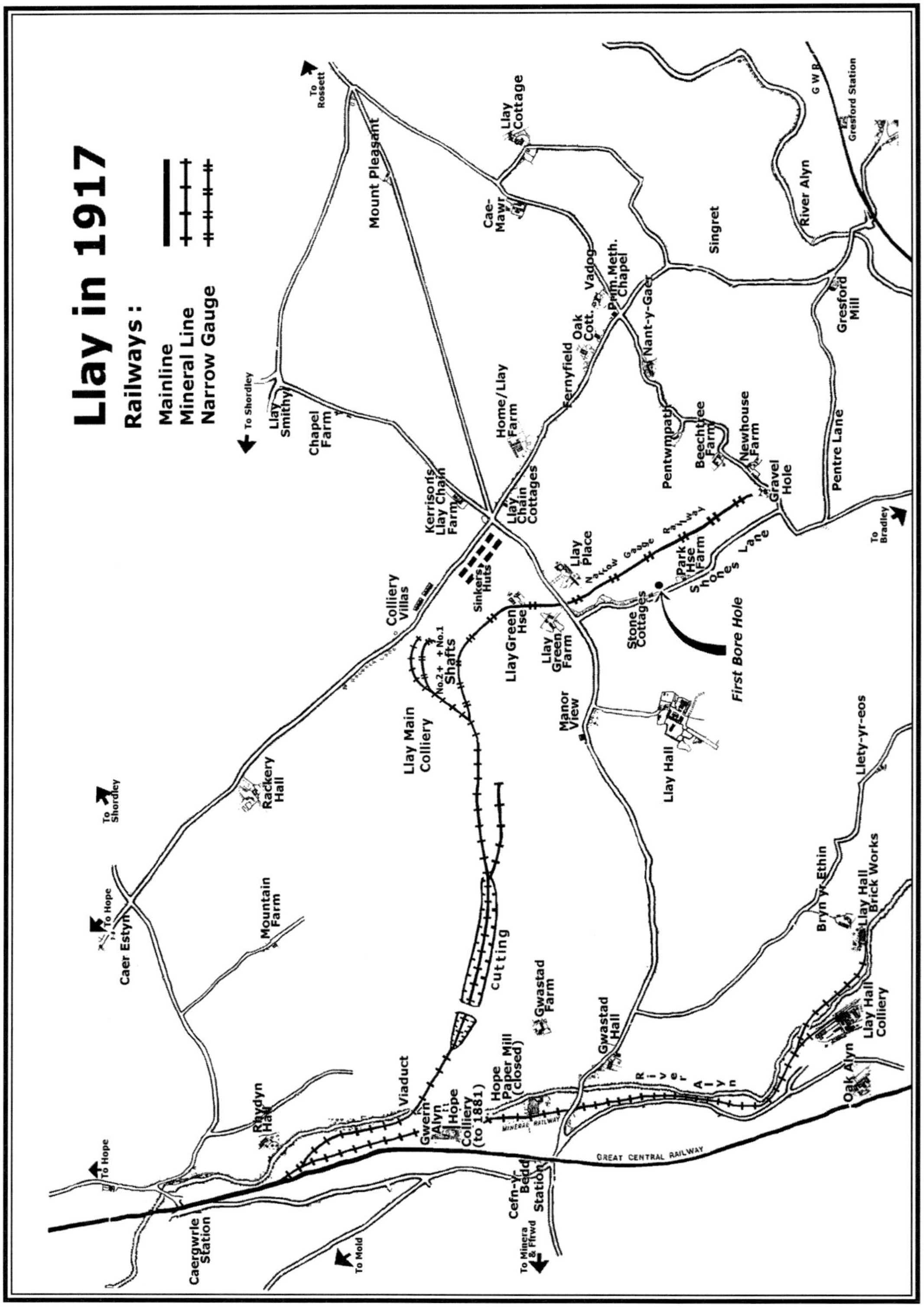

[Drawn by Michael Adams]

collieries working in 1880[4] includes those of Ffrwd, Gwersyllt, Llay Hall and Wrexham & Acton (at Rhosddu). At nearby Abermorddu, Hope (or Gwern Alyn) Colliery is also listed as working at this time, but the owners gave notice to terminate the mining lease in June of the same year owing to its unprofitability.[5]

The censuses of Llay between 1851 and 1871 record no coal miners or mining-related occupations and most working people were engaged in agricultural work. By 1881, this had changed. In April 1873, the works at Llay Hall was taken over by the Llay Hall Coal, Iron & Firebrick Company, its agent and chief engineer being Edwin Stanley Clark. He invested heavily in improvements which included a 1¾-mile branch railway to connect with the Wrexham, Mold & Connah's Quay Railway at Caergwrle. In the Llay census of 1881, John Thomas of Bradley was recorded as a 'colliery railway man', probably employed at Llay Hall Colliery as no other colliery railway existed in the locality. This census records that 19% of Llay males of working age were employed in colliery work, most likely at Llay Hall Colliery.

Llay Hall Colliery was situated on the River Alyn at Cefn-y-Bedd. Remnants of the colliery buildings and its chimney can be seen today. Although the works were in the parish of Gwersyllt, the land on this western side of the river Alyn belonged to the Llay Hall estate. The colliery is believed to have been started in around 1845,[6] but suffered from water ingress and the sinking of the shaft was not completed until 1877 by the Llay Hall Coal, Iron & Fireclay Company Limited.[7] The compant's engineer was Edwin Stanley Clark (1849–1900), a civil and mining engineer, who had been born in London in 1849. In 1873, he was living at Oak Alyn Hall, Cefn-y-Bedd as agent and chief engineer for the Llay Hall Colliery. He was instrumental in setting up several industrial ventures in the Llay area of the Alyn valley, some of which were more successful than others.

Around 1885, Edwin Stanley took on the Wilderness Brick Works which was located downstream from Llay Hall Colliery. By 1888, he needed to procure further finance and went into partnership to form the Wilderness Brick Works Company where his partner was Mr Russell Rea of Liverpool, a shipping agent, who later became a partner in the Llay Main Colliery Company, with sole rights to distribute coal from Llay Main. When the Wilderness Company was eventually wound up in 1898, a net loss of £7,000 was recorded.[8]

By 1896, Llay Hall Colliery, employing 276 miners and 84 surface workers, was managed by Samuel Young who lived at Rock Cottage on the Oak Alyn estate. In addition, there was a drift mine at the same site mining fireclay for the Llay Hall brick works.[9] Edwin Stanley Clark died on 10 January 1900 and was buried in Wrexham cemetery; the brass eagle lectern in Gwersyllt Church being erected in his

Edwin Stanley Clark and his family c.1889. Standing: Edward Stuart, Susan Muller. Sitting: Cecile, Edwin Stanley, Henry Denton, Lettie [Amanda Clark]

memory. After his death, Mrs Clark did not stay long at Oak Alyn Hall but moved to Wrexham and her eldest son Edward Stuart came home from Cambridge to take over the colliery.[10]

By the time of his death, Edwin Stanley Clark had established himself and his family as local benefactors and the main employers in the locality. Samuel Young, the colliery manager, was left £150 in his will. His household property included a collection of sixty-four paintings which were 'practically all picked up … for small sums from houses and dealers in the neighbourhood'.[11] William Michael Rossetti, chronicler of the Pre-Raphaelites and brother of the poet and artist, Dante Gabriel Rossetti, assessed this collection for the Board of the Inland Revenue as their valuer.[12] Clark had purchased the freehold or leasehold and their mineral rights on many local properties. His freehold estate was valued at £62,660 8s 6d (the equivalent today being nearly £6 million) and included Llay Farm (also called Home Farm, 116 acres), Llay Place estate (172 acres), Kerrison's Farm (6 acres), Rose Cottages, Beech Tree Farm, Park Farm (5 acres), Gravel Hole (24 acres) and minerals under 'the Madocks property' (Llay Hall estate) and under 'the Gwastad property'. All in all, this local estate represented a considerable part of the township of Llay and its leases would eventually pass to the owners of the future Llay Main Colliery.

The Clark children were tasked by deed of arrangement with the responsibility of carrying on the colliery business 'as before until the youngest child attains 21 in three and a half years' time, although it is probable that Llay Hall Brick Works (held in lease) will be given up, and the Wilderness Brickworks be sold'.[13]

The valuation of the estate hinted at problems of water ingress at Llay Hall Colliery, trouble which would eventually cause it to close in 1947, stating that 'the collieries on either side of it, Ffrwd and Westminster, are heavily watered'. The valuation also cast doubts upon any further possibilities for coal mining in the area stating that 'there is no proof that any minerals exist under the Llay Place Estate.'[14]

In the Middle Ages Llai, as it was then known, had been a land devoted mainly to agriculture, its peaceful meadows disturbed only by the hammering of fulling mills in the Alyn Valley. Records of the area in 1906 show that things had not changed much. At this time the Wrexham & East Denbighshire Water Company was extending its water mains into the Llay area and one of its officials commented:

> The district of Llay becomes each year increasingly popular with Tourists as a holiday resort, being strongly recommended by the medical faculty, owing to its dry and elevated position.[15]

Bill Millington (1894–1990) of Laburnum Cottage, Nant-y-Gaer Road, was a long-standing Llay resident and described the area in 1906 as:

> A straggling district with a cottage here and a small farm over there. No roads, just footpaths. No work other than on the railway and on the three large farms of Llay Hall (Mr George Lloyd), Home Farm (Mr J R Lewis) and Cae Mawr (Mr Thomas Alderman). There was no post-office in Llay but it didn't matter when there were no pensions or allowances to be paid out and the postman always brought a supply of stamps with him from Gresford. There were no telephones, no electricity and no piped water. People had to carry their drinking water from wells in the woods and fields.[16]

After Clark's death in 1900, ownership of the Llay Hall Colliery Company passed to the trustees of his estate and the management of it to his eldest son, Edward Stuart Clark (1877–1932) who was also a mining engineer. It was his instruction to sink a borehole that led to the discovery of workable coal at the Llay Main site. On 18 October 1906, Tom Barker, working on behalf of the Llay Hall Colliery Company, started to bore a hole at a point near the present junction of Third Avenue and Shone's Lane.[17] He found a small quantity of coal at a depth of 288 feet. Bill Millington's eye-witness account of this event, so significant for the future village, stated:

> Curiosity was aroused in the village when men and machines appeared on a field at the back of a house where Miss Jane Wynne had run a small shop for many years (Park (House) Farm, Shone's Lane). A borehole was to be drilled deep into the ground to find out if there was coal down there in sufficient quantities to warrant sinking shafts to get at it. Twist drills were used; there were channels in them and everything the drills passed was forced up to the surface. One of the men sent to carry this out was Mr Tom Barker who courted and eventually married my friend Charlotte Fidler (of Beech Tree Farm). The boring operation off Shone's Lane was a long slow job but eventually rich seams of coal were found at a depth of 800 to 900 yards.[18]

It took another two years before the Main coal seam was found at a depth of 2,373 feet on 4 September 1908.[19]

On 23 November 1910, a second boring was started to prove the continuity and dip of the seams. This borehole was located in the fields of Home Farm off the Rossett Road – the 'Straight Mile' and was called 'the Mount Pleasant borehole' by the colliery. Drilling ended here on 19 March 1911, stopping at a depth of 840 feet, the correlation of the coal measures having been proved. It became clear that at this place, a mile to the east of the Wrexham fault separating it from the workings of Llay Hall Colliery, there were workable quantities of high grade coal and, on 16 July 1911, a memorandum of association was drawn up between the Clark family members and the Rea family businesses to establish a company to be known as Llay Main Collieries Limited. This memorandum summarised the purpose of the company and in effect was the strategic blueprint for developing the colliery. It stated that the partners would 'buy collieries, mines, seams of coal … to carry in the business of colliery proprietors … to get and market coal and any associated minerals.'[20]

The Clarks covered their interests in the future colliery by taking out a series of leases which would at least recoup their initial outlay in drilling for coal under Llay. An indenture of 30 December 1911, between the Madocks family, owners of the Llay Hall Estate since about 1725, and under whose land lay the coal seams, and the Clarks, set up leases for the 'coal seams of 'Two-Yard', 'Crank', 'Brassey', and 'Main' and others under the lands situate in Llay.'[21]

It was apparent that there would be difficulties in raising coal from such great depths and that a considerable investment would be needed to fund the enterprise. The development of the Llay Main Colliery was beyond the means of the local entrepreneurs and the Clarks opened negotiations with a large mining company to take on the project whilst the family maintained a presence in the area. They continued as the owners of Llay Hall Colliery & Brick Works and in 1912, Edward Clark moved to live in Llay Cottage (sometimes called Llay Villa).[22]

The Rt Hon Russell Rea, Liberal Member of Parliament, merchant and ship owner, grandson

SECTION OF Llay Hall No. 1 Bore
National Coal Board, North Western Division
No. 5 (North Wales) Area

5

Exact Site Llay Place, Llay, Wrexham.
Latitude 53° 05' 40½" North
Longitude 3° 00' 00" West
Level at which ~~shaft~~ bore ~~drift~~ commenced relative to O.D. 293.5'

Date of sinking or boring 18th Oct.1906 - 14th Sept 1908
Sinker or Borer New Calyx Drill & Boring Co. Ltd Millwall.
One Inch Geological Map Sheet 121 (Wrexham)
Six Inch Map (County and Quarter Sheet) Denbighshire 21 SE
Bore put down for Llay Hall Colliery Co. Ltd.

Attach tracing from a map or sketch map if possible

NATURE OF STRATA: Geologist's Notes	NATURE OF STRATA: Borer's Journal	THICKNESS: Feet	THICKNESS: In.	DEPTH: Feet	DEPTH: In.
	Gravels and Sands	123	-	123	-
Base of Glacial Drift	Boulder Clay	23	6	146	6
	Red Marl	12	6	159	-
	Strong Blue Marl	7	-	166	-
	Variegated Marl	37	-	203	-
	Purple Marl	18	-	221	-
	Light Blue Shale	9	-	230	-
	Horizon 'B' Strong Grey Sandstone	21	6	251	6
	Dark Warrant	1	6	253	-
	Light Blue Shale	7	6	260	6
	Dark Warrant with Carbonaceous Flora	3	-	263	6
	Light Blue Shale	16	6	280	-
	Horizon 'C' Dark Warrant with Ironstone Nodules	8	-	288	-
	COAL	-	2	288	2
	Blue Shale	2	6	290	8
	Strong Blue Shale	7	4	298	-
	Blue Sandstone	3	-	301	-
	Strong grey sandstone with Iron Pyrites	4	-	305	-

Page from Tom Barker's notebook, 18 October 1906

Sir Arthur Basil Markham (1866–1916)
[Chesterfield Library P165/P7x7797]

of the Liverpool shipbuilder, Joseph Russell, already had connections with Llay Hall Colliery previously mentioned. In the autumn of 1912,[23] he discussed the details of the proposed colliery enterprise at Llay with Sir Arthur Markham MP.[24]

The Markham family were successful Victorian engineers who pioneered mechanisation in British coalfields and in the iron and steel and shipbuilding industries. On 25 February 1913, at the suggestion of Sir Arthur, Charles Edward Rhodes, one-time President of the Institute of Mining Engineers, reported to his fellow directors of the Hickleton Main Colliery Company board on a proposal to set up a colliery and village at Llay. The proposal included the involvement of the Rea Transport Company as a joint stakeholder and the two boards met on 13 May to discuss the formation of the new company and Llay Main[25] Collieries Limited was incorporated on 7 August. The first chairman of the company was Robert Armitage who, from 1906 to 1922, was a Liberal MP for Leeds Central and had extensive management experience in heavy industry.

There then followed a period of intense activity to create the infrastructure necessary to support the development of such a large undertaking. It became clear that a sizeable mine would be needed if there was to be any chance of making a profit. A workforce of around 3,000 men would be required to get sufficient coal over the coming years to cover the costs involved in sinking such deep shafts. The Markhams and their Staveley Company were used to such enterprises having already been involved in the founding and development of a number of mines and mining villages in Yorkshire.[26]

The land on which the colliery was to be built was leased from Mr E. M. Griffith for a term of 99 years from 1 July 1913,[27] and Lady Markham inaugurated the enterprise by cutting the first sod at the colliery site on Rackery Lane shortly afterwards. In September of that year, a trial well was started to test the ground and, at the same time, an order was placed with Markhams for two of their world famous winding engines.[28, 29] These large engines would be needed when the shafts were nearing completion but, for the initial trial sinkings, less powerful and more mobile winders would suffice.

Cochran steam boilers could produce enough power for small windings and for pumping operations when water was encountered during the sinking process. The photograph above shows two Cochran vertically-mounted water-tube boilers, one being only partially erected and not yet connected to any pipe-work. They may have been temporary ones used for sinking since their steam-generating capacity would not have been sufficient for general winding purposes.

The trial well on Rackery Lane in 1913. [Rod Challoner]

Cochran boilers at Llay Main, 7 October 1914. [Rod Challoner]

They could however have been permanent fixtures used as auxiliary boilers for other purposes such as small pumps. The operating pressure would have been about 100 psi and they would have had some form of insulation cladding, as would the pipe-work.[30]

R. Oswald Gardner – first manager of Llay Main Colliery in 1914 [Rodney Gardner]

The first colliery manager at Llay Main was R. O. Gardner who had been born in Workington, Cumberland in 1884, the son of another Robert who was secretary of an iron and steel company. By 1901, the family had moved to Abergavenny and at seventeen years of age, Robert Oswald was an engineering apprentice. He qualified as a colliery manager in south Wales in 1907 and by 1911 was working as a mining engineer at Askern, near Doncaster. Askern Main Colliery was being sunk at that time so it is probable that he was engaged there. He was still in Doncaster in December 1913 when his second child Guy was born, but in the early part of 1914 he moved to Llay. He is mentioned in an indenture of 15 April 1914 as being 'manager and agent'[31] and lived at Home Farm on the Gresford Road with his wife Beatrice and their two children.

There was one drawback with Oswald Gardner's appointment; he was a long-standing volunteer soldier and war with Germany was declared on 4 August. His military service prior to the First World War would appear to have been with the 4th Volunteer Battalion South Wales Borderers and, on 22 August, Oswald was posted as a lieutenant to the 3rd (Territorial Force) Battalion The Monmouthshire Regiment at their training camp in Northampton. He was promoted to captain on 23 November and was one of the officers commanding B Company. His unit landed in France on 14 February 1915 and during March, his battalion was in the front line with the 28th Division, near Ypres, Belgium.

On 7 May 1915, the German army was only two miles from Ypres and shells flew over the heads of the frontline Monmouths and pounded the city to rubble. On 8 May, a determined attack was repulsed by the Monmouths but at great cost. B Company was the most forward of all British troops on that day. They succeeded in stopping the German advance into Ypres, from where the route would have been open to the channel ports but in this action, Captain Gardner was killed, aged 31.[32, 33, 34, 35]

The second colliery manager at Llay Main was John Thaddeus de Seyfried (1887–1938). He achieved his Mine Manager's Certificate (1st Class) in 1910 when working in the Yorkshire coalfield[36] and, at about the same time, became a naturalised British subject (having been born in France). In 1911, he was living in Bolsover, Derbyshire and possibly engaged at the colliery of that name.[37] In 1913, he toured Germany, France and Poland for the Parliamentary Commission on Spontaneous Combustion in Coal Mines and subsequently collaborated on a report on the practicability of hydraulic stowage in British coalfields.[38] He had been the manager at Llay Main's parent colliery, Hickleton Main, and it is possible that he had already been appointed aacting manager in Llay in the autumn of 1914 when Captain Gardner was posted to France. de Seyfried was only 27 years old but was obviously a talented and well-respected mining engineer and who was to deploy all of his considerable skills in the making of the new colliery.

John de Seyfried oversaw the main development of Llay Main Colliery. He drew up detailed plans for the railway sidings, describing the track curvatures that would be needed; he designed shackles and bolts to hold the kibbles (large buckets)[39] used in early winding and monitored rates of freezing during shaft sinking. He married Alma C. Taylor in Liverpool in 1919 and died in Surrey in 1938, aged 51. By that time, he had become a successful entrepreneur as is testified in the 1933 *Colliery Year Book* and *Coal Trades Directory*.[40]

Hundreds of tons of building materials, bricks, timber, iron and steel supports and fastenings of all kinds were needed to build the colliery. Many bricks did not have far to travel as Llay Hall Brick Works was only a mile away; but manufactured iron and steel products, the girders and engines made by Markham, could only be brought to the site by means of a railway.

Llay is bounded by two main line railways. When the Shrewsbury & Chester Railway came to the east of the village in 1847, it opened up the rich mineral reserves of the Wrexham area to outside trade. To the west of Llay, the Wrexham, Mold & Connah's Quay Railway (through Caergwrle, Cefn-y-Bedd and Gwersyllt) opened in 1866. The colliery needed to connect to one of

N° 1 Winding Engine around 1920. Back: T. Blackwell – engine driver, R. Turton – engine wright. Front: J. T. de Seyfried – manager, Bill Wynne – engine cleaner. [Rod Challoner]

The Gwastad cutting, October 1914. The railway cutting near Gwastad farm on the Llay side of the River Alyn. A steam crane moves earth into side-opening Charles Baker & Sons wagons. Horses were used to move up empty wagons. [Rod Challoner]

these lines in order to export its coal but the Alyn valley barred the way on both west and east.

An indenture of 13 April 1914,[41] between the Great Central Railway (successors of the Wrexham, Mold & Connah's Quay Railway) and Llay Main Collieries paved the way for railway construction to begin and on 16 May 1914, Messrs Charles Baker & Sons, contractors, started laying standard-gauge rail track from the colliery site towards a connection with the main line near Caergwrle. The 1$^1/_2$-mile track from the sidings at Caergwrle to the colliery would require a viaduct to cross the River Alyn near Abermorddu and a cutting through some hilly farmland at Gwastad Farm.

Work on the colliery railway proceeded from both sides of the river. Brick abutments, built in the River Alyn to support the bridge superstructure, needed to take account the rise from the Gwastad side to the main line and an embankment had to be made leading up to the bridge.

The railway viaduct over the Alyn was completed on 29 July 1915.[42] Commenting on the photograph below, Paul Dally, a railway civil engineer wrote:

> The viaduct is of quite a modern design with deep main girders to support the rails and lots of lattice angle iron to give it strength and stability on the sharp curve and provide a safe walkway each side. I believe that they are building the embankment by raising its level a bit at a time and importing the fill in the Llay Hall colliery wagons. This would be a cheap method which did not require any major plant and would account for the significant difference in levels between the bridge and track.[43]

A cutting of around half-a-mile was needed near Gwastad Farm. In the census of 1911, the new tenant farmer at Gwastad farm was Thomas Pleavin, aged 26, recently married with a daughter only a few months old. Pleavin's neighbours at Llay Green Farm were Joseph and Harriet

Parry. These people would have known each other well as in the 1880s their families had farmed near to each other in Shordley, a few miles away in Flintshire. Land for the railway was needed on both of these farms. The cutting was on Gwastad land, but most of the railway and sidings took land from Llay Green. This amounted to 14.673 acres of the total of 17.981 acres of the Madocks' Llay Hall estate being taken for railway purposes. The Madocks family were compensated for their loss of earnings by being paid £62 12s 2d yearly rent and we are told that the occupying tenants were also compensated.[44]

The main-line connection to the colliery was completed in 1915 and materials could then be delivered in bulk to the colliery site. There was plenty of sand and gravel in the locality for colliery building and a narrow-gauge line was constructed to an existing gravel 'hole' about half-a-mile south of the colliery on Nat-y-Gaer Road. The line crossed the Cefn-y-Bedd road near Llay Place and, in the early 1920s, was also used to take house-building materials from the colliery into the developing village.[45]

> They used to take gravel up from the gravel hole and where we lived on Shone's Lane. (Park House Farm). There was a little field, part of the house. At the back of the hedge – the little engine used to go from there. I suppose we didn't have money for taking a photograph. I would have liked to have taken a photograph of it just passing along. [46]

Viaduct over the River Alyn from the Gwastad bank in 1914–15. Caergwrle castle is in the top left and below that, to the right, the new Llay Main line embankment may be seen leading up to the bridge. A steam pump is operating at the river side and to its left, a temporary bridge with narrow-gauge line has been constructed to carry materials over the river – a rail tub with aggregate can be seen to the left of the steaming vent pipe. {Peter Chadwick]

View towards Caergwrle from top of viaduct in 1915. The brick abutments are complete and the bridge is at its final level. The wagons on the track beyond have their doors open and are tipping colliery waste fom Llay Hall colliery onto the embankment. [Peter Chadwick]

From 1914, a small steam engine, nicknamed *The Coffee Pot,* moved materials around the colliery site on the narrow-gauge line. This locomotive was built in 1914 by Orenstein & Koppel of Germany and delivered new to Llay Main Colliery. Records show that the customer who ordered the loco was the Hickleton Main Colliery.[47]

Very deep shafts were needed to get at the Main coal nearly 2,400 feet down. At 13ft 2ins thick, this was the most important coal-bearing seam. A problem hampering the development of the mine was the presence of a thick layer of sand and gravel near the surface. This had been left by the last retreat of the ice sheet 14,000 years before and the sinking of the shafts had to take account of this difficulty. The solution was to freeze this unstable mass and then cut through the now solid soil, placing circular steel collars (called tubbing) to prevent the unfrozen sand from collapsing inward. In 1909, the mine owners had experienced this difficulty before in another of

The 'Coffee Pot' on the colliery site in 1914 [Rod Challoner]

their collieries, at Bullcroft near Doncaster.[48] There they had used a team of German workers to do the freezing.

This freezing process had been patented in Germany in 1883 by F. H. Poetsch and there were several German and Belgian companies who were experts in the field. At Llay Main, this specialised task was given to a German firm, the Rheinisch West Falische Company and, in July 1914, they started work but their job did not last long. On 4 August, Britain declared war on Germany after Belgium had been invaded and ten days later the freezing contract was withdrawn and the German workers interned, possibly at the Frongoch camp near Bala, but more likely at the large Knockaloe camp on the Isle of Man.[49] In spite of the war, sinking at Llay continued and the freezing work was taken up by Simon Carves & Company of Manchester, who were contracted on 16 December 1914[50] to sink the shafts to a depth of 300 feet, through approximately 150 feet of sand and gravel.

The method originally employed by Poetsch had involved the sinking of a series of bore-holes around the circumference of the shaft. These were lined with tubes down to the firm ground, and a freezing mixture of brine and ammonia made by the freezing machine was allowed to circulate in the tubes. Gradually over a long period of time, the cooling resulted in the ground around each tube being frozen, and the diameter of this circle of ice increased. The distance of one of these vertical tubes from the other was generally between 31 and 39 inches, so that when the columns of ice formed, they eventually joined up to form a wall of ice. The thickness of this wall of ice gradually increased until the whole of the ground within the shaft had frozen solid.[51] Ithel Kelly, one-time manager at Gresford Colliery, wrote:

Freezing units on top of N° 2 shaft (left) and N° 1 shaft in 1915. The hill of Bryn-y-Gaer (Caer Estyn) can be seen in between the two units with Hope Mountain on the left. [Peter Chadwick]

It was the first time that the freezing method had been adapted to sink through the glacial deposits in north Wales … to a depth of several yards below the depth of sand and gravel. After excavating the frozen material the shafts were then lined, tubbing consisting of cast iron segments bolted together to from a solid lining. To relieve the pressure of water behind the tubbing holes were left which allowed the water to flow into garlands and these into a sump from where it is pumped to the surface and used for colliery purposes.[52]

In February 1915, the building contractor made a start on the engine houses and stores. The contractors had their equipment in place by May 1915 and started work on N°· 1 shaft. By 7 January 1916, the frozen ground was well established and the sinking of N° 1 shaft began. Within a few months, the freezing, sinking and tubbing of N°· 1 to a depth of 260 ft was achieved and solid ground was reached where more conventional sinking methods could be employed to deepen the shaft.[53] N°· 2 shaft was started through frozen ground on 4 June 1916 and by 31 August 1916, solid ground was struck at 246 ft.

N°· 1 shaft was eventually frozen to a depth of 231 feet and N°· 2 shaft to 235 feet. At the surface, each shaft was enclosed in a housing of galvanised

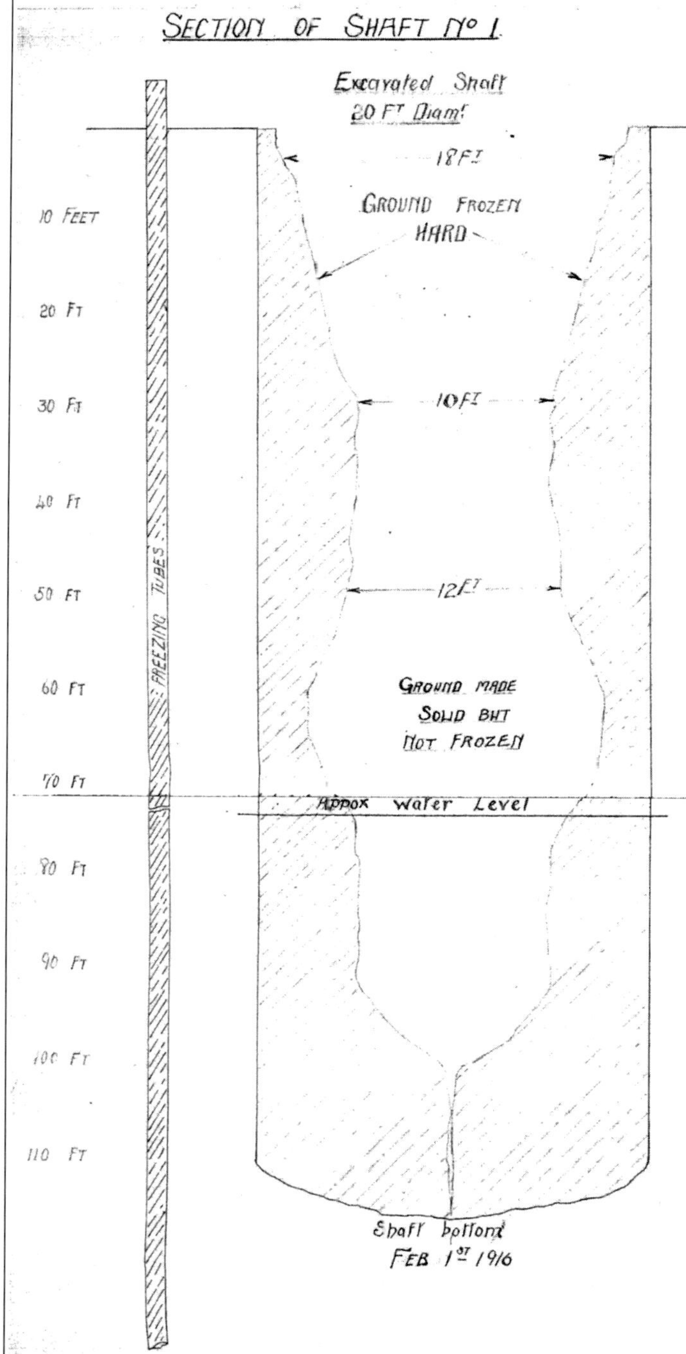

Redrawn by Michael Adams from an original sketch at FRO, FRO/CB/13/1]

Section of Shaft N°· 1 drawn by J. T. de Seyfried on 1 February 1916
The manager's diagram shows the shaft bottom at just over 110 ft at this time. Tubbing had not yet started.

Building N°. 2 Winding Engine House in 1917. In this photograph there is much activity. The concrete bases for the winding engines are complete. Notice the window frames on the left of the photograph. One bricklayer is setting bricks above a window frame on the lower right, but most of them are building the walls. At the rear of the building, the 'Coffee Pot' narrow-gauge engine is taking brick waste to a tip on the right.
{Peter Chadwick]

iron to prevent large icicles from being formed in and around the pit in wet weather as there was always the danger that one of them might break off and cause a fatality to men working at the pit bottom.[54]

Running water was expected to be encountered and work on N°. 1 shaft stalled when a feeder of water at 400 ft suddenly increased its flow to around 100 gallons per minute in December 1916. A pumping plant was installed and after an eight week delay sinking resumed.

In January 1917, the colliery received notice that in April all collieries would be taken over by the government as a temporary wartime measure and that sinkings at Llay and elsewhere would be stopped. Llay Main was not yet producing any coal and men were needed in the army, conscription having been introduced in 1916. There was plenty of work at existing collieries and mining was a reserved occupation. De Seyfried, concerned that key men would depart from Llay for good, wrote to the *Iron and Coal Trades Review Magazine* asking that Llay Main Colliery be not named in an article on the closing down of colliery sinkings as this would cause men to apply for jobs elsewhere. This request was agreed to and the colliery board met at the Royal Station Hotel,

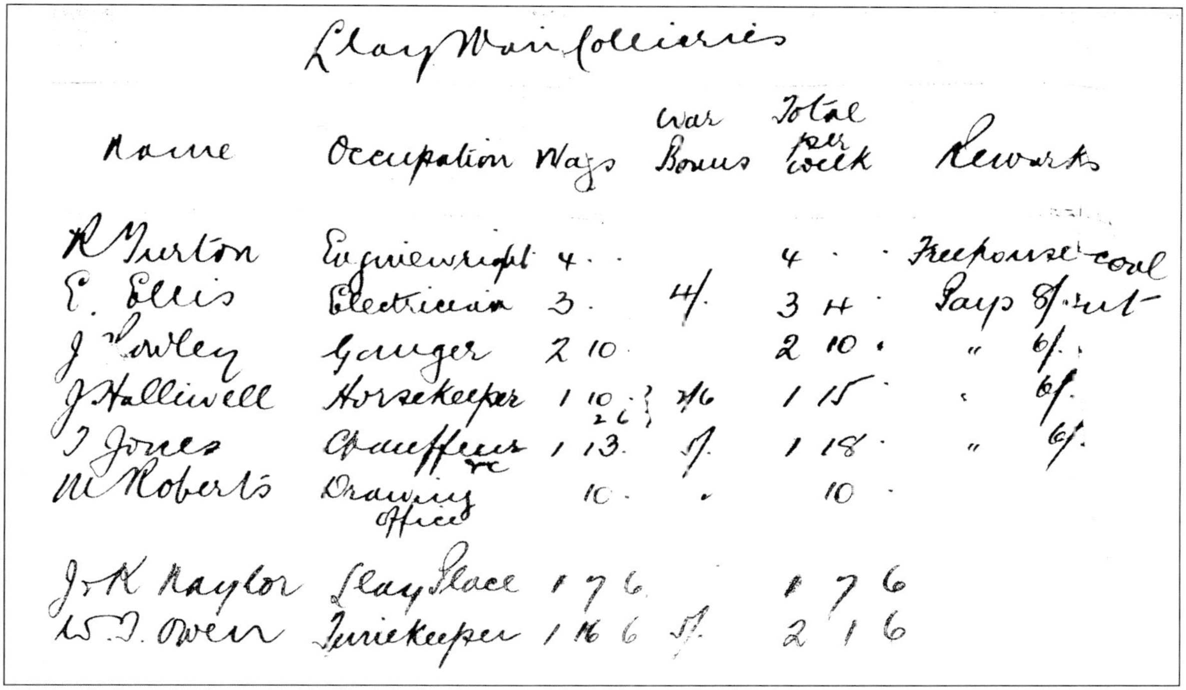

Llay Main Collieries

Name	Occupation	Wages	War Bonus	Total per week	Remarks
R Turton	Enginewright	4 . .		4 . .	Free house coal
E. Ellis	Electrician	3 .	4/.	3 4 .	Pays 8/- rent
J Rowley	Gauger	2 10 .		2 10 .	" 6/.
J Halliwell	Horsekeeper	1 10 . 2 6	7/6	1 15 .	" 6/.
T Jones	Chauffeur &c	1 13 .	5/.	1 18 .	" 6/.
W Roberts	Drawing Office	10 .	.	10 .	
J R K Naylor	Llay Place	1 7 6		1 7 6	
W. D. Owen	Timekeeper	1 16 6	5/.	2 1 6	

Workers wages in 1917. Mr Turton was in charge of winding procedures and oversaw the installations in the new winding house. The horse-keeper was needed as horses were used to move materials around the site. Llay Place was being leased by the colliery company from the Clarks and permission was given for its use as a clubhouse for officials from June 1917. [FRO/CB/8/5]

Sheffield on 29 January to consider the situation.[55] At that time, 95 men were employed at Llay and a list of jobs being done was supplied by de Seyfried to William Wilde at the colliery offices at Hickleton Main in February.

On 1 March 1917, St David's Day, the coalfields were temporarily taken over by government, being run by a controller of the Coal Mines Department of the Board of Trade.[56] At the end of March, de Seyfried wrote to Arthur D. Nicholson, Her Majesty's Inspector of Mines to give notice that 12 April was the date given by the Home Office for the suspension of operation of Nº 1 shaft and to ask for support in pleading for essential maintenance work to continue, to stop the pit from flooding.[57]

Nº. 1 shaft had reached a depth of 197 yards (591 ft) and Nº. 2 shaft a depth of 109 yards (327 ft) when the sinking had to be stopped for the time being. de Seyfried had to submit a list of colliery employees and found that he personally was needed elsewhere, his expertise being valued by the government. By 1918, he was in charge of the technical administration of the Coal Mines Control Agreement, and was a technical adviser on mining matters to the conjoint branch of the Inland Revenue and Home Office.[58] Twenty months were to pass before any further work could be attempted at Llay Main.

Sir Arthur Markham had made his wartime base at Newstead Abbey just outside Mansfield,

LLAY MAIN COLLIERIES . 19th, FEBRUARY, 1917.

LIST OF MEN EMPLOYED.

Engine-men:-	Winders.	3.	8/1.		
	Spare Winders. ...	2.	8/1.		
	Loco Man. ...	1.	5/10.		
	do. do. ...(spare)	1.	5/10.	(when not on loco, 5/7).	
	Pump-man.	1.	4/8.		
	Spare Engine-men.	2.	5/6.		
	Browett-Lindley Sets.	2.	5/11.		
Stokers.		3.	5/11.		
Assistant Stokers.		3.	5/5.		
Spare Stoker.		1.	5/7.		
			Foreman	Journeyman	
Blacksmiths.		3.	7/3½.	6/8½	
do. Strikers.		2.	4/6½		
Fitters.		3.	8/2.	6/4½	
do. Labourers.		5.	5/6.		
do. Boys.		2.	3/2.	3/3½.	
Electrician's Men:-	Assistant.	1.	6/6.		
	Lighting Set.	1.	5/11.		
	Labourer.	1.	4/6½.		
	Boy.	1.	10/-	per week.	
Carpenters.		5.	6/6.	6/2½.	
do. Labourers.		3.	5/-	4/9½	3/6.
Sawyer.		1.	6/3.		
Sundries:-	Shunter. ...	1.	5/3½.		
	Nightwatchman.	1.	35/-	per week.	
	Horsekeeper. ...	1.	30/-	do. do.	
	Chauffeur. ...	1.	33/-	do. do.	
	Office Boy. ...	1.	10/-	do. do.	
	Caretaker & Wife.	2.	27/6	do. do.	
Bricklayers.		5.	6/9½	6/3½	
do. Labourers.		4.	4/6½		
General Labourers.		24.	4/6½		
do. do. (Youth).		1.	3/1.		
Tipmen.		6.	6/11.	6/6.	

The Llay Main workforce April 1917. [FRO/CB/8/5]

from where he played a major role in the war effort by co-ordinating coal supplies to the armament factories.[59] In addition, he made strenuous efforts in Parliament to get underage soldiers returned from the Western Front, but to no avail. Some believe this endeavour put a strain on his already weak heart and that it led to his untimely death in 1916, aged 50.

For the fifty years from 1851 to 1901, the population of Llay had averaged around 500 people in just 105 homes. During that time, collieries had been opened in the area and the Llay census records show a steady increase in the number of workers associated with local mines. Before the colliery enterprise began among the lanes and parkland of the Llay area most of the homes were those of settled families, many of whom would eventually be drawn into working for the colliery or to servicing the growing village. The Tilston family had been blacksmiths at Llay Smithy since the seventeenth century and still live there to this day.

The census of 1911 shows 115 inhabited dwellings accommodating a total population of 573, seventy-one more than in 1901. An increasing number of men were employed in the local collieries, mainly at Llay Hall Colliery, but agricultural work was still the mainstay. Some combined the two and had a smallholding as well as working down the mine. William Wynne, a farm labourer, his wife Annie, sons William, Trevor and Tom and daughters Ellen and Jane, lived at New House Farm in the area then known as Pentwmpath. Like many other dwellings in the area, the farm was owned by the Clark family of Llay Hall Colliery.[60] Mary May Jones (Davies), known as 'Mrs Jones The Farm' was born in Cefn-y-Bedd in 1902 and in an interview in 1996 said:

> We came to live on Shone's Lane (Park House Farm) when I was 14. Old man Crewe lived in the cottages above us. There were two cottages there and we used to go to together with our buckets to get water from the well at Pentwmpath. We used to go to the fields to glean the corn with our pinnies turned up. I went with old Mrs Millington. They said we could have the pieces of corn. After they'd put the stacks up we could go and pick the corn and we'd take them home and we'd thrash the corn out and feed our chickens. We swapped farms with the Wynnes and came to live at New House Farm. Not that we had a big farm, it was more or less what my dad could do, because my dad kept his work in Llay Hall. He walked across the fields to Llay Hall colliery.[61]

Amongst the people mentioned by Mary May Jones was the Crewe family which was spread out across the Llay area: in Stone Cottages on Shone's Lane lived Siddy Crewe and her mother, Margaret, and father, John, a labourer working for the Urban District Council and at Rose Cottages, near Home Farm, lived Samuel Crewe, a roadman working for the Rural District Council, his wife Fanny, his sons Frank and Leslie and daughter, Gladys. Another branch of the family lived at Chapel Cottages on Chapel Lane – William and Rosanna Crewe and their children Margaret, William, John Henry, Daniel and Edward. William, the father, was a colliery labourer, possibly at Llay Hall Colliery. All of William's children were born in Llay, Margaret the eldest in 1897.

The Ankers were another family who lived in one of the three Chapel Cottages in 1911. James the head of the family was a coal miner born in Hope. His wife Frances and children Ernest (a gardener), James (a groom), Harold (a page boy), Gladys, Aylmer, Beatrice, Wilfred, Doris and Vera were all recorded as being born in Gresford which at that time included Llay. Leonard,

Maria, Cyril and William Ankers were baptised at Llay Main Mission room (see below) on 13 May 1919.[62]

Of the Parry family, Harriet and Joseph ran Llay Green farm as we have seen and Seth Parry was a coal worker living at Bradley Cottages. George Parry, a groom, lived at Croes Howell with his wife, Martha, and daughter, also named Martha. Bill Millington described George as follows:

> Mr Parry had been so many years a gentleman's gentleman that he had become a gentleman himself and he found it hard to relax. In voice, manners and bearing he was a gentleman. His daughter Patty married a man from Worthenbury and there she went to live.[63]

After years of quiet husbandry here, the Parrys were greatly affected when the colliery railway was built in 1914. They lost 13% of their farm land and experienced major disturbance from railway building which cut off easy access to many fields.

In addition to these established families, the development of deep mines in the locality attracted other people to the Llay area. By March 1911, deep coal measures under Llay had been proved and in the Llay census of the same year, there were four workers described as sinkers, one of whom was said to be at the United Westminster Collieries. The United Westminster & Wrexham Collieries began sinking Gresford Colliery in 1908 with the first coal being produced there in 1911. The other sinkers may also have been employed at Gresford. At Wilderness Farm, there were two erecting engineers in the same census. It is possible that they and a Charles D. Horne, a 'borer (well and prospecting)', lodging at Llay Chain Farm, were working on the Mount

Llay Green Farm. Harriet Parry feeding the poultry about 1910. [Greville Williams]

Rackery Lane – Colliery Villas and Sinkers' huts in 1914. The houses for key workers, Colliery Villas and Cottages, can be seen on the extreme left together with three hutments for sinkers across the road on the colliery site. The bases for the two winding houses are being prepared in the foreground. [Rod Challoner]

Pleasant borehole. The census also recorded two colliery proprietors living in Llay; perhaps they were interested in the new mine.

In 1913 work started on the trial well and there was a steady influx of workers after this time. By the end of 1914, progress was being made in building the railway and sinking shafts. Local accommodation was needed for workers engaged in these tasks and the first of the settlers' homes were Colliery Villas on Rackery Lane. These were for key officials and across the road from these, on the colliery site, were hutments for sinkers. There were altogether around eighteen hutments in two rows alongside Rackery Lane. These were used to house firstly the sinkers working for Simon Carves & Sons. Once the house building programme was underway in 1920, the huts became temporary accommodation for colliers and their families whilst their permanent homes in the new village were under construction. One of the huts was designated 'The Pavilion' and was used for many years as a social club. Another came to be used as the first Catholic church in the village and one was moved in 1925 next to St Martin's Church to become known as the 'Church Hut' and used for functions until it was replaced in around 2000. Thus, the first village development took place in the area called Llay Chain, near what is now the Crown Inn.

By 1914, further facilities had been installed at Llay Chain. Harriet Laura Bellis (née Platt) had moved to Rose Cottage in 1912. She was a daughter of Sam Platt, the chauffeur to Edward Clark, and described described the situation like this:

> Lots of people started to come to work at the colliery which had just started sinking so a shop was needed. Llay Stores it was called. Mr Percy Guest that was in charge of the shop went into the army. Mr J. Edwards of Caergwrle took it over for his daughter. It was a blessing not to have to goto Gresford. The letter box was inserted into the wall and a huge wooden hut was put there by Miss Sykes of Croes Howell where we could meet at night for games and she provided everything for it. but those rather rough sinkers started to spoil it so they had to close it.[64]

In those days, attendance at church or chapel was expected and the area underwent a series of religious revivals which resulted in packed houses at local places of worship. The established Church, as represented by Gresford and Gwersyllt parish churches, was the preferred place of worship for the Clark family and for senior figures of authority in the developing colliery.

In 1914, the only church in Llay was that of the Primitive Methodists on the crossroads of Gresford road and Nant-y-Gaer road. This tiny chapel, now a house, was called Ewle chapel in 1851, presumably because of its proximity to the *hewl* or *heol*, the Welsh for 'road'. This had been erected in 1836 and had an average congregation of around 60 people in 1851.[65] Bill Millington gives us an idea of what went on there in around 1914:

> The organist was Miss Jane Wynne, the elder daughter of Mr S. Wynne the steward. The organ, or was it a harmonium, was a very humble instrument. A Miss Olive Sykes ran a Bible class for teenagers on a Sunday afternoon. The piano was played by Miss Lucy Lloyd, who was a teacher at Burton School and a daughter of Mrs Jane Lloyd the local midwife.
>
> The building had seating for eighty people but I have seen many more get in and on some occasions chairs had to be borrowed from houses nearby in order for people to sit in the aisle which was very narrow and presented difficulties for Mr Samuel Crewe when he tried to get up amongst them to take up the offertory. The chapel was lit by paraffin lamps, two hanging over the aisle and two on the wall each side of the pulpit.
>
> Remember that in those days as stranger was rarely seen in Llay and it was only at the Chapel that people could meet each other and the chapel was the centre of social life in the village.[66]

Sinkers came from outside the locality, from Ireland, Yorkshire and Lancashire. On the whole, they were a fairly rough lot and the colliery founders saw to it that their spiritual needs were met by inviting the Navvies Mission Society of London to set up a church in Llay. The Society and its

Llay baptisms in Gresford Parish Registers, 1915–17.

Date	*Child*	*Father*	*Address*	*Trade or profession*
1915				
23 Jan	Annie	Frederick George Luker	9 Hutment, Llay Main	Engine driver
15 Aug	Jean	Edward Ellis	2 Villa, Rackery Lane	Electrician
26 Dec	Robert	William Benjamin	Manor View, Llay	Collier
1916				
3 Feb	Elizabeth	Charles Henry Coward	8 Llay Colliery Hutments	General Labourer
19 May	Benjamin	Benjamin Eaton	9 Hut Llay Colliery	Pit sinker
1917				
30 Mar	George	Herbert Roberts	14 Llay Main Hutments	
12 Apr	Martha Hebe	John Harris	1 Cottages, Rackery Lane	Fitter
12 Apr	Ivy	Miles Miller	7 Cottages, Rackery Lane	Fitter
30 Apr	William Eric	John Thomas Wynne	7 The Hutments, Llay	Collier
3 Oct	George Frederick	Henry Glover	1 The Huts	Pit Sinker
4 Nov	Florence May	Samuel Tydd	6 Llay Main Cottage	Collier
9 Dec	David Arthur Dempster	Andrew Dempster Brydon	Home Farm, Llay	Mining Engineer

lay preachers used whatever premises were available to improve the navvies' understanding of the Bible, and to lead them away from a culture of excessive drinking and immoral behaviour. Tom Cleverley was a Navvy Missioner. In 1911, he was at Dover ministering to workers widening the Admiralty pier.[67] He conducted the first service at Llay on 9 January 1916. Harriet Platt recorded that:

> A church mission hall was erected between the Chain and Rose Cottage. It used to be a nice friendly place and used to get packed. One had to get there early to get a seat. An old gentleman Mr Cleverly was in charge of it. He was called a mining missioner and would be moved about to wherever a coalmine was being sunk. Rev J. E. Williams used to come to take Holy Communion.[68]

2: Model Colliery and Village (1919–26)

The Controller of Coal Mines allowed sinking operations to resume at Llay Main at the beginning of 1919.[1] The colliery manager, John de Seyfried, having returned from his wartime duties, quickly made up for lost time and work on the sinking of N° 1 shaft recommenced in May and, at the same time, the permanent headgear was being erected.[2] By October, the headgear for N° 2 shaft was completed and sinking of this shaft had also resumed.[3] Work continued around the clock and a daily report of March 1920 (overleaf) gives an insight into the night-shift's activity.[4] Keith Folwell, the penultimate manager at Llay Main Colliery, interpretated this report:

> There would have been four shifts of six hours duration working in or about the shaft. The sixteen men may have included the winder driver and the banksman who would have been in charge of activities the top of the shaft. The usual sequence of events was that a pattern of drill holes was drilled down for about six feet, the holes were charged with explosive and blasted, the rock was hand loaded into a hoppit and hoisted to the surface. Then a lining was installed and the process repeated.

Colliery buildings at Llay Main, 1917. This photograph shows the cooling tower, N°. 2 winding engine house, power house and N°. 1 winding engine house. In the foreground, the freezing unit has been removed from N°. 2 shaft. On the extreme right the freezing unit of N°. 1 shaft has yet to be dismantled. [Rod Challoner]

The blasted rock was loaded into the hoppit by two concentric rings of men using shovels. If any of the outer ring of men threw rock onto any of the inner ring of men instead of the hoppit they took their place in the inner ring. It appears that during the shift 8 hoppits of rock were loaded and hoisted to the surface, 32 barrels of water were pumped from the shaft bottom into a barrel and hoisted to the surface and one support ring (number 30) was installed. The latter is assumed to have been a temporary support.[5]

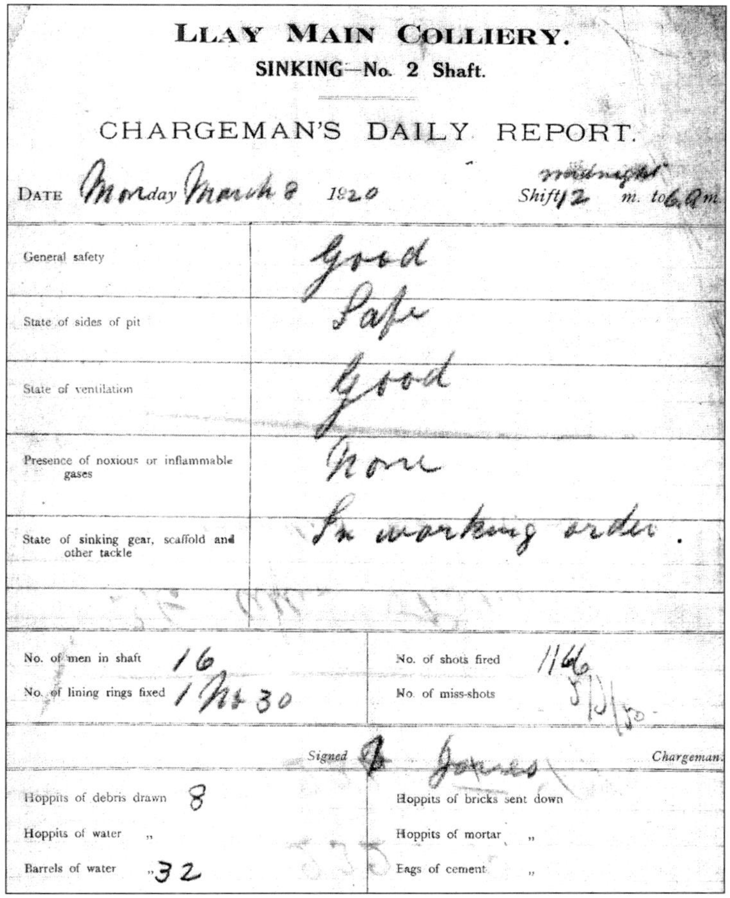

LLAY MAIN COLLIERY.
SINKING—No. 2 Shaft.

CHARGEMAN'S DAILY REPORT.

DATE Monday March 8 1920 Shift 12 midnight m. to 6 am.

General safety	Good
State of sides of pit	Safe
State of ventilation	Good
Presence of noxious or inflammable gases	None
State of sinking gear, scaffold and other tackle	In working order.

No. of men in shaft	16	No. of shots fired	11
No. of lining rings fixed	1 No 30	No. of miss-shots	

Signed J. Jones Chargeman.

Hoppits of debris drawn	8	Hoppits of bricks sent down	
Hoppits of water	,,	Hoppits of mortar	,,
Barrels of water	32	Bags of cement	,,

Progress report on the sinking of No. 2 shaft, 8 March 1920 [FRO/CB/13/1]

De Seyfried sent in regular progress reports to the colliery owners and samples of coal were analysed, revealing that the quality of the coal varied from seam to seam. Letters from the County Analyst's Office in Darlington to Rea Ltd, in May 1920, confirmed that 'sample 188 is a steam coal of high quality, sample 190 TD is of average quality as a steam coal'.[6]

With the colliery nearly completed, a large workforce was needed to extract the coal. When the sinking of the colliery started in 1913–14, a few houses had been built on Rackery Lane. Mr Turton, the engine wright, had lived at No. 1 Villa until he left for Chirk in 1920, possibly in order to work at Ifton colliery. The provision of housing for the workers and their families was seen as a priority and the new village was built on parkland at the former Llay Place estate.

The colliery proprietors, Hickleton Main Colliery Ltd, had previous experience of establishing new settlements to house their workers. Llay Main colliery was going to be large and to ensure sufficient manpower, amazingly a town of 30,000 people was planned. House building started in earnest in 1920, but the original plan was modified and the size of the settlement reduced, possibly because of a decline in the world market for coal. Even so, as late as 1922, there was still talk of a small town of 2,850 homes and a population of 15,000.[7]

The style and layout of the houses were heavily influenced by the colliery owners' experiences elsewhere. Sir Arthur Markham had been involved with the establishment of Woodlands Model Village, built for Brodsworth Colliery (Doncaster) in 1907–09 and Carcroft New Village

*Colliery Cottages on Rackery Lane c.1925. A busy scene as miners return home. On the left, Owens' paraffin cart from Gresford makes steady progress towards two young ladies in the centre, and a boy and girl manoeuvre a pushchair towards the colliery. A cart with household goods at N*º *7 announces new arrivals at Harold Dunnico's house. [Doreen Monslow]*

(Doncaster) established between 1912 and 1914 for miners working at Bullcroft Colliery.[8] The Markhams were enlightened employers, who believed that good living conditions would help to develop a healthy and stable workforce and miners and their families should receive better education and engage in activities to further their spiritual needs and social responsibility.[9] These were the underlying principles upon which the design of the village of Llay would be based. Like Woodlands and Carcroft, Llay was regarded as a model colliery village and on some maps of the 1920s, the name 'Llay Model Village' appears.

In 1917, the government had set up a committee called the Housing (Building Construction) Committee. Under the chairmanship of Sir John Tudor Walters, it was asked to 'investigate the questions of building constructions in connection with the provision of dwellings, for the working classes in England, Wales and Scotland'. An influential member of the committee was Raymond Unwin, partner and brother-in-law of Barry Parker, the architect and designer of Llay. Unwin influenced the Commission to consider the houses of working people as a collective entity, a community, not just as dwellings.

On 23 March 1904, Barry Parker (1867–1947) and Raymond Unwin (1863–1940), both regarded as pioneers of town planning, had been appointed consulting architects to Letchworth, the first Garden City. Unwin was responsible for the layout while Parker specialised in design. Later, Unwin went on to a distinguished career as Principal Inspector of Town Planning and, in 1918, became Chief Architect at the Ministry of Health and as such would have approved the plans for the new village of Llay. How did such an eminent architect as Parker get involved with designing the village of Llay? It could be said that his long association with Unwin may have been significant as the latter had worked at the Markham's Staveley company as an engineer, working on the development of mining townships.

Barry Parker was a devotee of the socialist Arts and Crafts movement and a prominent member of the 'Garden City' movement. He was a Quaker and his work was driven by concern for the working man and his family. His plan took into account the need to develop a communal spirit in the village as a stabilising factor for the future inhabitants. Llay was going to be more than just a place to exist in. Living there would involve its inhabitants in activities to develop the community; they would work and live 'with the cohesion of a single entity'.[10] Churches, social clubs and village organisations would be central to the development of this sense of community, but public houses would not be welcomed. The Crown Inn on the crossroads near the colliery, at the beginning of Rackery Lane, did not open until 1929, nine years after the houses in First Avenue had been built.[11]

Barry Parker – architect of the model village of Llay [© First Garden City Heritage Museum]

The landscape of Llay proved to be the ideal site for a village. Its well-drained, flat fields and gently rolling countryside were easy to build upon and the watercourses of the river Alyn and the Nant-y-Gaer brook were natural boundaries. It could be said that this open aspect laid the foundation for the development of a harmonious settlement of miners and their families. Some believe that the ribbon type of housing development of the south Wales coalfield, produced by the need to follow deep valleys, was partly to blame for labour problems in these coalfields and the reason for the failure to develop an appropriate community spirit in these mining villages.[12]

On 15 April 1920, two years before any coal was raised at the colliery, the Llay Housing Association was formed and the building of the first 200 homes for the miners began on 26 May. The building contractors were J. P. Linnell of Prestatyn.

> Vast quantities of building materials were brought by rail to the mine. From there, bricks, timber and other supplies were sent to the building site by horse and cart, lorries and by a narrow gauge railway.[13]

Plans for the village and for the various different house styles were drawn up for the Llay Housing Association by Parker, working for the Housing and Town Planning Trust. The chairman of the latter was Sir Tudor Walters, who was also a director of Llay Main Colliery Company. In May 1920, Sir Tudor sent a letter to Wrexham Rural District Council stating that the trust had a contract for the erection of a first instalment of two hundred houses at Llay which were '… to be completed as rapidly as possible and it is anticipated that the houses would be ready for occupation by the end of November [1920].[14]

An article in the *North Wales Chronicle* fostered the idea of a 'miners' utopia' being created at Llay.

> The Llay Housing Association has come into being. The men who own the colliery are funding the capital for the Housing Association ... The company has a scheme for 200 houses nearing completion. Mr Smillie and others have painted a sombre picture of bleak hillside mining villages where the dwellers live cheerless lives in squalid hovels. By contrast the new village will be a miners' paradise. The site of the new village is a really charming piece of country. It is only in winter when the trees are bare that it is possible to see just the top portion of the colliery stack. The houses are designed in seven different types ... the total number of houses that are going to be built cannot definitely be stated ... a second lot of 200 is under consideration.[15]

In June 1920, a description of the Llay community appeared in the *Wrexham Leader*:

> One must be inspired with the spirit of Christopher Columbus to discover Llay (says a writer in the *Daily News*) ... a Wrexham postman confessed he did not know of such a place ... Today, Llay is but a little hamlet of a few widely scattered cottages and a few lines of wooden hutments in the midst of some of the most luxuriant verdure to be found in the whole land. The shafts and paraphernalia of a pit-head appear almost as impudent intruders. Actually they are heralds of a commercial enterprise which is to retain for a century or two an industry which in this quarter of north Wales otherwise would die from exhaustion on 50 or 60 years time.
>
> At present accommodated in the hutments are 150 miners. Altogether about 2,000 houses are to be erected, and of these 200 are to be completed this year. It is to be the creation of a model village with ample 'lung spots' each house built on the most up-to-date and approved plan. There will be playing fields and a village institute. The site today is a fine open private park, but soon its fringe of towering trees will ring around a garden village of miners and Llay will have found a place on the map.[16]

Some of the original houses were designed to have no back doors, but this idea was dropped after opposition from Wrexham Rural District Council and the miners' representatives.[17] The Housing Association was owned by Llay Main Colliery Ltd, and on 30 July, a large portion of the village lands passed to it from E. Stuart Clark.[18] The colliery houses were built in three phases. The first pase lasted from 1920 to around the end of 1922. The second from 1923 to 1924 and a third, smaller, phase was completed between 1924 and 1925. Each house had an inside toilet and bathroom, unusual for workers in those days. Houses were built at eight per acre, which meant that each 'cottage' had plenty of garden space to encourage workers to grow their own vegetables or keep poultry.

Some of the avenues were given names associated with local farms or places, but the larger avenues were numbered. This seems to have been the practice in some of the other purpose-built Yorkshire mining villages in the owners control.

> The houses were owned by the colliery owners and let only to colliers in the early years of the pit. Near the mine were two rows of sinker's huts in a line finishing near the Crown Inn. Once sinking had been complete they were occupied by families waiting for their house to be built. The first hut was a clubhouse for the workers, the landlady being a Mrs Scott. One hut was used as a community centre.[19]

House building had started in 1920 before the pit sinkers had finished their task. Some Irish

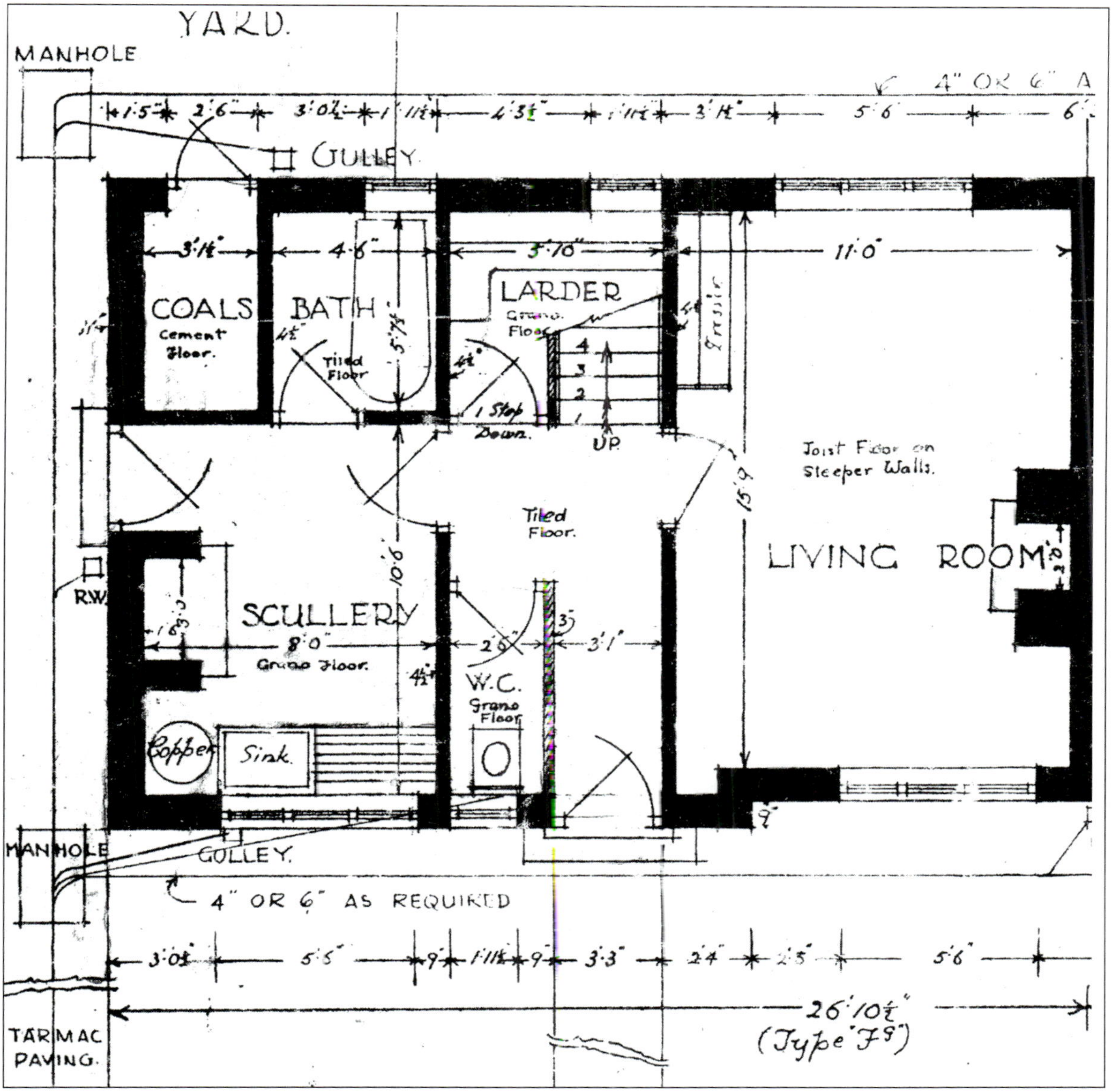

Llay House plan, ground floor, Type F 'g' cottage (left hand side of block of four)

sinkers were housed in the huts on Rackery Lane and they were known to be a tough lot. Trouble broke out on 29 August, 1920, when three Irishmen, Michael Gallagher and John and Brian Lavin, visited huts tenanted by Richard Scott. A disturbance lasting several hours occurred which involved the smashing of crockery, an assault on Scott's sister and the theft of Mrs Scott's pony and trap. In their defence, the men later said that they had been supplied with whisky, stout and beer by Mrs Scott, and had been drinking there all day. One of the accused said he had been struck on the head by a pint pot and that Mrs Scott was herself drunk. After hearing five hours

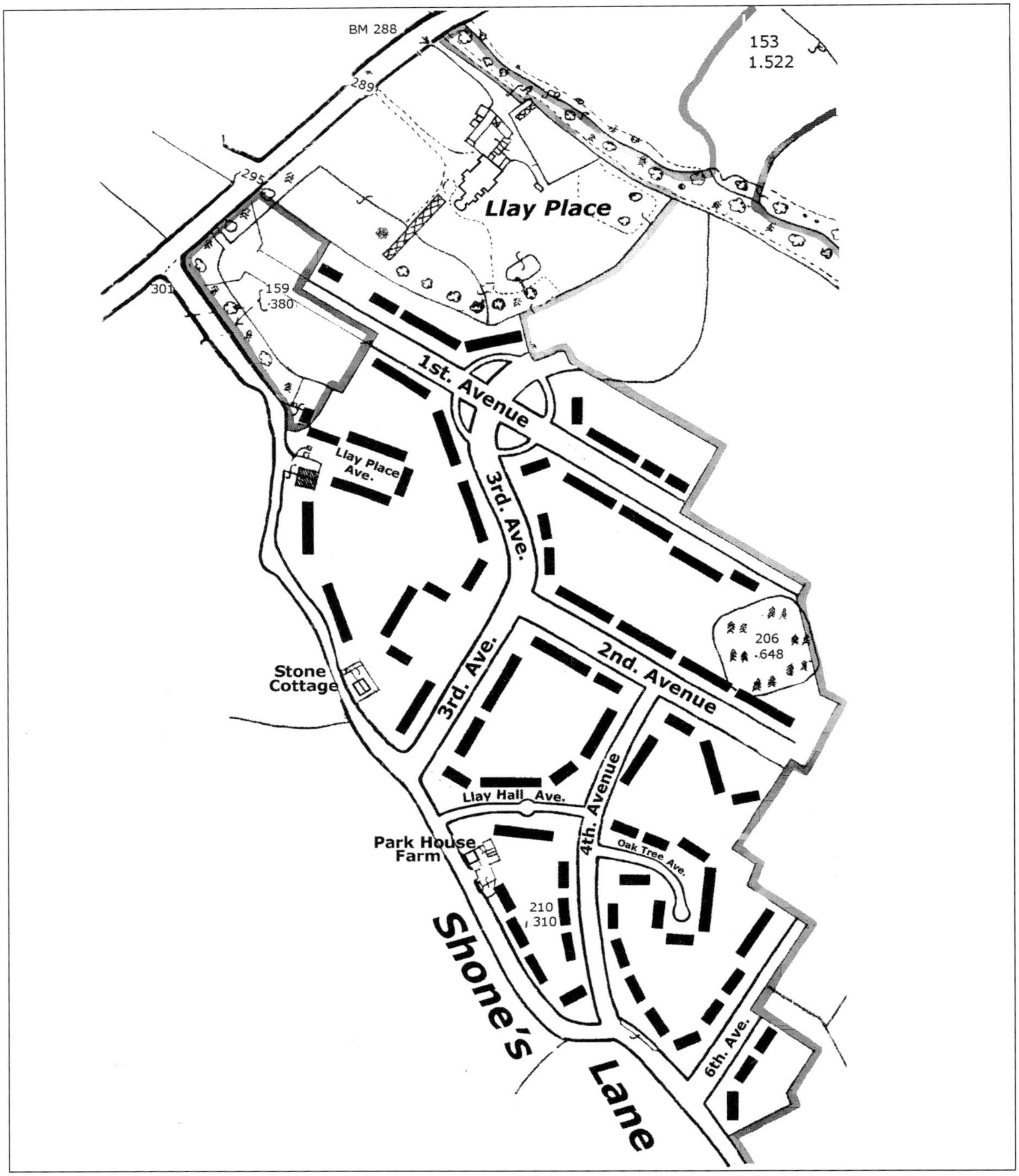

Llay Model village – plan of first phase of 200 houses 1920[20] *[Redrawn by Michael Adams]*

Llay – house building in Second Avenue in 1920. 'Titch' of Llay Hall Farm with his horse and cart stands in front of some newly-built houses. The presence of curtains indicate that the house on the left is already occupied.
[Greville Williams]

of evidence, the magistrates decided to fine Gallagher and John Lavin 20 shillings each. The police brought a charge against Mrs Scott for selling whisky without a licence. Inspector Rees and his police officers searched the huts and found beer in casks and bottles, and receipts for whisky bought by Mrs Scott. She was subsequently fined £2 and her husband, Richard, £3 with an advocate's fee of £2 2s.[21]

Llay was the only purpose-built mining village in north Wales and would have had the feel of a 'frontier' community in the early 1920s. Law and order was a priority for the village founders and PC Benjamin Lloyd, with his wife Sarah and sons Benjamin and George, was installed at No. 1 Second Avenue, his rent being paid by the Chief Constable. Lloyd was reputed to have kept a gun:

> We came to Llay in 1922. I lived in First Avenue until my father [Charlie Jones] became steward of the first miners' institute [at Llay Place] where we lived until my father became landlord of the new built Crown Inn in 1929. Every Friday, Tom Jones, the colliery chauffeur in the '20s, would drive Mr Barlow, a dapper little gentleman, to the bank in Wrexham to collect the miners' wages, accompanied by Lloyd the policeman who, it was said, was armed with a revolver.[22]

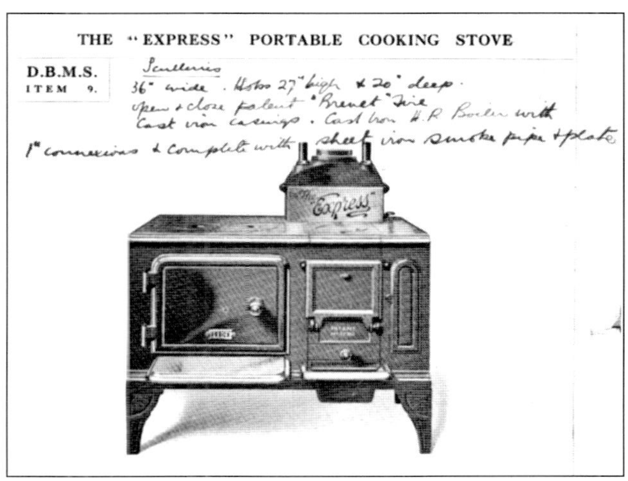

Kitchen range installed in Llay houses.[23]
[Herbert Gaskin]

Llay policemen had their own way of dealing with potential sources of trouble:

> After Lloyd the policeman came PC Stan Evans, a young chap. One – Sophy, the local 'baddie' boasted how he would put Evans in his place. PC Evans heard of this and one of the first things he did was to take Sophy on the Pant Mawr and on a field opposite the cemetery gave him a good thrashing. Evans was a boxer pre-Police. No more trouble from Sophy'.[24]

Miners were attracted to the new village from far and wide, but the colliery company's policy was, whenever possible, to recruit locally and most families migrated the short distances from established mining villages such as Leeswood, Brymbo and Coedpoeth. People of different languages, religions and customs were thrust together in an endeavour to form a new village and to establish a successful colliery.[25]

In August 1920, the 'Main' coal seam was struck in N°. 1 shaft at a depth of 2,496 feet, and on 13 September, the 'Wall and Bench' seam was proved at a depth of 2,709 feet at N°. 1 shaft. In September, the sinking of N°. 1 shaft was completed at a total depth of 2,715 feet[26] and the manager ordered 2,886 feet of winding ropes for this shaft in October.[27]

In March 1921, collieries came out of post-war government control and there followed a three-month strike because of the mine owners' refusal to match the pay the miners had been receiving during the period of government control between 1917–21. In Llay, the effect of this strike must have been marginal as no coal was being produced at that time. The issue of employers demanding their workforces to work longer hours for less pay resurfaced at the pit in 1925. For now, a report on the developing colliery in a local newspaper struck a note of optimism:

> Up to the present the company have sunk one shaft down to a depth of 900 yards, the other will be completed soon after the present stoppage in the industry comes to an end 'but the dip in the gradient of the seams will delay development for another twelve months.' In order to get a return on their outlay the colliery will have to reach an output of a million tons per year – which would mean employment for 3,000 men. The plant is as up-to-date as it can be. The colliery will be equipped with the latest mechanised haulage 'there will be no ponies. The miners lamps will be electric.'[28]

By May 1921, the colliery was nearing completion and the village was expanding rapidly. One of the colliery owners, Sir Charles Markham, director of the Doncaster Collieries Association, decided to take a personal interest in proceedings and took up residence at Oak Alyn, Cefn-y-Bedd, once the home of the Clark family. When the N°. 2 shaft (upcast) was completed in July of that year, at a depth of 810 yards (2,432 ft),[29] de Seyfried calculated the winding depth to be 777 yards (2,331 feet) with the headgear height of 23 yards (69 feet).[30]

It was essential that a shared sense of belonging should arise in order for the settlement to achieve stability. The village needed to develop its own identity. Institutions were soon founded which would enhance the value of community life. In 1922, there was still talk of a small town being built at Llay:

> The new garden village at Llay Main is being developed by the Housing & Town Planning Trust who have plans for 2,850 homes, 200 of which are already built with another 200 under construction. The pit

Cooling tower, N°. 2 engine house and headgear. LMS and Llay Hall Colliery wagons bear a load of pit props ready for the next phase in developments underground. The many bricks in front of the headgear bear witness to its recent construction. The headgears were 85 feet high and made of lattice steel by Markham & Co.

employs 3,000 and the village has a population of 15,000. Sir Tudor Walters is Chairman of the Housing & Town Planning Trust. Walters was formerly a fellow Liberal MP to the late Sir Arthur Markham.[31]

In 1922, the first-phase houses were supplied with electricity when a cable was laid across the Cefn-y-Bedd road from the colliery.[32] Until 1950, only direct current could be supplied and it had only enough power to provide for a small number of electric lights in each home. Few other appliances could be used. When coal was being wound up the pit, the lights in the houses would dim considerably. That was, however, only a minor inconvenience and families were glad to pay the 9d a week charge.

> We moved out of Highfield (Wrexham), candles, a paraffin lamp and tin bath into a new house with two fires, four bedrooms, indoor toilet and bathroom. My mother pressed the light switch down as she went in and the lights came on. 'It's a miracle,' she said. [Herbert Henry Jones, Pit Deputy][33]

Initially, some of the rents were too high for miners to pay and a few of them were summoned for non-payment of rates. One man said he earned 26s 3d per week but had to pay 16s 5d of that for rent, water rate and 'unemployment'. The rent of the house was 12 8d. Another had a rent of 17s 2d a week. He was told by the magistrates that the rates must be paid and replied, 'And my children must have food'. One miner was supported by the Llay Presbyterian minister Revd J. Lewis Evans who told the court that it was impossible for him to pay the rates.[34]

The village infrastructure was improved when a post office was provided.

> LLAY MAIN – POSTAL FACILITIES
> A new sub-office will shortly be opened in the new village where stamps and money orders can be obtained. A savings bank will also be instituted in connection with the office. Mr E.G. Haines of Gresford has been appointed sub postmaster. There will not be a telephone or telegraphic exchange at present

N°. 34 First Avenue – the village's post office, 1922 [Glenys Price]

but should the necessity arise these will be provided.[35]

The colliery owners encouraged the development of sporting activities in the village. On 5 August 1922, Llay Sports were held on the Rackery Lane fields that were owned by the colliery. An account of it shows how the colliery and village combined to put on a major event. Hundreds of people turned up from surrounding villages to watch running – the over-50s event being won by J. Naylor of Llay with no opposition, and Mrs Edge of Llay won the married-ladies race. A two-mile cycle race was won by J.W. Roberts of Hope. The Caergwrle brewery of Lassell & Sharman gave a prize to W. Matthews of Gresford for wining the most events. There was also a stretcher competition where teams from local collieries were tested on first aid and judged by Dr Harrison of Gresford – Westminster Colliery were the winners. It was then that Dr Harrison started ambulance (first aid) classes in Llay on behalf of the colliery company.

A close relationship grew between the colliery and the village, the former being always available to help with social events. A 'treat' was held at Rackery Hall in August 1922 for pupils of the Church in Wales Sunday School which exemplifies such co-operation.[36] The treat had been an annual event since 1917 when it was described by Ena Dean of Rackery Farm:

> The house itself was cleaned from top to bottom as well in case it was wet and preparations has to be made indoors. In the event it was a lovely sunny day. 'What shall we do with the children afterwards?' Dad and Mr Cleverley went to the colliery manager and asked what materials could be borrowed for the afternoon. The answer was 'ropes and planks and anything within reason.'
>
> Now along the drive from the road to the farm there were trees with branches extending over the

lawn. Mr Cleverley had some special boards cut to size to make seats for swings. He borrowed some ropes and chains from the colliery, had holes bored in the seats and fixed them as swings to the branches. There were three or four fir trees, a couple of cherry trees and a walnut tree for the little ones. What about tables? The colliery manager said, 'Take all the timber you need' so father made some trestle tables and set them up on the lawn. We had to go to school when some of the preparations were made and it was marvellous to come home and see see-saws and swings all ready for use.

The day came, the children assembled and the Treat got under way. It was marvellous. Then who should arrive but Miss Allington Hughes from Gresford. She came like a ship in full sail with clothes baskets full of small prizes and presents. She seems to have spent her life getting presents and giving them away. One haughty mother said, 'Would you believe it! Can't we do anything or arrange anything without Miss Allington Hughes turning up?' Everyone laughed. All Miss Allington Hughes said in that connection was 'Why wasn't I told all about this?' One wonders how she found out?

And so the children all had presents too and prizes for winning the games they played. It was a beautiful day. We never had to go into the loft or into the house at all. How many children were there? Forty or fifty perhaps. A lot were sinker's children. Most were, in fact. It was good for those who didn't know religion as we did. The Chapel children heard about it some weeks before and came to the Mission the week before the Treat in order to get a ticket. It was just like a big show. Rackery Lane was full of people from Caer Estyn, Caergwrle and Llay. Many just came to look.[37]

Although it was half-a-mile from the new village, the Pavilion hut on Rackery Lane continued to provide good service in 1922 and was used for dancing classes, dances, whist drives and the Ladies Sewing Guild fancy dress ball. A male-voice choir was formed with Llewellyn Powell 'a noted baritone singer' as its conductor. It too held practices at the Pavilion. A choral society, started and conducted by Mrs Bessie Clark, wife of Edward Stuart Clark, gave a concert at Croes Howell Hall in March 1922. The Crewe family were involved, taking part in the singing as well as loaning a piano. Stuart Clark chaired the proceedings and said that the concert was to raise funds to buy a piano for the Society.[38]

Other village organisations started during this time were:

Llay Presbyterian Young People's Christian Guild (1923)[39]
Llay Presbyterian Scouts (1922)[40]
Llay St John's Ambulance (1922)[41]
Llay Nursing Association (1922)
Llay Branch of the British Legion (1923)[42]
Llay Main Colliery Silver Band (1924 possibly 1923)[43]
Llay Cricket Club (*c.*1923)[44]
Llay Bowls Club (*c.*1922)[45]
Llay Tennis Club (*c.*1923)

The colliery company was keen to develop a community with high spiritual and moral values and suitable sites were granted by the colliery company for this purpose. In 1921, as the first phase of house building was nearing completion, new churches were being planned:

Proposed new places of worship – the development of the Llay district is causing different religious

Llay Tennis Club c.1926. Robert John Roberts (R.J.) is in the front row with Elsie Lloyd his future wife. Eddie Ivor Jones is in the back row. Photograph taken at the first Miners' Institute at Llay Place. The courts later became the site of the secondary modern school. [Beryl Baigent]

bodies to think of needing ample provision for its religious requirements. The Church in Wales, the Presbyterians, and the Primitive Methodists each propose to erect new places of worship, suitable sites having already been granted by the colliery company for the purpose.[46]

Most miners were of the Nonconformist tradition and Trinity Presbyterian Church (initially called Park Church) was the first permanent church to be built in the new village. The foundation stone was laid on 11 July 1922 and a temporary building was placed on site. Trinity opened on 23 November 1922 and services and Sunday schools, in both Welsh and English, were held there until the opening of Glanaber Welsh Presbyterian Chapel on Nant-y-Gaer Road in 1925.

Trinity Church played an important part in the life of the village. The main part of the chapel had seating for around 200 people and either side of the main hall were four classrooms. With a kitchen and a large hall it at the rear, it was ideal for concerts and meetings of all kinds.[47] It was used as an infants school before the Council School was built in 1926, and the schoolroom was used for coroner's inquiries into miners' deaths at Llay Main Colliery – including the inquest on the Llay disaster of December 1925. Miners played a prominent part in the running of the church – in 1922, Richard Jarvis was superintendent of the Band of Hope and William Parrott superintendent of the Sunday School. The church's fortunes mirrored that of the colliery and membership declined to a handful of faithful adherents by the mid–1960s. The church closed in 1969.

Trinity Presbyterian Church. The foundation stone may be seen in the wall near St Martin's Mews – the site of the church. [Herbert Gaskin]

By April 1922, the equipping of N$^{o.}$ 1 pit for winding was completed and the first coal was raised.[48] A report in the *Colliery Guardian* of June 1922 stated:

At Llay Main a new pit is rapidly nearing

completion. Already, several hundred men are engaged and when developed it will be the biggest pit in North Wales, employing over 2,000 men.[49]

A small quantity of coal was raised in 1922, but production began in earnest in 1923. It was machine cut and loaded onto conveyor belts by hand. The first collier to enter the mine is said to have been Ed Berry, who was ever after known as 'No. 1'. Coal tubs were moved along the haulage system by relays of stationary engines powering endless ropes. Full tubs were called 'piechers' by some.[50] No pit ponies were ever used and electric illumination was in use from the start.[51] Ten years after it was founded, the colliery company was no doubt relieved to get the pit working. The company details are recorded in the 1923 *Colliery Year Book and Coal Trades Directory* as follows:[52]

Llay Main Collieries Ltd
Registered Office: Rotherham
Annual Output: 300,000 tons
Class of Coal: Gas, Household, Steam
Other Information: Just putting coal on to the market. Output at present 6,000 tons per week, rapidly increasing
Chairman: Robert Armitage, Farnley Hall, Leeds
Directors: G. C. H. Davy, Smeaton Manor, Northallerton
William Humble,[53] Skellow Hall, Doncaster
Alec L. Rea, 20 Water Street, Liverpool
Sir J. Tudor Walters, 4 Stone Buildings, Lincoln's Inn, London, WC2
General Manager: W. L. Halpin
Secretary: Walter Hazard
Agent: W. L. Halpin
Manager: G. B. Tristram
Employees under ground: 1,150
Employees above ground: 400

According to a booklet (which was produced for a joint visit of the British Association and the north Wales branch of the National Association of Colliery Managers on 18 September 1923), No. 1 shaft was designated the 'downcast' shaft through which cool, fresh air was to be drawn and passed around the workings to the foot of the No. 2 shaft, the 'upcast' shaft, whose head would have to be enclosed and connected to a ventilation fan by a passage called the 'fan drift'. Any coal raised by this shaft would have to pass through air locks at the pithead and the insets (underground entrances to the shaft) so as not to short-circuit the air currents. As a result, the intention was to use mainly No. 1 shaft for coal raising. The 'Rheolaver' washery was noted for its efficiency and treated 100 tons of raw coal per hour. It separated the shale and waste from the different sizes of saleable coal. The Cooling Tower had a capacity of 240,00 gallons of water per hour. A reservoir was constructed across Rackery Lane which had a capacity of 1.5 million gallons of water.

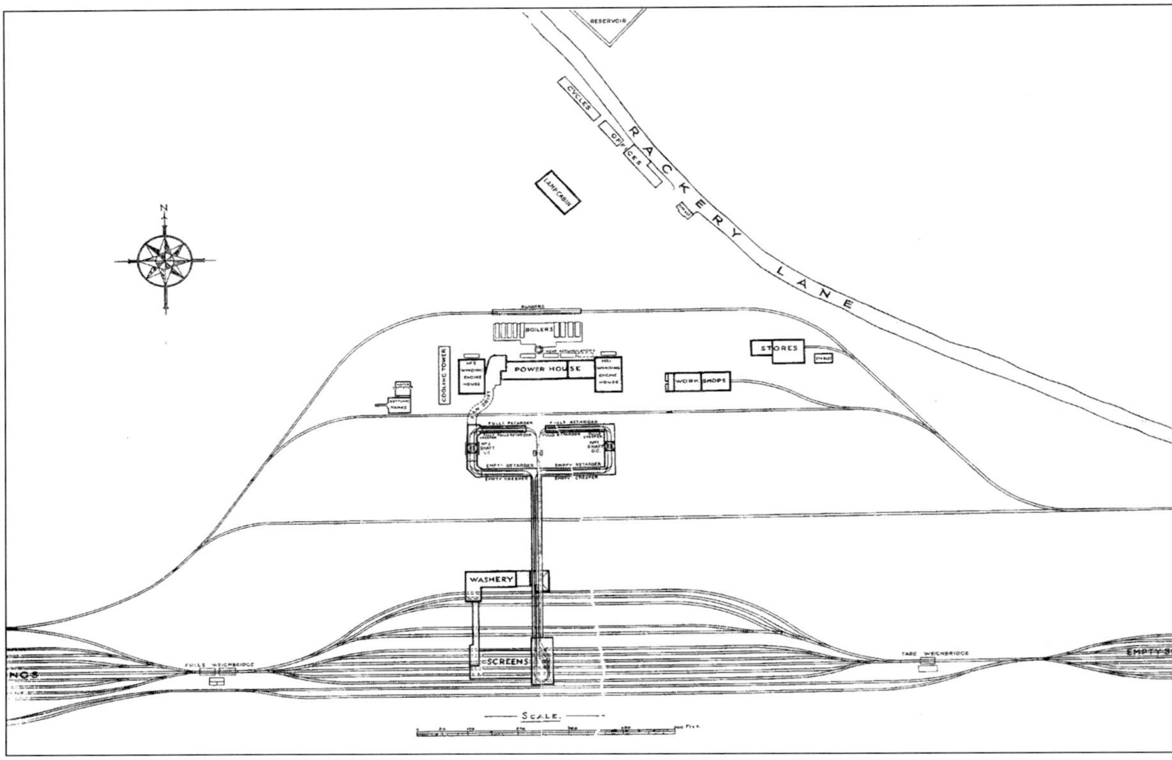

Llay Main colliery surface layout 1923[54] *[Jan Wood]*

The Brassey (otherwise called 'Quaker') seam was 48 feet above the Main Coal and the Two Yard seam was another 48 feet above that. Ideally, the seams would be worked in descending order so that the effect of mining in one seam would have minimum effect on mining in the others. At Llay, the reverse happened, resulting in worse mining conditions in the upper seams than would otherwise have been the case.[55]

During the interwar years, the coal industry suffered from massive overcapacity. The British share of the world coal market dropped from 59% to 37% and there was increased competition from other coal producing countries and from cheaper alternative energy sources. Before 1914, demand for coal had been rising at an annual rate of 4%; after the war, British exports of coal plummeted whilst domestic demand remained stagnant. It was in this climate of retreating coal sales that Llay Main started operations. Despite that, after the first coal was raised in 1922, the output from the Two Yard, Quaker (sometimes called Brassey) and Main seams rapidly increased and the local situation seemed far from desperate as the mining village began to take shape.

By April 1923, the following houses had been built: those in First Avenue (apart from some at the top on the west side), Second Avenue, Third Avenue, Fourth Avenue, Sixth Avenue, Llay Hall Avenue, Llay Place Avenue and Oak (Tree) Avenue.

The population of the village was sufficient to merit the building of a school, but the local education committee was slow to provide one and the first village school was opened in the

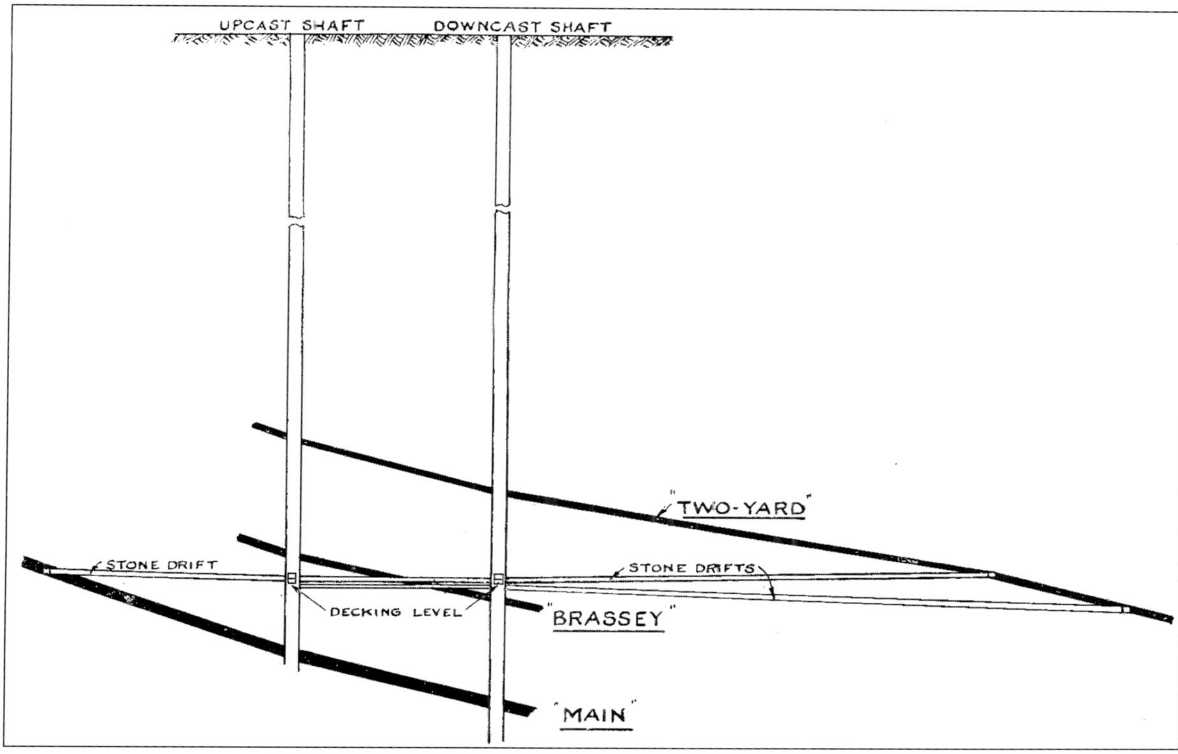

Section view of Colliery workings, 1923. This view from the side of the workings shows the dip of the three seams. *[Jan Wood]*

Plan view of Colliery workings 1923. This view shows the main underground workings as seen from above. *[Jan Wood]*

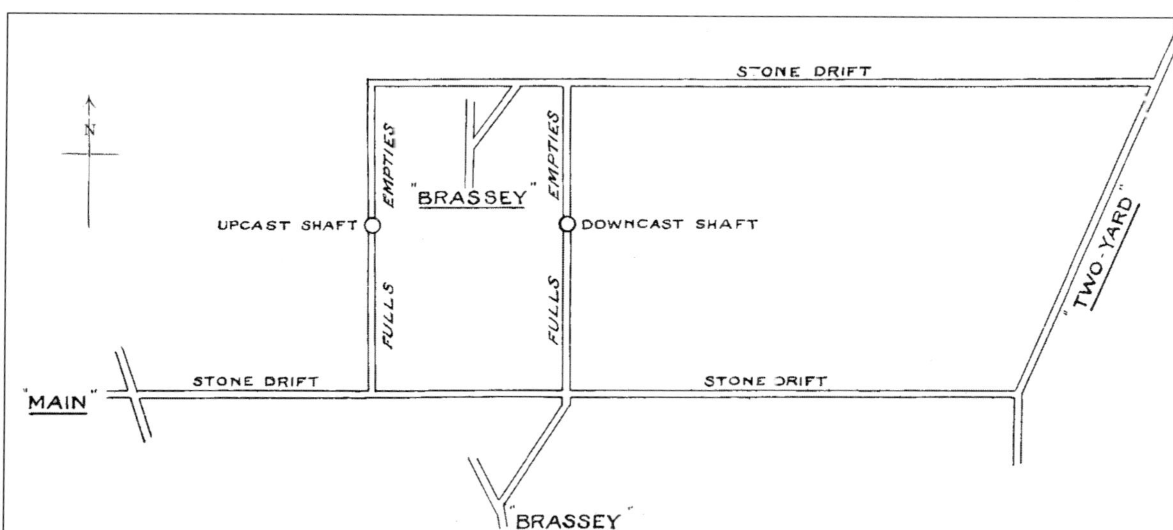

The Power House at Llay Main 1923.

The photograph shows the two generator sets and a regulator in the foreground. The nearest set is driven by a Bellis and Morcom high-speed twin crank, vertical, compound steam engine. The alternator is a relatively slow speed (probably around 300 rpm) salient-pole type manufactured in Bradford. There is a fly-wheel between the engine and the alternator and the unit on the end of the drive shaft is the DC exciter supplying the current for the field coils seen projecting from the inner wheel-like frame of the rotor. The exciter output would have been regulated from one of the units in the foreground.

The second set is a turbine alternator with a similar excitation arrangement as the first. The speed would have been 1500 rpm and the manufacturer possibly English Electric. It may well have been a mixed pressure turbine, using low pressure exhaust steam from the winding engines when available and high pressure steam from the boilers at other times. The turbine would have exhausted into a unit located below where the steam met with cold water and was condensed thus producing a vacuum of around 13 psi which augmented the inlet pressure of the turbine. The condensed water was then returned to the boilers.

Output from both sets would have been 3 phase AC, probably at 2200V and 50 cycle/sec. This seems to have been a popular voltage in the coal industry around that time. Rough estimate of ratings: Bellis set probably 250 kW, turbine set probably 1000 kW.[56] *[Rod Challoner]*

Methodist and Presbyterian churches. Olive Rogerson Williams, daughter of Edward Williams, of 3 Second Avenue, was the first pupil entered in the register on 9 April 1923. Seventy-seven pupils were admitted on the first day, their ages ranging from almost 5 years to 9 years. By the end of the month, there were 106 pupils on the roll, with just three schoolteachers appointed viz: Ceridwen Williams, aged 22; Elsie Lloyd, aged 19 (photograph figure 35) and Blodwen M. Turner, aged 19.[57] Of the three, Ceridwen (or Ceri) Williams is assumed to have held the role of head teacher as she was the only certified teacher. Facilities in the chapels must have been far from ideal, but a start had been made on the education of the village children.

Llay Main Screening Plant 1923. This screening plant was built by Messrs Plowright Bros, of Chesterfield and contained four tipplers, four picking belts, each 99 feet long, for steam, gas, house coal and nuts. Located 450 ft from the shafts. Gantries conveyed tubs to and from the screens.[58] Picking out rock and dirt from the coal was a hard job. No women were employed in this work at Llay, but Mrs Finney, wife of Albert Finney, Nant-y-Gaer Road, had been a 'pit-brow lass' in Lancashire.

> *The wagons would go to the top. From there they'd go into a revolving drum and all the coal would drop down to the conveyor belt below. There would be the screenhands picking out all the rubbish and throwing it on one side. Picking the stones from the coal was a very menial job done by surface workmen taken on specially for the job. Very often you'd get underground miners disabled in some small way – they'd take work on the screens just to get work. The pay was much lower and that (coal) was broken up eventually and thrown into the washer to be washed and sized and came out as slack or slack or doubles or various sizes of coal.*
>
> *Then the wagons came underneath and were loaded from the top by chutes, all according to the wagon [size]. They would stand there for about 3 to 4 hours to get the water out because you were sending coal to somewhere like John Summers, 20 or 30 wagons a day. When they got there they'd weigh them and by the time they'd got there 10 or 20lb of water had dropped out and there was always a complaint about excess weight.[59] [Jan Wood]*

At the colliery, coal was at long last being wound and the workforce increased to around 1,800 men. Recreational facilities for the off-duty miners became a priority and as a result the bowling green was laid out at Llay Place, a house which had a chequered history. Built in 1865 by James Hassall Ffoulkes (JP and High Sheriff in 1874) on the site of an earlier dwelling and used as his family home. It was later owned by the Clark family and was used as a preparatory boarding school for boys when the lease passed to Llay Main Colliery in 1917. The Clarks were to give not less than seven months notice to A. H. Morrison, the headmaster, whereupon 'the lessees shall be at liberty to convert and alter the said dwelling house into colliery offices or an institute.'[60] The bowling green was opened on Thursday, 8 June 1923, and an inaugural game of doubles was

The First Aerial ropeway c.1923. Initially the ropeway worked at fifty tons per hour but this was increased to ninety tons per hour in the 1950s. In the photograph full 'Llay Main' wagons are waiting to be despatched. Wagons were of either ten- or twelve-ton capacity and a variety of them would be found on site: [Rod Challoner]

> *In those days different people owned wagons which you had to pay for. You hired them. They came into the colliery yard. If they were there for 2 days you had to pay 2s 6d per day demurrage charges on wagons which didn't belong to the colliery like LMS, Brymbo Steel, Summers, Gateby Colliery, Hickleton Colliery. We used to have a man, full-time, going round booking every wagon in. They came in in hundreds. When you're getting 3,000 or 4,000 tons of coal a day … there's some coal to get away in 10 ton wagons.*[61]

played between W. L. Halpin (the managing director of the colliery), paired with Dr Morris Jones (the Llay doctor), against Revd J. Lewis Evans (the Presbyterian minister) and Mr Edward Stuart Clark.[62] The house itself was to be converted into 'an institute for employees' during the winter of 1923/4 and Charles Jones was appointed as steward and moved there from First Avenue with his wife, Jenny and son, Dyfed.

A seven-and-a-half-acre field at Llay Chain (near The Crown public house) was bought for use as football, cricket and hockey pitches. Fields near the Gwastad were also pressed into service as football pitches. The first Llay team was that of Llay Rangers[63] and a Llay Main football team, eventually to be based at the Institute, was entered the Ffrith and District League during 1921–2 but had difficulty fulfilling its fixtures because, as the club chairman put it, 'Owing chiefly to the working hours of Llay Main Colliery, it is most difficult for many of our players to turn out at match hours.'[64]

Competition to get into any of the sporting teams was strong:

> … you had to be a Yorkshireman and a deputy to get in the cricket team in the twenties! Although, I wasn't old enough then anyway. But a man named Mr Craddle was the captain, of course, he was the colliery manager! Then they found out they were getting beaten too often, so what did they do? Well, they got jobs going for good cricketers at Llay Main! That's the reason we got men from Pontblydden, Brymbo, Gwersyllt, we got the men, mostly electricians, foremen, fitters, et cetera, we had a good team to finish up, like. Much against the Yorkshiremen, they didn't care much for it because they weren't getting picked. The village Vicar, Bransby Jones, he was the star man in the team. [Mr D][65]

In August 1923, Llay Main's parent company, Hickleton Main, showed faith in their investment by increasing their capital, issuing £750,000 of 6% debenture stock to pay for developments at Hickleton, Brodsworth, Markham Main and Llay Main.[66] By this time, development of the model village for miners and their families was well under way and, in an age of desperate unemployment, Llay Main was an attractive prospect and colleagues from other colliery villages in the Wrexham area joined them in working at the new pit, many walking to work whilst waiting for a house in the village.

A second phase of house building started in 1923, extending the village towards the area then known as Pentwmpath, taking in Pentwmpath Farm, Laburnum Cottage, Beech Tree and New House Farm. Contractors for these houses were Jones & Co. of London,[67] who were given exact instructions on all aspects of their task by the architects from the Housing and Town Planning Trust acting for the Industrial Housing Association, a company set up by the colliery owners and others to build 12,000 colliery houses in Britain.[68] The typewritten specifications included:

The Lamp Room at Llay Main in 1923. The equipment for the lamp room was supplied by Oldham & Sons, Denton, Manchester.[69] There were 1,800 lamps in 1923, with capacity for a total of 3,000. The lamps were charged electrically by two Metrovick motor generators from a separate room.[70] [Jan Wood]

The first miners' institute – Llay Place in 1923. [LLHSA]

Provide a stone or slate shelf in the larder
Form brick and tile door surrounds
Cover roofs wit best second quality grey Welsh slates
Supply and fit in each garden 4′ by 4′ wrot (planed timber) deal clothes posts
Internal doors are to be Columbia Pine four panel doors
Finish walls of Living rooms with 3 1/2 ft by three quarter inch moulded chair rail
Finish walls of Living rooms and Parlours with 1 1/2 ft by 1ft moulded picture rail
Supply and fix in each house a dresser of the length shown from floor to ceiling … groove shelves for plates.
For plaster – the hair to be the best long, clean, black hair. The coarse stuff to be three parts of sand to one of lime and hair.
Kitchen ranges – fit Yorkshire ranges ('Express' added in ink)
Electric light – connect to the company's main and lay on up to house meter. Allow £7 10s per house for internal wiring and fittings
Supply in each scullery a standard pattern sink, white glazed inside and buff glazed outside
Supply in each bathroom a standard pattern cast iron bath
Supply and fit in each w.c. a standard pedestal w.c. apparatus with trap and two gallon flushing cistern.
Paint – distemper to be of one coat 'Duresco' to approved tints. (These were buff for house types F, Fg, Fgo and terra cotta for house types G and F82). No thinning materials of any kind are to be allowed on the job.

Llay Pals Football Team, 1923–4 This team played on the 22-acre field at Gwastad Farm. Back row : Albert Peters (trainer), Ted Evans, Bob Thomas, Norman Williams 'The Butcher', Teddy Lloyd, –?–, Geoff Jones 'Moors', Joe Ralphs, Dick Hughes. Middle row: Jack Taylor, Tom Sheldon, Jack 'Capper' Jones , –?–, Herb Hughes, Jack Hughes ('The Crown'), Jack Ralphs. Front row: Trevor Jones ('Rent Man'), Whit Ankers, Ben Reid, Glyn Roberts, Tommy Ivor Davies. [Graham Hughes}

> Garden walls – dwarf front brick walls 2′ 9′ high above ground level with return ends up to entries through houses. Capped with half-round bricks.
> Gates to be in oak with heavy pattern wrought iron latch.[71]

By March 1924, the second 200 houses were nearing completion and there was still optimism that many more would be added. It was felt important that there should be some differentiation between the houses. First Avenue was to be the main entrance to the village with a wide, tree-lined avenue with a view directly to the Anglican church. Houses here were larger than others and were meant for colliery officials and village dignitaries.

In March 1924, a new colliery manager, Edward Albert Hughes, was appointed and he and his wife Jennie came to live at Nant-y-Gaer Hall. Some professional classes came to the new village to live side-by-side with their clients. The electoral register of 1924 records that Dr Morris Jones lived at 9 First Avenue, Revd Bransby Jones (the Church in Wales priest) was at 26 Second Avenue and the Presbyterian minister, Revd J. Lewis Evans, at 31 Second Avenue. The doctor and religious leaders played key roles in helping to develop the new community. In the same year Robert John Roberts came to teach at the Council School and to live at 19 Shone's Lane. 'R.J.' spent his entire teaching career at Llay, where he was a faithful member of the Welsh Presbyterian Chapel and was well liked by all.[72]

The school, still being held in the Nonconformist chapels, was reorganised and a mixed or 'upper' department was added, opening on 15 September 1924 with W. Ernest Williams in charge as the temporary headmaster. He would remain in that post until the new school was built in 1926.

The new mixed department opened up to older pupils living in Llay, but who until that time had been attending at Gresford, Gwersyllt, Abermorddu, Hope, Burton, Cross Street or other local schools. The numbers were added to as each new house was finished and colliers from Wrexham, Coedpoeth, Leeswood, Cefn, Brymbo and further afield took up residence. During the first week, 144 pupils were admitted. These were added to on the 1 October when 21 pupils moved up from the lower school, leaving 126 pupils on the books of the 'lower' department. A total of 291 children were being taught in cramped conditions and the head teacher sought the opinion of the education authority as to the maximum number of pupils which could be accommodated.[73] Classrooms were separated by sliding partitions and the noise from one class could easily be heard by the neighbours which must have been a considerable distraction for both staff and pupils. In spite of this, the more able pupils were entered for an examination to gain a place at the Wrexham Grammar Schools, permission being granted to use the minister's room as a classroom for scholarship pupils. In October, the school log records what was to be a constant refrain over the years: '16 Oct 1924: A decided fall in the attendance today – many boys being engaged in harvesting potatoes. Number present: 170 morning 167 afternoon.'[74]

From the early days at the colliery, all employees at Llay were expected to be members of a trade union.[75] The relationship between management and union was generally sound; Hugh Hughes, the secretary of the North Wales Miners' Association said that the owners fought hard for their point of view in any negotiations over wages or conditions of employment, but once agreement had been reached and signed, the management could be relied upon to 'carry it out loyally.'[76] A typical negotiation occurred in 1924 when the manager, E. A. Hughes, was concerned about the excessive amount of dirt being filled into tubs. The union met to discuss the company's intention to give the men 14 days notice that they intended to abolish the miners' allowance of 25lbs which was added to the beam of the weighing machine to compensate for the dirt sent out.[77] The same meeting, held at Llay Main Colliery Offices on 6 May 1924, discussed fixing a price for North Brassey 'hand-got (pick and shovel) conveyor loaded coal'.

A miner's wages depended upon the type of work in which he was engaged and the nature of the seams. Seams had different prices and there was also a different price for 'hand-got' and 'machine-got' coal and for its haulage. To complicate matters even further, in addition to day-wage men and contractors, there were datallers, day-wage men who serviced the hewers' work. Colliers worked in 'sets', groups of about five men, each of which was allocated a section of the face and pay was dependent on the weekly output of the set. The hardest workers were paid more wages and anything that caused delay to the set's hewing, e.g. not enough props available, was treated with disdain. The following wage list is taken from the time-book:[78]

Week ending 25 October 1924

David Sides	5 shifts	£2 4s 11d
John Sides	5 shifts	£2 5s 0d
David George Sides	5 shifts	£2 5s 0d

First Avenue – Industrial Sunday parade 1929. These parades were initiated by Rev Bransby Jones around 1923. The procession wound its way through the village and was followed by a service, to which an eminent preacher was invited. Left to right: colliery officials, choir members, Edgar Williams (organist), Archdeacon W. E. Williams (Gresford), Mr *Page (manager Merediths' Stores), Revd W. Eyton Lloyd (Llay curate). John Gaskin, The Archdeacon of Montgomery, Tom Gaskin with crucifix. [Herbert Gaskin]*

Edward T. Sides	6 shifts	£2 12s 6d
Joe Fisher	5 shifts	£2 4s 11d

Dead Work

4 yards ripping at 7s 9d
4 yards ripping at 6s 9d
3 strechers at 1s Cd
1 casting out at 6s 4d
3 of dirt at 8d

I am indebted to Keith Folwell for the following interpretation of the above:

It would appear that the time sheet refers to a group of men working in the same set engaged on a particular task. In this case there were generally four men working in the same set, two on afternoon shift and two on day shift or night shift. In those days there were five afternoon shifts per week and six shifts each on day or night shift.

David and John Sides worked the afternoon shift and David George and Edward T. Sides worked the day or night shift. However, Joe Fisher was the substitute for one shift for David George Sides – probably on Saturday.

In addition to the requirements of the particular job these men carried out additional work called dead work which was paid for as a price per yard of advance or per timber set etc. Dead work refers to work performed outside the normal contract. Driving is usually associated with tunnelling in coal, ripping is the enlargement of an existing road, stretchers are timbers between the walls of a tunnel or roadway, casting out is shovelling material (coal or stone) to a place where it can be loaded onto a conveyer or into a tub and was paid for at a flat rate of 6s 5d per shift, payment for dirt was 8d per unit.

I do not know what these units were but it could have been an additional payment per ton or per tub for handling dirt rather than coal! It is not clear why the total pay/man/per shift varied in some cases but was probably due to different deductions for such things as tools, explosives etc. Actual earnings/shift for each man in the set would have been identical.[79]

At about 1.15 a.m. on Friday, 5 December 1924, an explosion occurred near the 17s face of the North Two Yard District. Two men were working on the face, about 200 yards on the return side of the N°. 17 gateway, when they heard a slight noise and felt a difference in air pressure which was followed by a cloud of dust. Three other men working on a roadway about 300 yards from the explosion had a similar experience. All five made their way out towards the shaft.[80] It was soon established that nine men had been killed. Three hundred men were working on the night shift, mainly engaged in repair work. Had the accident occurred during the day shift, coal-getting would have been in full swing and around 180 men would have been in the vicinity of the explosion.

The first bodies to be found were those of Isaac Evans, a hauling-engine attendant, and John William Hughes, a filler. They were close to a compressed air hauling engine and both were badly burned. Close to the bodies were two electric safety lamps lying on the floor, both of which were still working, but a flame safety lamp (N°. 324) that was hanging nearby, was extinguished. Twenty yards further were found the bodies of William Ernest Williams, a fireman, and John Humphries, a road repairer. The fireman's safety lamp (N°. 506) was found two yards further up and was not lit. Close to him there was a low-tension firing battery and the end of a shot cable, two yards away. The battery key and a detonator box, containing seventeen detonators, was found close to the bodies. The cable was afterwards found to extend about twenty yards to the N°. 17 face where one or more shots had been fired in the ripping, five yards back from the coal.[81]

Several rescue teams were now available and in due course all the bodies except one were found within the next thirteen yards or in N° 6 gate to the left. The ninth body was recovered the following day from under a roof fall. Williams had probably been sheltering in a slight recess next to a chock while he fired the fatal shot and had been able to move a short distance after the explosion.[82]

Geoff Bellis, a colliery secretary at the time of the incident, said:

> I was there all day long. I spent most of my time with Harry Gabriel – going to Mrs Jones's on Rackery lane, the chauffeur's wife. She was making sandwiches and pots of tea all day long and this Gabriel and me were going across to the pit top and sending it down to the rescue teams until I don't know what time. The last thing I remember is going on the telephone. I was taking calls saying 'Yes there's been an explosion here, some have been killed, how many I'm not sure. There was a big headline next morning in the paper neither confirmed nor denied – the number of men killed is unknown.[83]

The men killed were:

Isaac Evans, aged 19, of 45 Garden Place, Mold.
Joseph Reginald Evans, aged 35, of The Cottage, Abermorddu, who was married with two children.
Robert Percival Evans, aged 32, of Oak Mount, Cefn-y-Bedd (brother of Joseph Reginald Evans).
Thomas Charles Fletcher, aged 43, of the Bridge Inn, Mold.

NORTH WALES GUARDIAN, FRIDAY, DECEMBER 5, 1924

Appalling Mine Disaster.

Explosion at Llay Main: Nine Victims.

Relief Fund Opened: Mayor of Wrexham's £50.

North Wales Guardian, *5 December 1924. [LLHSA]*

> Edward Henry German, aged 15, of 14 Springfield Terrace, Rhosddu. He was found dead sitting by his haulage engine with his hand on the lever. The report in the *North Wales Guardian* of 5 December 1924 stated that he was 'a cheery youngster who was much liked by his workmates' and in the words of one who knew him, 'he seemed to have died with a smile on his lips.'[84]
> John William Hughes, aged 22, of 35 Shone's Lane, Llay.
> John Humphries, aged 53, of Maeshafn.
> Henry Jones, aged 36, of 6 Oak Tree Avenue, Llay. He was married with one child.
> William Ernest Williams, aged 41, of 6 Fourth Avenue, Llay. He was the fireman of the district and was married with seven children aged from 20 to 2 years old.

The local clergy did all they could to comfort the bereaved families and Revd Bransby Jones (Anglican), Revd J. Lewis Evans (Presbyterian) and Revd R. Lewis Jenkins (Primitive Methodist) visited them in their homes.

The inquest into the men's deaths was held at the colliery between 22 and 24 December before Llewellyn Kenrick, Coroner for East Denbighshire, who was assisted by assisted by D. H. F. Matthews (Senior Inspector of Mines) and A. D. Nicholson (Divisional Inspector of Mines, Lancashire, Cheshire and North Wales Mines District). Representing Llay Main Colliery were H. E. Allen (secretary of the North Wales Coal Owners Association), Sidney L. Criddle (the new manager at Llay Main) and Arthur G. Price (undermanager). Representing the miners' interests were the North Wales Miners Association's solicitor Cyril O. Jones, Thomas Rowlands (President), Edward Hughes (General Secretary), Hugh Hughes (Financial Secretary) and others. Evidence was taken from the following witnesses:

> Wilfred Slater Hayes, head lamp man
> Samuel Challoner, timber man
> Edward Albert Hughes, colliery manager
> Herbert Glyn Davies, surveyor
> David Harold Dunnico, head ambulance man
> John Charles Williams, night overman
> John Matthews, night overman

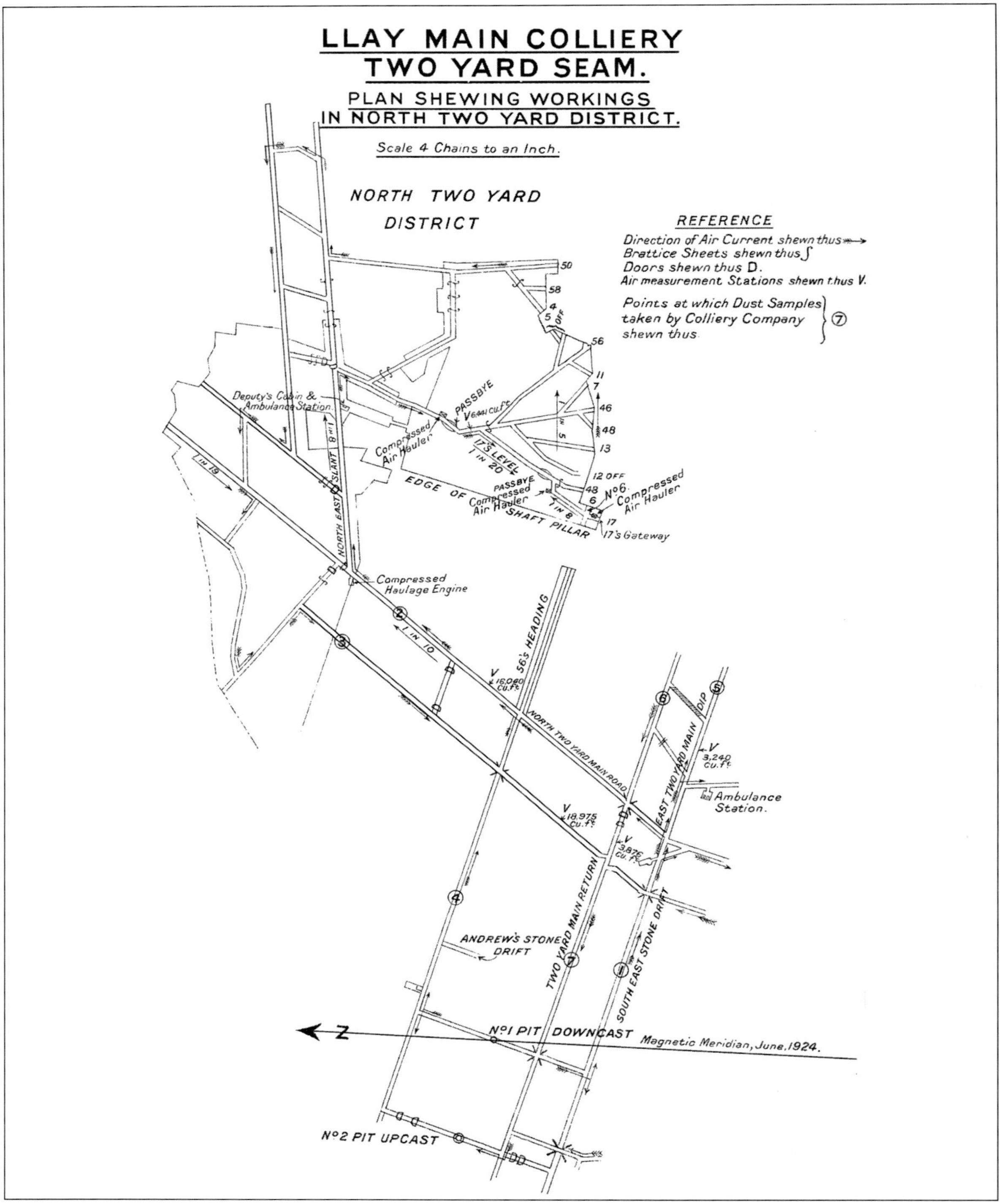

Plan of the Two-Yard Seam workings in 1924. [North of England Institute of Mining and Mechanical Engineers]

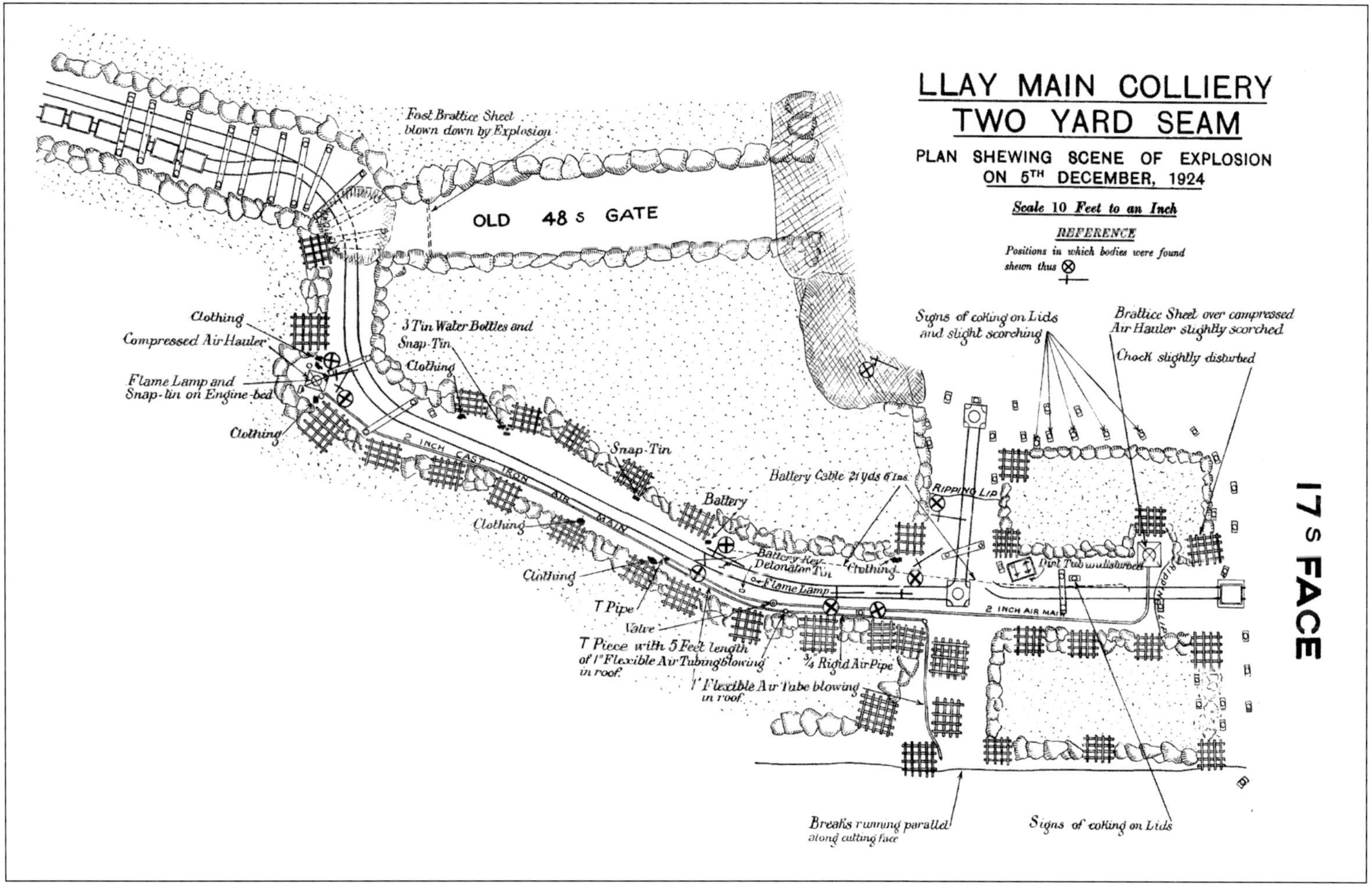

Diagram of the accident scene 5 December 1924. (Locations shown are referred to in the text.)
[North of England Institute of Mining and Mechanical Engineers]

Charles Richardson, 12 Third Avenue, fireman of afternoon shift
Dr Morris Jones, who certified the causes of death as carbon monoxide (known as afterdamp) poisoning and the effects of the explosion
John David Matthews, lamp man
Alfred Davies, lamp man
Henry Charles Owens, storekeeper

The proceedings were opened on Saturday afternoon and the Coroner's opening remarks included his view that 'They all lost their lives instantaneously and in the same manner' and that he therefore would take the evidence regarding the death of the deputy (William Ernest Williams) and to 'assume that I have heard the evidence with regard to the remaining men.'[85]

The first two witnesses called were Samuel Challoner and Harold Dunnico. Challoner, a timber man, said:

> I came to the lamp station and examined the lamps and then we went down to the Two-yard seam. I saw William Ernest Williams (the fireman) at the pit bottom. He told us to go to the two trucks of girders – about 400 or 500 yards from the pit bottom. He told us to load these two trolleys … we went about 80 yards below the place where the accident occurred and we waited about a quarter of an hour, waiting for wagons to put some debris in … We were there a short time and heard a shot and a rumbling in the roof – it was a quarter past one in the morning. We went in the direction of the pit bottom for assistance. We came back along the South N° 10 where the accident occurred and me and my partner saw Ellis Hughes and I advised him to go up and see for further help.[86]

On reaching the pit bottom Sam Challoner met Harold Dunnico, the head ambulance man, who was doing his rounds. They returned to thr 17s face to find out what had happened and see what could be done. In his report to the coroner Dunnico said:

> I went in with Challoner afterwards and removed some tubs, and then we saw a gas lamp lit on the engine. That was in. We got to the fall and removed one or two pieces of debris and got through about two or three yards the other side of the fall and saw a lamp. The fall was between two and three tons. We got through the fall under the girder. We went after about five yards – the lamp was three yards away – we saw an electric lamp – lit. The next thing we found was a body which was about a yard and a half away – nearer the fall. It was Isaac Evans. He was dead. I knelt down to examine the body because it was covered in dirt. I just had a look at it, to make sure, and I thought he was dead, and I told the others to clear out now and take the lamp, and we would see the officials. I did not move any bodies at all. I just examined the first one and came out and reported what happened. I did not know how much danger there was further ahead, and discretion was the better part of valour.[87]

The other witnesses were called and some recalled to clarify certain points of fact. In the end the jury returned the verdict that death was caused by carbon monoxide poisoning, together with shock due to the explosion. The official report into this incident, entitled *Report on the Causes and of the Circumstances attending the Explosion which occurred at the Llay Main Colliery, Wrexham, Denbighshire on the 5 December 1924*, was written by Arthur D. Nicholson, HM Divisional Inspector of Mines and presented to Parliament as Command Document 2365 in 1925. It covered ventilation issues, explosives and shotfiring, stone dusting and safety lamps. He concluded that a shot in

Llay Main Colliery underground officials at Nottingham in 1930.(Names in heavy type were witnesses at the coroner's inquiry.) Back row: E. Williams; P. Hughes; J. S. Love; D. Davies; E. Thomas; G. A. Folwell; ***J. Matthews****; U. Davies, J.B. Ellis. Third row: J. Evans; J. Morris; S. Gilham;* ***J. C. Williams****; R. Roberts; T. Price Jones; Parry Davies. Second row: W. H. Pritchard; E. Barnes;* ***D. H. Dunnico****; A. Hardy; H. Pevah; W. Rogers; D. C. Owen; L. Davies.Seated: R. J. Roberts; R. Robinson; T. W. Mottram (manager); H. O. Ball; A. Davenport;* ***H. G. Davies****.*

the 'bind' coal at the right side of Nº 17 gate had been fired and that the coal got down was mostly cleared so that a new 'backover turn' into Nº 6 could be laid. After this, a breaking-in shot in the metal above the 'bind' coal was fired at the right side of the gate. Firedamp (mainly methane gas), which had accumulated in the roof cavity formed by this second shot, was ignited by the firing of the third shot which in turn ignited a larger amount of firedamp which had accumulated in the open break by the shaft pillar on the high side of Nº 17 gateway. This latter gas had emanated from the Powell coal, 12 feet above the 'Two Yard', seam having got in by the break alongside the shaft pillar. The night overman, John Charles Williams, brother of William Ernest Williams, the shot firer who was killed in the disaster, and Charles Richardson, were emphatic that there had been no gas in the district on the two shifts before the explosion. Firedamp had been been reported in the North Two Yard District on 16 and 26 November, and in both cases, was found on the right, or higher, side of the Nº 17 gateway, against the shaft pillar. On these occasions compresed air, used to drive the haulage engines, was used to ventilate the break near the shaft pillar. It was an easy way of overcoming a difficulty but no 'brattice' (ventilation control) was erected to supply extra air to the break. Nicholson suggested that the clearing of the gas by using exhaust air on the 16 November had lulled the men into a false sense of security and that this was inadequate.

> I am satisfied that if a brattice sheet had been erected at N°. 6 gate and another at N°. 17 gate, the ventilation of the high side where the roof break existed would have been much more adequate. The canvas doors or sheets in the N°s. 46 and 48 gates should have been doubled. The fast side corner at the face of N°. 17 was the highest point in the whole district, and if gas was to be found in the district, this would have been the most likely place to find it.[88]

Immediately after the disaster, the Mayor of Wrexham, Councillor Owen. E. Rickman, opened a Relief Fund with £50 and hoped to raise a four-figure sum by Christmas. Arrangements were made for banks in Wrexham and the Borough Treasurer's Office to collect the donations. Concerts were organised at venues in the Wrexham area. Local bands, choirs and soloists performed at the Glyn Cinema and the Select Picture House, and the proprietors of the Derby Cinema in Caergwrle gave the total proceeds of an evening's performance.

Coal mining was an extremely dangerous occupation and deaths at collieries in the Wrexham area were not infrequent. A letter to the *Wrexham Leader* of 2 January 1925 from 'T.H.R. of Southsea' asked for general relief for all fatalities (not just disasters) and stated 'the dependents of the man killed in Gatewen this week should be treated the same as the dependents of those unfortunate men of Llay Main.' The same newspaper reported that the Mayor's fund 'was provisionally closed on Monday last, the amount being £1,137' – not much for the widows and fatherless children to share. One wonders why the fund closed so soon, less than one month after the catastrophe? On Christmas morning, a united service was held in the Presbyterian Church conducted by the pastor Revd J. Lewis Evans, assisted by W. Crewe and T. Millington of the Methodist Church.

To date, there is no memorial to the miners who were killed in the Llay Disaster of 5 December 1924.

After ministering to the needs of his parishioners during the crisis, the Revd Bransby Jones had a new church as a focal point for their worship. On Saturday, 21 February 1925 the Church of St Martin was consecrated by the Archbishop of Wales and Llay became a chapelry of Gresford Parish.[89]

Interior view of St Martin's Church c.1950. *[Graham Hughes]*

Primitive Methodist Church, Second Avenue, stone laying c.1923. [Greville Williams]

The new church was designed by R. T. Beckett of Treuddyn and was built by Peter Edwards of Dodleston on a prime site, directly facing First Avenue. The foundation stone was laid on Sunday, 11 November 1923, by Kathleen Francis Allington Hughes of Gresford. As with the Presbyterian and Methodist Churches, the land was donated by the colliery company.

In Second Avenue, the Llay Methodists also had a splendid new church. By the end of 1925 their pastor, the Revd R. Lewis Jenkins was given his own chapel. The Primitive Methodist Church, or 'The Prim' as it was always called, came under the Chester Methodist second circuit and many of those who preached there came from that city. The Methodists preached strict temperance and members were encouraged to 'sign the pledge' not to touch any alcohol. Samuel Crewe and his family were great supporters of this church from the time when services were held at the tiny Ewle chapel on the Gresford road.

When still recovering from the disaster, the colliery faced another crisis as increased foreign competition from more efficient collieries led to a further downturn in coal exports from Britain while the domestic market remained static. Throughout the industry, wages made up two-thirds or three-quarters of the cost of the coal, which meant that employers attempted to cut costs by asking the workforce to work longer hours for less pay.[90] At Llay Main, the colliery owners requested that the men accept a reduced 'price list', the document which summarised their pay for different tasks. On Tuesday, 26 May, a meeting of 1,000 Llay miners at the pit appointed a deputation to negotiate on the new price list, but the whole committee was summoned to meet the manager and William Humble, one of the directors of the Llay Main Colliery Company Ltd. Hugh Hughes, the General Secretary of the North Wales Miners' Association, said that, 'The Llay Main Committee had received nothing less than an ultimatum.'

Negotiations, which began on 27 May, were concerned with the proposal to fix an inclusive price for work on the 'Brassey' and 'Two Yard' faces.[91] Hugh Hughes spoke to Arthur Cook, Secretary of the Miners Federation of Great Britain and asked about national support for the Llay men. He was told that the National Executive Committee had decided not to take up the 'question

William Horsley Humble, director of Llay Main Colliery. Humble was said to be concerned about the welfare of the miners and about safety. He was also a director of Doncaster Amalgamated Collieries.[95] *[Nick Humble]*

of local troubles'. As 510 collieries had gone out of production since January 1924, each district would have to overcome its own local difficulties.[92]

The average rate of pay at the coal face in Llay Main was 13s 6d per shift. Miners were being asked to accept a 50% reduction – 6s 9d per shift. They were told that the company was losing 3s per ton and was prepared to take a loss of 1s a ton because the colliery was only at the development stage. The miners committee rejected the proposal, but decided to negotiate with the colliery owners. Hugh Hughes said that at Llay Main the output per shift was 2 tons 10 cwt compared with 1 ton 12 cwt for the average in north Wales pits – an increase of 18 cwts per man shift at Llay.[93] On 8 June, the Llay Main colliers met and decided not to allow their representatives to negotiate with management on the price reduction and the colliery was closed by the owners on 13 June.[94]

The distress caused to families was immediate as there were no unemployment payments available. Application was made to the local authority to pay relief to the families of unemployed men and by early July, F. T. Cheatham, the relieving officer, had received 120 applications for relief from married men who were out of employment owing to the temporary closure of Llay Main. It was unanimously decided to pay 10s to the wives, plus the children's allowances (8s 6d for the first child, 5s for the second child, 4s for the third and subsequent children) The relief was to be in kind but the

Wrexham Leader, *19 June 1925. [North Wales Media Ltd]*

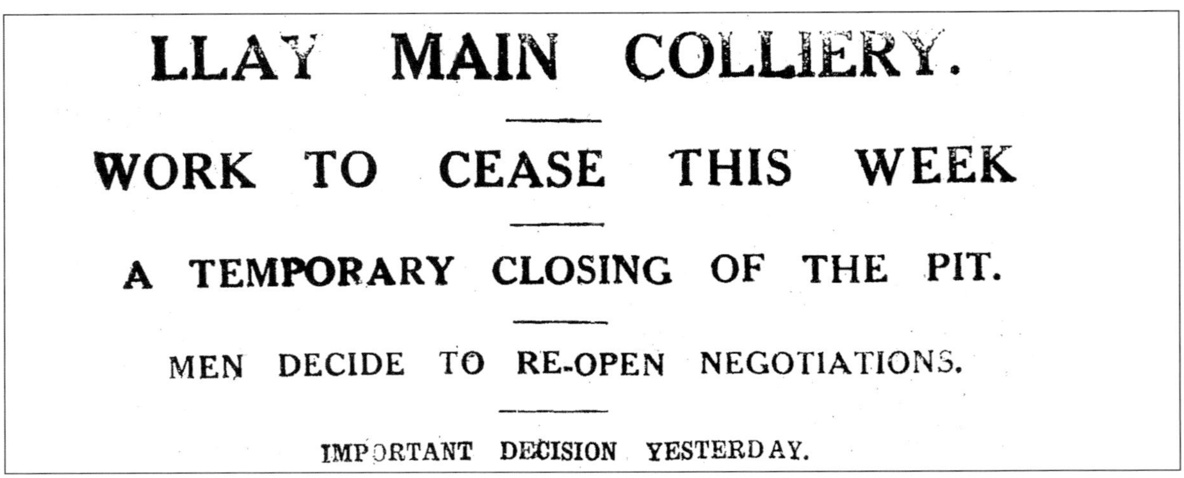

LLAY MAIN COLLIERY.

WORK TO CEASE THIS WEEK

A TEMPORARY CLOSING OF THE PIT.

MEN DECIDE TO RE-OPEN NEGOTIATIONS.

IMPORTANT DECISION YESTERDAY.

recipients could obtain it at shops of their own choice. The relief paid was, however, to be recoverable from those who received it.[96]

On the morning of the 30 June, Llay schoolchildren were fed for the first time in the Pavilion, one of the sinkers' huts on Rackery Lane which had been converted into a social centre in around 1918. The school log stated that the 'Headmaster did not arrive in school for afternoon session until 2.15 due to having to attend to the feeding of children at the Pavilion.'[97]

> Owing to the industrial situation, the outlook in the village is daily becoming more serious. Through the efforts of Dr R. Morris Jones and Mrs Jones, a band of willing workers have secured the pavilion, and have converted the same into a soup kitchen, which has been welcomed by many. Appeals for subscriptions to carry on the work have been circulated in the district, and up to the present £40 has been handed to Dr R. Morris Jones, who has volunteered his services as treasurer. The need for further contributions, whether in money or kind, is great.[98]

On the evening of 30 June, an open-air public meeting, under the auspices of the Labour Party, was held in the Market Square, Llay, to discuss the question of unemployment benefit. A special platform for speakers had been erected from which addresses were given by Wesley Hooley, E. Hodgkinson and Mr Haynes 'the Post Office'. A letter had been forwarded to the Minister of Labour. It was proposed to invite Mr C. P. Williams, MP, to speak at the next meeting which was to be held within a few days.[99] On the same evening, the school managers met at the Presbyterian church. Present were: Dr G. Harrison, JP; Miss K. Allington Hughes, JP; Dr R. Morris Jones; Mr Richard Jarvis and the Revd J. Lewis Evans (correspondent). Discussion centred around the industrial situation and the managers were unanimously in favour of bringing into operation the Act for providing meals for school children. They foresaw a worsening situation and the voluntary effort of feeding the children as rapidly becoming exhausted. They stated that '… the area from which voluntary contributions can be gathered is very limited. Ninety-five per cent of the community are unable to contribute.'[100] The reply from the Ministry of Labour to the local Labour Party was swift and to the effect that the day-wage men, who were not involved in the dispute, had their claim to unemployment benefit approved but were only entitled to benefit for 4½ weeks. About 750 colliers failed in their applications because they alone were involved in the decision to reject the new price rates.[101]

Early in July a demonstration of around 500 miners marched from Llay to Wrexham to draw attention to their plight. Led by the colliery band and with the village priest the Revd Bransby Jones and the village doctor, Dr Morris Jones at the head of the procession. They moved on to the workhouse and demanded to be admitted as they had no means to be fed at home. The workhouse managers asked them to await a decision on their unemployment benefit, but the Llay miners entered the workhouse nevertheless as a gesture of defiance.[102]

On 13 July, the headmaster, William Ernest Williams, was informed by Denbighshire Local Education Authority that they did not intend to make provisions for either food or footwear to needy cases. In those days children could not attend school without footwear. On 28 July, the headmaster noted that, 'owing to the industrial dispute the number on books shows a daily decline.'[103] Voluntary efforts were redoubled and concerts were held in Llay and Wrexham to support the distress fund.

A further public meeting was held by the Labour Party on 5 August, again in the square opposite St Martin's Church. The speakers were: Robert Richards (the prospective Labour candidate for East Denbighshire); Mr Emlyn Rogers, BA, Bangor; W. Hooley, Llay and A. R. Davies, Rhos. A large crowd was present to hear the speakers deal with the minimum-wage question and that 'A most successful meeting terminated by singing 'Guide me, O Thou Great Jehovah' to the tune *Rhondda*.'[104]

Families continued to leave the village and, when the schools reopened on 3 September, it was noted that a large number of children were absent having left the district owing to the closing of the colliery. The attendance was down and in many cases due to children being without footwear. On 11 September, falling pupil numbers caused Classes VI and VII to amalgamate under the charge of R. J. Roberts. The number on registers continued to show a daily decline due to the industrial situation.[105]

There seemed to be no end to the crisis as, on 18 September, a further meeting of the colliers of Llay Main held at the Pavilion unanimously resolved not to return to work on the terms offered by the owners. The pit had now been idle for thirteen weeks.[106] Owing to the delay on the part of the Education Authority to provide footwear for children to attend school, a clog fund was inaugurated by the school teachers and on 19 October, 127 pairs of clogs were distributed for needy cases. These were provided by the Llay Voluntary Relief Fund.[107] The crisis was not to last much longer and on Thursday, 29 October, a ballot at the pithead was held resulting in an agreement to return to work. The men had agreed to accept the newly negotiated price list.[108] A letter from Sidney Criddle, the new mine manager, informed Mr Matthews, HM Inspector of Mines, that 'I am pleased to tell you our pit will be resuming work on Sunday night, 1 November.'[109]

The winter of 1925/6 was exceptionally snowy and getting about proved difficult. By February 1926, the low attendance of pupils at the Council School was being blamed on 'minor illnesses due a certain extent to the poor footwear worn by many children and the deplorable state of the roads.'[110] The roads were so bad that children could not get up to the Mission Room at Llay Chain for cookery lessons. It would be some time before the New Road to Wrexham was built, but at the colliery a major change was about to occur.

In March 1926, the Carlton Main Colliery Company, owners of a number of collieries in the South Yorkshire coalfield, including Carlton, Grimethorpe & Frickley Collieries, bought the shares of Llay Main Colliery from the Hickleton Main Colliery Company. The reasons for the sale are not clear, but market conditions were unfavourable and, after one lengthy strike at Llay, there was the threat of another of possibly greater length in the air. Having invested so much capital in the enterprise (£1 million had been spent in the sinking of the pit), could the Markham companies have recouped their outlay after only three years of production? The *Colliery Guardian* stated:

> The Llay Main Colliery, the biggest pit in North Wales employing 3,000 men, is sold by the owners Hickleton Main to their neighbours Carlton Main Colliery Co Ltd and their subsidiary Rea Ltd. This will enable Hickleton to concentrate their operations in the south Yorkshire coalfield.[111]

Earlier, in 1919, the Carlton Main Company had already taken a controlling interest in Rea

Ltd, the Liverpool coal factors who had a large stake in Llay Main.[112] Apart from the new directors, colliery personnel stayed as they were and the manager, E. A. Hughes, remained in his position. Not long after the change of ownership, the colliery was again involved in a long stoppage of work.

In June 1925, the National Coal Owners' Association (NCOA) announced that they intended to reduce the miner's wages. The Trades Union Congress (TUC) stated that they would support the miners in their dispute and the Conservative government was forced to intervene to avoid a general strike. This they did by providing a subsidy to bolster the miners' pay, but this was to last for only nine months. A Royal Commission, the Samuel Commission, was set up to look at the problems in the mining industry and its report came out in March 1926. The conclusion was not favourable to the miners as it proposed a reduction in wages. In the same month, the NCOA tabled new terms of employment which included an extension of the seven-hour working day, district wage-agreements and a reduction in the wages of all miners. Depending on a variety of factors, the wages would be cut by up to 25%. There would be no negotiations, if the miners did not accept the new terms they would be locked out of the pits from 1 May.

In line with all other collieries in the country, work stopped at Llay Main at 9 p.m. on Friday, 30 April.[113] On 1 May, the TUC met and declared that a General Strike, 'in defence of miners' wages and hours', was to begin. Despite desperate attempts to reach agreement with the Conservative government and the mine-owners, the strike went ahead.

Colliery officials in front of N° 1 shaft in 1926. Throughout the strike of 1926, colliery officials worked to maintain the underground workings although no coal was produced. Billy Biggins (top left) was the assistant engineer. Tom Price Jones is in the middle row seventh from left. Dick Williams is in the front row fourth from left. [Michael Adams]

On 4 May, the Llay Strike Committee held a meeting at the Holly Bush in Cefn-y-Bedd at 11 a.m. to decide on the arrangements for who would work to keep the pit sound. The following Saturday, 8 May, Labour Day, the Llay miners held a demonstration when, led by the colliery band, they marched to Wrexham. The route took them through Cefn-y-Bedd, Gwersyllt, Rhosrobin, Rhosddu then via Grosvenor Road, Regent Street, Hope Street and High Street, to the Beast Market.[114]

The next day was designated as an Industrial Sunday by St Martin's, and the Revd Studdert Kennedy, otherwise known as 'Woodbine Willie the Chaplain of the Trenches', gave a powerful oration from the pulpit. The content of his message is not known, but it left its mark on the miners leaders who were present. The preacher was known to have Conservative views and Albert Jones, the Llay miners' Llay Lodge President, described the event as being a 'wash out'. Albert recorded in his diary that on 10 May, 'Woodbine Willie held a small meeting at Llay Pavilion at 10.30 p.m. to 11 p.m. to explain the mess he made on Sunday on Political Propaganda in the Pulpit re Strike.'[115]

On 12 May, the General Strike was called off, but the miners continued to be in dispute. At Llay names were taken at the Pavilion of those miners who would eligible for the small amount of union pay and payouts started on 14 May. The Wrexham Board of Guardians increased the amount of relief for wives and children which was distributed in kind by the Salvation Army from Hightown Barracks in Wrexham.[116] During May, Arthur Cook, Secretary of the Miners' Federation, travelled to a number of pits in Denbighshire and Flintshire and attracted large crowds with his rhetoric in favour of strike action.[117]

The strike had affected all workers in the major industries and transport. The trains had stopped running and some teachers could not get to Llay school. Once more, children needed to be fed and their experience during the 1925 strike helped the school to implement the necessary arrangements. The Llay Voluntary Relief Fund was established and a soup kitchen was set up at the Pavilion where meals for children were served by the teachers who had also set up a fund for footwear. The school log records that on 2 June 'Provision of Meals for Necessitous children' was put into operation 'owing to the poverty prevalent due to industrial crisis'. Eighty children were supplied with dinner in school, prepared by voluntary workers and served by the staff. Breakfast was provided at 8.30 a.m. and dinner at noon. As the days passed, so many children attended for feeding that up to two hours were taken up for the mid-day meal.[118]

A slight distraction for the Llay union men was provided by the visit to Wrexham of HRH Prince Henry, Duke of Gloucester. Two permits were delivered on the 9 June for officials to see the duke open the new Wrexham & East Denbighshire War Memorial Hospital on the same day. A deputation of union men asked for relief to be paid out in Llay instead of Wrexham and this was granted with the first payments being made on 17 June.[119]

On 21 June, the miners' Seven Hours Act was suspended for five years and the following month the mine-owners announced new terms of employment for miners based on the 8-hour day. The miners were furious about what had happened and the strike continued.

The office staff had to do the work demanded by the Management, such as watchmen, stokers in the boiler house, cleaners in the power house and the servicing of miners' lamps in the lamp room. Jobs to which I was directed included the stoke-hole; pushing full tubs of coal into the tipplers where the contents were unloaded onto a moving conveyor belt below for deleterious material to be extracted by other office staff. I should say that some coal getting was carried out by the underground officials for colliery consumption. Other work I was detailed to perform consisted of oiling the winding wheels on top of the headgears; examining the water pumps in the sump and one inset in the shaft side some 50 or so feet below the surface winding level.[120]

The villagers did their best to cope with the crisis. A series of open air concerts was held in the Market Square:

Another open air concert, was held on Thursday evening, at the Market Square, under the auspices of the Industrial Christian Fellowship. Mr Haynes, the Post Office, presided over a large audience, and the Rev B. Jones accompanied the soloists. The Llay Main Colliery Silver Band were in attendance, under the conductorship of Mr James Smith. The band opened with a quick march 'Always Ready,' and a miscellaneous programme was sustained … More artistes are required to support these free concerts, and those who wish to take part are requested to communicate with Mr Robert Thomas, 18 Second Avenue.[121]

At this time, their children were missing school in order to pick coal from the colliery waste. Many did not have footwear. At the end of the month, William Ernest Williams ended his work

Llay School Infants Class in July 1926. This photograph was taken outside the Presbyterian church which was used as the infants school at this time. The teacher on the right is Miss Luke. Gordon MacDonald is on the back row second from the left. The Hilton twins Eileen and Norma are in the middle of the second row and Percy Rogers is third from the left on the front. The boy on the extreme left is wearing clogs, but most others in this row have boots. [Gordon MacDonald]

as temporary head teacher at the school. A new school had been built and would be ready to receive pupils after the summer break.[122]

The strike wore on and, at the beginning of August, there were thoughts of bringing out the 'doggies' (haulage foremen) and the company offered to discuss new prices for 'Main' and 'Two Yard' hand-got conveyor coal. This came to nothing and it was ruled in order for the 'doggies' to carry on work. The unity of the miners was sorely tested and in desperation some decided to accept the poor terms and return to their pits. In some collieries miners were made better offers to tempt them back to work and at Llay Main, on 11 August, there was an unexpected offer of favourable terms from the management. The Llay miners were offered the maintenance of a seven-hour day and no reduction in pay.[123] Some returned to work, but others were still against any settlement and there was friction between the two groups on 12 August after the first shift's winding. The Strike Committee decided to hold a general meeting on Saturday, 14 August to deal with this and settle any outstanding issues. This mass meeting at Llay included speeches by Hugh Hughes, the miners' agent, J. Williams and M. Forshaw who explained who explained what might happen next and the miners present decided to stand firm and carry on with the strike.

By now, families were in a desperate situation. Children were being sent to live with relatives out of the area especially to those with non-mining occupations. Under these dire circumstances, men continued to drift back to work. On 16 August, Albert Jones was on picket duty until 3 p.m. to persuade any 'blacklegs' to turn back. The next day, feelings were running high at the pickets and the pithead meeting was broken up by the police who allowed a short speech by Robert Jones, the Llay union delegate, and those who were working voted to stop. On 26 August, he was sent to the Soviet Union – there had been reports of Russian money being available for the miners strike funds.[124]

The degree of hardship being experienced by families is exemplified by the parents' inability to provide for the basic needs of their children. The new Council School at Llay first admitted pupils in August 1926, but this event was set against a backdrop of misery.

> Several mothers came up during the week to explain the absences of their children viz. their inability owing to strained circumstances to provide footwear. Twelve children were given vouchers entitling them to boots through the generosity of Mr Aston of Wrexham.[125]

The creation of a purpose-built, all-age school in Llay had been first mooted in June 1921. Land for building the school was bought from the Llay Housing Association at the same price they paid the colliery company for it[126] and the school was designed by Walter. D. Wiles, the county architect, and built by W. E. Samuel of Wrexham. The quality of the stone (from a quarry at Grinshill in Shropshire) used for the building was called into question at a discussion by the Denbighshire Education Committee on 14 May 1925, where it was said to be inferior to Cefn stone. The meeting, however, concluded that the Grinshill stone was to be used as:

> They were spending money on cutting stone on a school not expected to last beyond the life of Llay Main Colliery – and that was 80 to 100 years.[127]

The new Council School first received pupils on 31 August 1926 and the school log book stated

Staff Llay Council School, 1926

William Evan Williams	Headteacher	
Mr Mulvey	Certified Male Teacher (CMT)	Class VI
Owen Jones	CMT	Class IVa
Mr R J Roberts	Uncertified Male Teacher	Class IIIa
Miss Ethel Jones	Certified Woman Teacher (CWT)	Class V
Miss Morse Jones	CWT	Class IVb
Miss Mary Luke	CWT	Class VI
Miss Mildred Edwards	CWT	Class I
Miss Bertha Williams	Uncertified Woman Teacher (UWT)	Class IVb
Miss Woodfine	UWT	Class II

– 'the Teachers and children re-assembled at the New Schools at 9.a.m. on August 31st.'

During September, the pickets continued to be set at the colliery and meetings were held at the Presbyterian Church, now available in the daytime as its role as the village school had ended. Terms were offered and rejected. A mass meeting of the North Wales Miners' Lodges was held at Gwersyllt on Saturday 11 August but, by the end of the month, there was still no consensus. The union admitted that they had failed to stop others from working and support for strike action seemed to be ebbing away.[128]

Only sixty-four families received a relief payout at Llay on 9 October and the union decided to pay out 5s to those who were ineligible for it. There was a mass meeting to stop the pit from working and it was reported that 1,500 stopped work at Llay Main on Tuesday, 12 October.[129] The previous day, the Revd J. Lewis Evans, the Llay Council School Correspondent, had visited the classrooms to distribute boot vouchers.

The formal opening of the school took place on Wednesday, 20 October 1926, under the chairmanship of William Aston. Speeches were made by James Darlington (Chairman of the LEA) E. Jenkins (County Schools Inspector), William Evan Williams (Head Teacher), Revd J. Lewis Evans, Dr Harrison (Chairman of School Managers), County Councillor Miss K.

DENBIGHSHIRE EDUCATION AUTHORITY.

LLAY COUNCIL SCHOOL.

OFFICIAL OPENING OF NEW COUNCIL SCHOOL, ON WEDNESDAY, 20th OCTOBER, 1926, **at 3 p.m.**

The Managers extend a cordial invitation to

............Albert ...... + ...

to the Opening Ceremony to be performed by

JAMES DARLINGTON Esq., G.M., Chirk.

(Chairman of the Denbighshire Education Committee),

Chairman:—WILLIAM ASTON, Esq., Wrexham (Chairman of the Buildings Committee).

Miss K. ALLINGTON HUGHES, J.P.; Dr. GEORGE HARRISON, J.P. (Chairman to the Managers); and J. C. DAVIES, Esq., M.A., J.P. (Secretary and Director of Education), will take part in the ceremony.

TEA at 4 p.m. Kindly supplied by Miss K. Allington Hughes J.P.

R.S.V.P. by 18th October to—Rev. J. Lewis Evans, Llay, Wrexham.

A bus will leave Wrexham for Llay at 2.30 p.m. on Wednesday.

Llay Council School – invitation to attend the opening ceremony. This was sent to Albert Jones of Pant Mawr, who was a Llay Parish Councillor and President of the Llay Lodge of the North Wales Miners' Association. [Mel Jones]

Allington Hughes, JP, and William Waite representing the colliery. The invited guests were entertained to tea by Miss Allington Hughes. Later, the premises were thrown open for inspection to the public.[130]

The official opening of the new school heralded a time of recovery for the colliery and the village and by mid-November 1926, more of the Llay miners had returned to work. This appeared to have made an unexpected impact on the health of the 407 village schoolchildren:

> There have been daily occurrences of illness among the children lately. Nurse Harrison, who visited on Friday morning, put this illness down to the fact that, now many of the fathers are working, the children are better fed; and consequently reaction sets in.[131]

A miners' meeting held at Llay Pavilion on 20 November, concluded with a decision to get the best terms possible at the colliery and work was resumed on Monday, 22 November. To all intents, the strike was over at Llay. In spite of this, on 26 November, the colliery owners, now the Carlton Main Colliery Company, informed Hugh Hughes of the NWMF that there could be no settlement with Llay Main until he and his district committee had settled for a general resumption across the district.[132] Three days later, Hugh Hughes asked for a further meeting with the Llay Main Colliery Company to discuss the terms which they were prepared to offer under the Coal Settlement on fixing the price for hand-got conveyor face coal in the 'Main' Coal and 'Two Yard' Seam.[133] On 4 December, the NWMF declared an end to the dispute in their region.[134] Finally, on Thursday, 30 December, at a general meeting on the Pit Bank, the Llay miners agreed to the company's terms.[135]

These were hard times for the new village, the mine disaster of 1924 having been followed by long strikes in 1925 and 1926. The hardships proved unbearable for some and they left the village and their excellent houses. The village, which had only recently begun to fill, rapidly emptied again. Around 100 families left and returned to Lancashire or Yorkshire or emigrated. Eli Green's parents moved to Llay from Ashton-in-Makerfield but 'as a result of the Great Strike of 1926, and the subsequent lockouts, my parents decided to migrate to Australia.'[136] Those who stayed tried to help themselves as best they could, but for many people poverty became a persistent reality. Geoff Bellis witnessed these times at Llay:

> In those days labour was very hard to get and Llay Main Colliery paid a few coppers above the local rate to attract people there. The top rate was 5s 9¾d for non-contract workers. If they worked five days a week they were lucky. Very often there'd be 'no work tomorrow'. The rent was taken out of their wages before they got their money so they were going home with a pound in their pocket for a week's work. I can't believe it. Can't believe it. They were very poor. I can see kids now with nothing on their feet and quite ragged in the early days. We had the 1925 strike at Llay, it lasted six months and was over prices. Like all strikes it was over more money. But eventually they went back … worse off really – they didn't get anything at all from it.
>
> And then the 1926 national strike – another six months strike. Llay was a very poor place, very poor. But they kept their heads high, fantastic when you think of it. One particular family, Stapleton, he had two kids in Grove Park at that time and I can see them now, properly dressed, a credit to them really, yet he was getting peanuts. But they got to Grove Park, and that's typical of the mining industry. Fantastic people, fantastic. Couldn't do enough for anybody.[137]

3: The Growth of the Mining Community (1927–38)

Following the strikes and associated troubles of 1926, the colliery and village of Llay made significant progress. This was a period of great productivity at the mine and a time when the village finally overcame adversity to develop into an organised and happy community.

In 1927, the coal industry faced substantial problems – costs appeared too high and capacity was excessive; labour was said to account for 75% of costs.[1] Nevertheless, there was sufficient confidence at Llay Main's parent company, the Carlton Main Company, for them to buy Hatfield Main Colliery Co. Ltd of Doncaster early in 1927, a pit that was still in operation in 2010. It then owned Grimethorpe, Frickley, South Elmsall, Brierley, Ferrymoor, Llay Main and Hatfield Main. The combined output of these collieries was around four million tons per year. Some of the Carlton Main directors became familiar names at Llay. Kenyon Wake was the chairman and other directors were J. J. Addy, Roland Addy, Douglas Vickers, Harold Carleton Walker and Sidney Gill.[2] Carleton Walker was the nominated chairman of Llay Main Collieries Ltd and his visits to the colliery involved him being picked up in his Rolls Royce at Rossett station. This car was garaged at the pit entrance and was only used for ferrying him to the mine. Bill Manktelow was his chauffeur.[3]

Previous disagreements between management and men were put aside and in 1927 wage negotiations were conducted with goodwill on both sides. A meeting between management and men on 11 April 1927 agreed to raise the price for 'Main' hand-got coal from 2s 1½d per ton to 2s 4d per ton, and this was signed by the managing director, Sidney Gill, the manager, E. A. Hughes and Arthur Price, undermanager. For the workmen, Hugh Hughes, the miners' agent, signed and for the Llay Main Lodge (branch of the miner's union) the signatories were: Albert Jones, the chairman; Robert Jones, the delegate and John Hughes, the lodge secretary. The colliery price list for 1927[4] covered prices for:

- Hand-getting and machine-cut conveyor faces in the 'Two Yard' and 'Brassey' mines.
- The dirt agreement of April 1927 (in 1924 the union had successfully negotiated against the proposal to drop this).
- Prices for getting, driving, ripping, benching in the 'Main' Coal Seam.

By November 1928, 3,000 men were employed at Llay Main which was the largest pit in north Wales.[5] The equipment and methods for getting coal at Llay were known to be first-class for their time and production figures matched expectations. On one day in November, the workers produced their best daily figure of 4,596 tons of coal. At the same time, the other pits in the Carlton

Workshop workers 1927. Leslie Crewe is second from the right front row. Leslie was interested in first-aid work and won several competitions. By 1929, he was an ambulance man at Llay Main working under his brother-in-law, Harold Dunnico. In April 1929, he examined a miner with an old wound to his hand. He advised him to see his doctor immediately. This advice was not heeded and the man subsequently died.[6] *[Pauline Crewe]*

group produced: Hatfield Colliery 4,261 tons per day whilst Frickley Colliery's best daily figure was 6,005 tons, the world record at the time.[7] Another record was made at Llay Main when, for the week ending 22 December 1928, the colliery achieved its highest ever weekly output at 22,872 tons of coal.

On 7 November 1928, St Martin's Church Hall and Institute was opened, situated next to the church on the land now occupied by the Llay Resource Centre.[8] A Mr Cass was installed as manager and he lived at the Institute with his family. For much of its existence – it was demolished in 2003 – it served as a youth club and cinema. The land was donated by the Llay Main Colliery Company and the building was erected on the site at a cost of approximately £6,000. The opening ceremony was performed by Mrs Edwards, the wife of the Bishop of St Asaph, and Sir Watkin Williams Wynne. A bus was laid on from Wrexham, travelling via Gresford and Rossett to bring people to the opening ceremony.

The cinema opened two days later and the first film shown was the Buster Keaton silent comedy *The General*. There were two houses held, the first at 5.00 p.m., and the second at 7.30 p.m. The following year saw the first occasion when Llay school children went to the cinema as a Christmas treat.

> Preparations were made for the Christmas Treat. This took place on Thursday 4.15 to 7.30 and passed off without any untoward incident.The children were entertained to tea, received gifts and were admitted to the local Cinema where suitable pictures were shown. All these were provided for by funds contributed to by the Llay Colliery Co. Directors and Staff, Miss Allington Hughes, the School Managers and the Teachers.[9]

This was an annual event for many years. The cinema programme was changed every Monday, Wednesday and Friday from this time, right up to the time that it closed in around 1960.[10]

St Martins Church Hall (Institute), 1928. [Peter Chadwick]

> I worked in the colliery offices at Llay Main before nationalisation. The staff were picked and allocated jobs outside of their general work. The Church and the Institute, they were under Harry Ball, he was like the head of the village and involved with whatever went. The insurance clerk was one of the top grade men, he ran the cinema in Llay Main, belonging to the Church Hall. One chap, R. L. Goss, he was secretary of the Gardening Society, as I say, Ted Davies ran the picture house. Now when Ted went on holidays I used to take over and see to the finance side, see that the tickets were issued out and balancing the cash. So you were tied into the mining village. This was the thing, you had other jobs outside of your main job. [Mr J][11]

The next year another innovation came to the village with the arrival of a radio set at the school. The school log of 7 October 1929 stated that the 'wireless set was tried in No. 1 room on Tuesday afternoon. The reception was slightly better, but not sufficiently clear for the words to be understandable. The head teacher fears it will not be a success.'

Not all of the Llay colliers had a home in the village. Unemployment, which made men keen to find work, and transport developments, which made it easier for them to travel, meant that the company did not have to house all of its workforce. About a half of the Llay Main workers commuted to the pit from old mining villages within a ten-mile radius of the pit.[12] In 1929, the colliery company used its influence as a large employer to persuade the Wrexham Rural District Council to construct a housing estate to the south of the colliery village. In the same year, these workers produced the record annual output for Llay Main when 1,037,592 tons of coal were raised in $264\frac{3}{4}$ days – an average of 3,923 tons per day. Unfortunately, with so many miners working at the colliery, the number of accidents began to increase:

> We had so many killed in the pit. I remember my brother-in-law, he was the head ambulance man, and we were there together he and I. And one week, it started on the Monday – there was a man killed on the Monday, and five were killed in that week. He was going away on holiday on the Saturday and he said 'You'll have to deal with it' he said to me. 'Righto' I said, 'Harold you get off on your holiday' … and there were five killed – Oh it was terrific. [Leslie Crewe][13]

Harold Dunnico was born in Bolton in 1897, one of nine children. In 1911, he was a grocery assistant and, when war came, enlisted in the Royal Army Medical Corps, serving in France between 1915 and 1918. He was made head ambulance man at Llay Main Colliery and on his appointment had the use of the a Sunbeam motor ambulance, which had been purchased in 1922. It would not be too strong a statement to say that some colliers and villagers owed their lives to his prompt actions. In addition, in his spare time he produced many of the village pantomimes and is remembered as being well-respected by his colleagues and fellow villagers.

Harold Dunnico in the colliery yard c.1931. *The new pit-head baths building is in the right background and to the left is the Lamp Room. Harold Dunnico is driving Sam Platt's car which is a side-valve, JAP-powered Morgan Aero of 1928/9 vintage.*[14] *[Pauline Crewe]*

The Carlton Main Colliery Company was less ambitious than its predecessor and sought help in developing the new village. The company applied to the Welfare Fund, raised out of a levy on every ton of coal raised in Britain, for money to build the colliery baths, the first to be constructed in north Wales. These funds were used to erect the Miners' Welfare Institute and to lay out the Recreation Ground. The Miners' Welfare Fund had been set up in the 1920s under the provisions of the Mining Industry Act and funds were raised from a levy, initially 1d per ton of coal produced, and after 1926 a levy of 5% of coal royalties.[15] When the baths were opened in 1930, a memorial tablet was installed to commemorate the event.

MINERS' WELFARE FUND. COLLIERY PITHEAD BATHS

> These baths, erected by the Miners' Welfare Committee in pursuance of the Mining Industry Act, 1926, were opened and handed over to the Trustees on the 9th August, 1930 by E. Shinwell, Esq., Secretary for Mines.

Emmanuel (Manny) Shinwell, later Lord Shinwell, was a member of the first Labour government under Ramsey MacDonald. After the opening ceremony, the onlookers were then given a conducted tour of the facilities. Miners and their families were further invited to look around the next day.[16] A booklet was produced for the opening which contained detailed instructions on

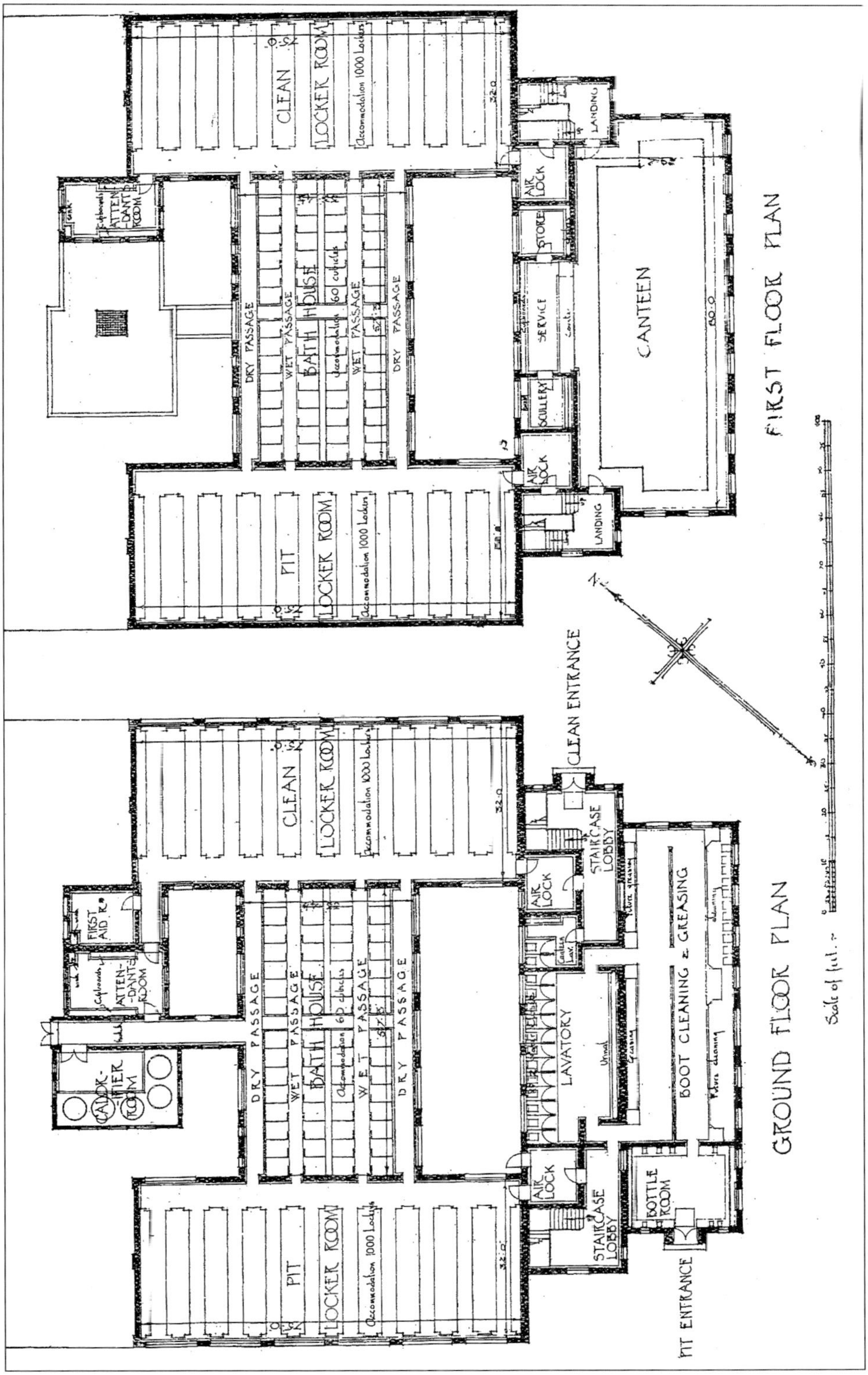

Llay Main Colliery Pithead Baths floor plan. [LLHSA]

how the baths were to be used. To avoid the spread of 'athlete's foot' the men were encouraged to make sandals so as not to walk around in bare feet, 'all that is necessary being two pieces of wood, shaped roughly to the sole of the foot, and a piece of webbing or strap, nailed across the top, under which the front part of the foot is passed.'

The plan of the building which is issued with this pamphlet, illustrates clearly how .the, clean-clothes and pit-clothes locker rooms are separated, the shower-bath cubicles occupying the centre of the building between them. There are 1,000 clean-clothes lockers, 1,000 pit-clothes lockers and 60 cubicles on each floor.

Instructions for bathing: At the end of his day's work each man enters the bath-house by the pit-clothes entrance. In the pit entrance, as already mentioned will be found, the boot cleaning and greasing apparatus, as well as drinking fountains and special taps for filling water bottles. The boot cleaning apparatus consists of rapidly, revolving brushes to remove the dirt prior to greasing. All that is necessary for greasing the boots is a quick rub round with the brush, taking care to be as economical as possible with the grease, so as to avoid carrying any of it into the building.

On arriving at his pit-clothes locker, each man undresses and hangs his clothes up on the hooks. Pit boots may be slipped into the place provided at the bottom of the locker, hang on one of the side hooks, or placed in the racks provided underneath the seat (if left on the bottom of the locker, and not as suggested as above, they are liable to get too dry). Then the door should be shut. If the door of the locker is not shut, the heat for drying the clothes will not pass through them, but out through the open door. The latch of the door is fitted to take a padlock, which a rnan can provide for himself if he so wishes. Then using his towel for a covering if desired, (or a bath slip which can be obtained from the Attendant) and taking his soap-dish with soap in it, he proceeds to the bath cubicle in the section allotted to him. There is a fitting in the bath cubicle to take the soap-dish. Finish your wash with cold water and you will not catch a chill. The openings in the wall leading to the bath cubicles will have numbers painted over them, indicating the locker numbers allotted to that particular section. There will be no congestion if each man uses only the section allotted to him. The golden, rule, therefore, is 'Follow these instructions for the benefit of others.

After bathing, with his towel round him or wearing his bath slip, and carrying his soap dish, each man goes through the nearest opening to the clean clothes section. When he is dressed, he should leave his wet towel, bath slip and soap-dish in the clean locker ready for the next day.[17]

The baths were viewed as a huge benefit to the collier and kept as much coal dust as possible from his home.

They were a boon to the housewife and the men, yet there were some who would not use them. A charge of 6d (22p) per week was made. The men had to provide their own soap and towels but these were sold at the baths fairly cheaply. One of the first actions of the Coal Board at the Vesting Date was the abolishment of that charge.[18]

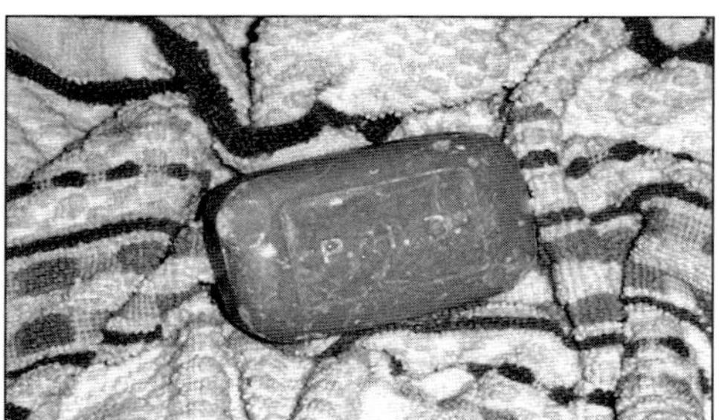

Pit Head Baths towel and soap, 2010. Towels and soap could be bought at the baths. Some of these are still around today and are in good condition after nearly fifty years. The soap bears the marks 'P.H.B.' (Pithead Baths).

> They were a Godsend. We were adverse to accepting the baths at Llay Main, but we came to realise that they were a Godsend at work and home. They had the false idea that they caused bad backs and sent you baldheaded, and all those silly things.[19]

The Main coal was developed from the shaft bottom by headings, but by 1930 the maintenance of these roadways had become so expensive that the method was abandoned. About 1,000,000 tons of workable Main coal outside the shaft pillar were thus 'sterilised' because the principal haulages and airways traversed this area and the seam was about eight feet below the floor of the roadways. About 1930, long-wall working was adopted and roadways were re-ripped two or three times. Advancing long-wall working was the best method of getting coal from the Main seam at Llay. Large panels of coal were taken out by removing all the coal between two headings (roadways being pushed out away from the pit bottom). The following routine was developed:

> The lower six feet of the seam was filled out in the normal way on to conveyors. The waste coal was then broken down by coal bursters and also filled on to the conveyors. This exposed the batty (fissured) roof which collapsed regularly in the wastes and provided sufficient dirt to allow strip packs to be built 10 to 12 yards apart.[20]

The ingress of water was a big problem at the neighbouring Llay Hall Colliery, but this did not occur at Llay Main where inbye pumps were unnecessary. Water from glacial deposits drained into both shafts, but this was collected and about 30,000 to 35,000 gallons per day was fed into a water lodge at a depth of 700 feet and pumped to the surface.[21]

The dip of the seams to the east required drifting – the driving of inclined roadways – and the construction of a number of levels to get the coal out. The more profitable coal lay nearer the shafts and, in the early years of the colliery, they made good profits.[22] As time went by, and seams

Llay Main Colliery Offices c.1930. This is one of the few remaining colliery buildings. This housed the general offices and the wages office. Miners collected their pay packets from a series of eight to ten small windows around the left hand side of the building. [Peter Chadwick]

Llay Welfare Institute Management Committee, 1931. Back row: –?–, J. C. Williams, –?–, T. H. Bayley. Middle row: –?–, –?–, –?–, R. Jarvis, –?–, –?–. Seated: E. Tilston, –?–, E. Bithell, –?–, H. O. Ball, T. W. Mottram, R. Robinson, D. Holmes. [Llay Miners' Welfare Institute]

were worked out, quality coal lay further away and required complicated haulage arrangements.

Miners wages had dropped after the failure of the 1926 strike but by 1929, wages at Llay Main were reasonable. John William Morton moved from south Yorkshire and started work there as a collier on 29 August 1929 and lived in Fourth Avenue. He was paid 7s 6d per day. On 25 February 1930, he was involved in an accident when a roof fall damaged his back and was off work until July of that year, returning to do 'light work'. There was a big incentive to return to work as his compensation was reduced by 50% on 21 July. His weekly wage was then made up of 'Light work – £1 10s 0d plus 15s 5d compensation.[23] For sick miners, being on compensation, 'on the compy', was not an easy option. For deserving cases, some help was given by workmates who would make a small donation when collecting their pay.

> If someone was sick – they [workmates] would stand one each side [of the pay queue] with caps and they would collect money from people's wages.[24]

A club for colliery officers had been opened near the colliery in one of the old sinkers huts, next to another used as the Catholic Church. Some recreation for the miners was provided at their Institute at Llay Place, the snooker tables were particularly popular. As the range of leisure activities grew, the club became too small to accommodate them all and a much larger building was planned.

John William Morton with sons Desmond, Harry and Kenneth c.1931. The family was photographed during a walk around the back lanes north of Llay village. Sunday walks after church or chapel were popular with villagers in the years before television. 'Then there was the 'monkey's parade', we walked up the straight mile and back again. Sunday night for young people, just like the promenade!' [Mrs P.][25] *[Leri Morto]*

In 1929, an application was made to the Miners' Welfare Fund for capital to build a new Miners' Welfare Institute with sports facilities and a playground. The land was bought outright from the Madocks' Llay Hall estate for £2,338 and the Welfare trustees appended their signatures to the conveyance document. Thomas Wilfred Mottram of Nant-y-Gaer, the colliery manager, and Henry Oswald Ball of The Vadoc, the colliery secretary, signed on behalf of Llay Main Colliery Company. Thomas James Hughes of 33 First Avenue, checkweighman and Thomas Henry Bayley of 9 Third Avenue, sawyer, signed on behalf of the colliery workers. The same conveyance stated that the Miners' Welfare Fund was administered locally by the North Wales District Welfare Committee and that they had allocated a sum of £20,000 to the Llay trustees for the building of Llay Miners' Welfare Institute and Recreation Grounds.[26]

The architect of the 'Welfare' (as it came to be known) was F. A. Roberts of Mold, and the style of the building is now said to be 'a late survival of Edwardian Baroque'.[27] The grounds were developed as the main building was taking shape and the groundsman appointed to look after the facilities was Ernest Ankers. A tennis court, cricket and soccer pitches and two bowling greens were soon under way. The Miners' Institute was opened on 20 June 1931 by Robert Richards MP.[28]

During the early years, the Welfare was only allowed to sell intoxicating liquor on the ground floor. The colliery company used its influence to ensure that the bar would not open on a Sunday and insisted that women were only allowed in the unlicensed part of the building. Some people remember how Harry Ball, the Company Secretary and head of the colliery office staff, would mobilise the clerks who worked under him to turn up and vote down proposals for change at the Annual General Meetings.[29]

Laying the bowling greens at Llay Miners' Welfare Institute in 1929. These men also laid the cricket pitch and the tennis courts. It is thought that the foreman, Andrew Kerse (on the right) worked for the Halifax landscaping firm of Conway's. On completion he stayed in the area and was made a life member of Llay Miners' Welfare Institute.[30] *Note the three colliery spoil tips in the left background. [Llay Miners' Welfare Institute]*

Children's Recreation Ground, 'The Rec', in 1931. This was built as part of the Miners' Welfare Institute development and opened by Miss Allington Hughes JP, on 9 August 1930.[31] *It was the largest playground in the Wrexham area and became a favourite place for Llay children to meet up. The Rec was popular throughout the district and families from outlying villages would bring picnics and spend a day here in the summer. The superintendent in the photograph was the father of Ceridwen Williams, head teacher at the Council School. [Llay Miners' Welfare Institute]*

Llay Miners' Welfare Institute, c.1935. [Llay Miners' Welfare Institute]

At Llay Main, the colliers recorded the highest daily output for the pit at 4,616 tons on 18 March 1932.[32] In spite of this success, these were difficult times for Llay. The Wall Street Crash of 1929 had ushered in the collapse of the global economy and the years of the Great Depression. By 1932, unemployment among Welsh insured males had reached 42.8% and the country was among most economically depressed in the world.[33] The market for Llay coal became uncertain but, despite unemployment threatening the pit, union membership remained high with 2,779 on the books of the Llay Lodge.[34]

> During the depression short time working was prevalent, a blast on the hooter signified no work for the next shift. There was much poverty in the mining areas as will be seen by the following example. An underground worker earning about thirty-six shillings (180p) for a full week's work, would be left less than one pound after deductions for health insurance, doctor, rent and associated charges. To anyone with an elementary grasp of arithmetic it would be obvious that they would have great difficulty in making ends meet, yet they held their heads high and maintained some dignity. Do not forget that surface workers were paid less than underground workers generally. As a class workers in the mining industry are second to none.[35]

Collieries are dangerous places at the best of times and the colliers' work underground was enshrined in the articles of the Coal Mines Act 1911 which dealt with safe working practices. These rules were augmented by local bye-laws appended to the document. The fourteen Llay Main bye-laws signed off by Sidney Criddle in 1925 had not altered by the time Thomas Mottram signed them in 1933. The following are some of the by-laws:

> Fourteen days notice to terminate employment was to be given by employer or employee.
> Employees should attend on time, 'perform a full and fair day's work' and not leave early.
> Employees should not fight or quarrel or create any disturbance or use abusive language in the Mine.
> Employees should not be in a state of intoxication, take any intoxicating liquor into the Mine.
> All wages shall be paid and payable weekly upon the Friday.
> Miners and underground workmen shall, as far as is practicable, go down the pit in rotation as they arrive at the pit bank, and at the times stated in the notices on the pit bank.
> Every person employed shall do any work of a temporary nature as required by any Officer or Official of the Mine, but shall be paid for such work.
> No person employed shall change or take any time-board, mottey or token belonging to or used by any other person.[36]

Breaches of the rules were sometimes met with court appearances which doubtless served as a warning for colliers to obey them. In 1928, E. A. Hughes, the colliery agent and manager, brought a number of charges against some Llay miners. On 20 March, Thomas John Johnson of Leeswood was fined £1, with £2 15s 1d costs, for having a cigarette in his possession. On 19 June, Edwin Hughes of Caergwrle (engine driver) and Norman Williams of Rhosddu (haulage hand) infringed regulation 19 of the Act in that they were asleep in the mine. The punishment was 5s costs, but no fine was imposed. A more serious charge of the same date was that against William Edwards of Broughton, another haulage hand, who was accused of endangering life in the pit by omitting to put a stank prop in front of some tubs.[37]

In 1929, Thomas Wilfred Mottram had taken over as colliery manager from E. A. Hughes, who retained his duties as colliery agent. Mottram came from a mining family, his father, Thomas Harry, was a mines inspector and his elder brother, Charles Douglas, was a lecturer in mining at Birmingham University.[38] Mr Mottram, who would become the longest serving manager at Llay Main, was known for his zeal in pursuing better safety measures at the colliery.

The poor safety record of the coal industry was one of the most important considerations in its being taken into public ownership. In no single year in the annals of British mining history has the number of men killed in a single disaster, however large, ever exceeded the number taken in incidents that involved individuals and small groups of workers.

In its early years, Llay Main Colliery had a poor reputation for safety, perhaps due to the fact that a new and often inexperienced workforce had to cope with the harsh and unfamiliar conditions caused by mechanised working.[39]

> I don't think that Llay Main conditions were anymore dangerous than any other pit. But perhaps it was starting on automation more than the old fashioned pits, and the work was much faster I believe. But we must always remember that Llay Main was a big pit. The local pits perhaps had five or six hundred men, while Llay Main was employing two to three thousand. Your accident ratio would seem more in those conditions.
>
> They had a first class ambulance room and attendants and they would give you all the treatment that was necessary. If it was serious you'd be taken down to Wrexham Hospital for further attention.[40]

As a result of working at Llay Main many men suffered serious injuries or lost their lives. As well as the losses resulting from the 1924 explosion, there were many others injured in lesser-known circumstances. Under Mottram, the company made safety a high priority, encouraged miners to join the St John's Ambulance Brigade and sponsored teams in first aid competitions. Llay Main had a safety officer long before other pits of the area.[41]

The first fatality at Llay Main[42] occurred during the sinking operations on 4 April 1916 when Frederick Atkins, aged 37, was killed by the collapse of a steel roof, possibly the roof of one of the refrigeration plants. The following tables show the number of deaths during the years that the colliery was operating and the names of those who were killed.

By far the most common cause of death was a roof fall and 34 fatalities were due to this problem. Ten men died as a result of being crushed between tubs or killed by runaway tubs; seven deaths were put down to a collapse of face coal. There were eight surface deaths and two of these occurred when men were crushed between coal wagons. Between October 1927 and December 1932 the Main coal was worked simultaneously with the Quaker (Brassey) and Two Yard seams in the same area. This proved to be both dangerous and costly.[43] Five of the ten deaths in 1929 were caused by roof falls. In August, Mottram wrote to W. J. Charlton, HM Divisional Inspector for Mines, stating that in the case of the fatal accident to Robert Price Griffiths in July, there were not enough roof supports.[44]

It is clear that some of these accidents were brought about by substandard mining practices. Poor safety procedures were also to blame, machinery was left unguarded and victims sometimes caused their own downfall by malpractice as a result of poor training. Mottram was determined to get to grips with these issues he said:

> Re compensation accidents due to hands being taken into pulleys and from wires cutting hands. Re need to arrange with Dunnico (Head Ambulance man) and his Assistants … that he finds out from the person injured which rope and which pulley is concerned.[45]

His concern was unfortunately prophetic as in October, Thomas Williams, an oiler, had been drawn into a pulley whilst oiling. In a letter of 16 November to T. Boydell, HMI, Mottram confirmed that the accident was caused by 'a haulage return wheel which was not kept securely fenced'.[46]

Safety was a problem on the surface as well as underground and in November, Frank Jones a washery loader was run over by wagons. The manager asked R. G. Evans, the colliery chemist, who was also responsible for surface workers, to look into the incident and Evans replied that, in an effort to 'try to cut down still further the number of accidents, I have made W. T. Jones responsible for 'Safety First', it being his duty to report on defective fences etc, and report on all accidents.'

> Fatal accident to F. Jones on the surface 13th November. The above man worked under the supervision of a foreman named Stuart Gunning. If the deceased had been seen pushing at the buffer before the

Annual numbers of fatalities at Llay Main Colliery.

Year	*Deaths*	*Year*	*Deaths*
1922	0	1945	0
1923	0	1946	1
1924	10	1947	0
1925	1	1948	1
1926	7	1949	1
1927	3	1950	0
1928	5	1951	1
1929	10	1952	1
1930	7	1953	1
1931	2	1954	0
1932	6	1955	0
1933	3	1956	0
1934	2	1957	0
1935	1	1958	1
1936	1	1959	2
1937	1	1960	1
1938	1	1961	1
1939	2	1962	0
1940	3	1965	0
1941	0	1964	0
1942	1	1965	0
1943	0	1966	0
1944	2		
		TOTAL	79

Fatalities at Llay Main Colliery

Atkins, Frederick, aged 37?, 1916
Cartwright, P. H., aged 59, surface hand, 1940
Clutton, Benjamin, aged 19, haulage hand, 1928
Davies, Joseph, aged 61, ripper, 1928
Davies, Norman, 1928
Davies, George William, aged 44, collier, 1932
Davies, Edward, aged 38, collier, 1934
Davies, T., aged 64, labourer, 1951
Davies, D., aged 54, ripper, 1958
Edwards, Samuel, aged 32, collier, 1929
Ellis, W. C., aged 32, collier, 1946
Evans, Frank or Francis, aged 54, collier, 1931
Evans, Joseph Reginald, aged 53, 1924
Evans, Isaac, aged 19, 1924
Evans, Robert Percival, aged 32, 1924
Evans, Moses (or Moss), aged 18, taker off, 1927
Fenny, Henry, aged 44, collier, 1926
Fletcher, Thomas Charles, aged 45, 1924
Flynn, Birkacre, aged 21, surface foreman, 1929
Garston, Ernest, aged 41, miner, 1930
German, Edward Henry, aged 15, 1924
Griffiths, Robert P., aged 56, repairer, 1929
Hannaby, James Robert/Richard, aged 41, repairer, 1929
Harrison, R. George, aged 20, haulage hand, 1926
Harrison, George, aged 35, collier, 1924
Hughes, John Ellis, aged 27, loader, 1930
Hughes, O. A., aged 48, shotfirer, 1959
Hughes, John William, aged 22, 1924
Humphries, John, aged 53, 1924
James, W., aged 49, collier, 1944
Jones, William, aged 54, collier, 1928
Jones, Frank, aged 23, washery loader, 1929
Jones, Davis(d) William, aged 55, collier, 1930
Jones, Oliver, aged 39, ripper, 1930
Jones, Isaac, aged 39, collier, 1930
Jones, Hugh Owen, aged 67, ripper, 1933
Jones, Joseph, aged 56, collier, 1933
Jones, Joseph, aged 44, collier, 1939
Jones, T., aged 52, collier, 1940
Jones, R., aged 50, collier, 1940
Jones, Emlyn, aged 48, collier, 1953
Jones, Henry, aged 36, 1924
Jones, George, aged 28, collier, 1926
Jones, E. A., aged 54, collier, 1926
Jones, Edward, aged 55, byeman, 1926
Jones, William, aged 32, collier, 1932
Kelly, David Morgan, aged 53, railman, 1932
Matthews, E., aged 44, deputy, 1959
Mathias, John Edward, aged 33, coalcutter, 1932
Matthias, J., aged 44, collier, 1942
Miles, Joseph, aged 42, collier, 1929
Morgan, Samuel Edward, aged 17, haulage hand, 1929
Morgan, Thomas, aged 47, dataller, 1936
Morris, Pryce, aged 49, collier, 1927
Morris, Samuel, aged 55, collier, 1930
Moss, John Francis, aged 44, belt attendant, 1934
Murray, John Alfred, aged 23, haulage hand, 1929
Owen, David Charles, aged 64, deputy, 1938
Peters, Thomas, aged 43, metalman, 1930
Powis, Arthur L, aged 36, collier, 1926
Prydden, William, aged 60, collier, 1925
Richardson, Thomas, aged 55, collier, 1926
Roberts, John T., aged 23, screenhand, 1928
Roberts, Isaac, aged 39, collier, 1929
Roberts, Thomas James, aged 31, corporal, 1931
Roberts, T. L., shotfirer, 1949
Smith, Oswell Rees, aged 33, collier, 1933
Steen, L., aged 42, collier, 1960
Tattum, Joseph Herbert, aged 56, collier, 1932
Thomas, Lewis, aged 44, deputy, 1927
Thomas, H. S., aged 45, washery, 1961
Tudor, D., aged 52, collier, 1937
Williams, Thomas, aged 54, oiler, 1929
Williams, George Samuel, aged 16, screens attendant, 1932
Williams, E., aged 44, ripper, 1939
Williams, William Ernest, aged 41, shotfirer, 1924
Wineyard, Wilfred, aged 23, tippler attendant, 1948
Wynn(e), Thomas Lewis, aged 38, repairer, 1935
Wynn(e), John Lewis, aged 38, repairer, 1935
Wynne, T. B., aged 43, collier, 1944

matter would have been reported ... it is not the practice to attempt to move wagons by pushing at the buffer ... every effort is being made at this colliery – surface and underground – to improve the standard of discipline required.[47]

On 6 December 1929, R. J. Hannaby was killed whilst riding in a tub, having hit his head on the roof. Mottram wrote to Charlton that he intended 'prosecuting the men who were illegally riding when Hannaby was killed'. Charlton was equally keen to improve safety matters at Llay and undertook regular inspections of the pit.

Re inspection by Mr J. T. Shaw and Mr Evan Williams of 12th December 1929 reporting breaches of the Coal Mines Act 1911 requiring' one additional refuge hole required on 236 dip between 222 and 223 levels and no refuge holes provided on the inbye lengths of 100 yards on 224 level and 70 yards on 221 level. Section 28(4) of the act – the report of the night fireman for the oncoming day shift was not full and accurate – did not report the presence of an accumulation of firedamp in 224 bottom side. A flame test showed 3% methane ... I look with apprehension on the firing of shots in this district below 223 conveyor face, having regard to the conditions.[48]

These were matters that the manager needed to address urgently. As the year drew to a close, Mottram took his chemist's 'safety-first' idea a stage further by installing safety officers in the colliery, mainly to check that men were observing good working practices. One miner said:

Mr Mottram, the manager, he was very safety conscious, he started these 'safety corporals', the first one was Ernie Garston. The young lads would come down the pit and they'd be a week or ten days under him. And the first thing he'd say: 'Let me see your fingers'. I said, 'What do you do that for, Ern?' 'I want to see if they smoke, ' he said, 'I want to tell them of the danger of taking cigarettes and matches down the pit.

For about ten days he'd have 'em going up and down, going round the pit getting them used to the atmosphere, then he'd release 'em to wherever they were wanted on the haulage. And Mottram started that, 'safety corporal' he called him, 'safety officer' it came to, but he was definitely the man that started that round here. [Mr S.][49]

In October 1932, Edward Stuart Clark, the founder Llay Main Colliery, died at Seaford in Sussex. After relinquishing control of Llay Main Colliery in 1913, he had remained as managing director of Llay Hall Colliery Company.

He was 55 years of age and was educated at Rugby, and afterwards studied at the School of Mines, South Kensington. Up to the time of his last illness he was actively engaged in the management and direction of the work at Llay Hall Colliery, Cefnybedd. He saw the development of the North Wales coalfield and with his co-owners bored for coal on what is now the Llay Garden village. The body was brought home from Sussex by rail on Monday evening to Wrexham, and was afterward conveyed to St Martin's Church, Llay, where a brief service was conducted by the Rev. Gore Rees. The funeral took place on Tuesday afternoon, when a service was held at St Martin's Church, Llay. It was very largely attended. It was conducted by the vicar of Gresford, the Rev. Edwyn Jones, who was accompanied by the Ven. Archdeacon Williams, Chirk (formerly of Gresford), the Rev. S. A. Jones (Gwersyllt), the Rev. W. Eyton Lloyd, (Esclusham, formerly of Llay).[50]

Leslie Crewe in the entrance of the Ambulance Room, c.1932. He is trying out a Siebe Gorman Spirelmo smoke helmet of which every colliery had to have one, whereas breathing apparatus proper (Proto sets) were only allowed at the rescue station. It consisted of a foot bellows, around 50 yards of hose, and fed fresh air from the bellows, through the hose, to the helmet. The 'windows' open outwards when in fresh air, any excess pressure is vented out the very top, you see a relief valve. It would be used for very short distance work, mainly sealing off fire areas in irrespirable atmospheres, or for quick snatch rescue use in sumps and blind headings. They were seldom ever used and then only by trained rescue men.[56] *[Pauline Crewe]*

In the summer of 1933, Llay Main Collieries Ltd acquired Hafod Colliery from the Ruabon Coal & Coke Co Ltd. Hafod had closed as a result of the depression and in August steps were being taken to re-open it.[51] At the end of 1933, Llay Main had an annual output of 900,000 tons of gas, household and steam coal and employed 2,000 below ground with a further 450 above ground.[52] The Carlton group's profits were well supported by Llay Main so that the net profit to 31 March 1934 was £66,286 and a 3% dividend was paid. Profits from Llay Main Collieries Ltd were applied to the repayment of loans for the development of the pit.[53] Such profits being made by mine owners were due to the toil of those working in extremely dangerous places. Miners risked life and limb on a daily basis and in 1934 twelve Llay men lost their lives in the Gresford Disaster.

At 2 a.m. on 22 September 1934, an explosion occurred in the Dennis section of Gresford colliery, hardly a mile from Llay Main. Virtually every single person working in the Dennis section was killed, apart from a few persons working near the pit bottom, and one deputy and five men who managed to escape from the 29s district.[54]

Two hundred and sixty-one Gresford miners were killed, plus three rescuers and, a few days later, one surface worker. The event devastated the local mining community and the bitter memory of it lives on with each annual ceremony of remembrance. Three issues still rankle with the surviving relatives of those killed in the disaster:

1. The lack of clear conclusions about the causes of the explosion
2. The apportionment of blame[55]
3. The decision not to retrieve the bodies of the miners from the places where they fell.

Feelings of disgust with the colliery owners were exacerbated with the public knowledge that when widows and children received the dead miners' pay packets, they found that they had been docked a quarter of a shift's pay for their failure to complete the shift.

The names of 28 of the victims were read out by the Gresford vicar in a service at Gresford Church on Sunday 31 September 1934.[57] These men of the parish of Gresford included twelve from Llay. The Llay men killed were:

Ralph Evans, 135 Pentre Lane
Alfred Holt, 155 Pentre Lane
Henry John Houlden, 25 Second Avenue
Daniel Hughes, 23 First Avenue
Robert Edward Jones, 119 Pentre Lane
William Sidney Lloyd, 172 Pentre Lane
Henry Peters, 114 Pentre Lane (left a widow and nine children)
E. L. Rogers of 18, New House Avenue
William Henry Roberts, 105 Pentre Lane
Stanley Stratford, 5 Ninth Avenue[58]
Norris Williams, 118 Pentre Lane
Morgan James Yemm, 39 Seventh Avenue

The story of the Gresford Disaster has been well documented[59] and I shall add to it here only to try and account for the actions of the Llay rescue teams on 22 September 1934.[60]

All attempts to rescue any of the remaining men believed to be alive were barred by a ferocious fire that had broken out in the roadways to the Dennis section and by the large quantity of poisonous gases in the area. In the confusion following the explosion, it took some time for a rescue attempt to be organised. The men of the Gresford rescue teams were first on the scene but later, the Llay Main No. 1 rescue team was also sent down. Two members of this team, together with a Gresford rescuer who was guiding them, were killed by gas inhalation.

At around 4.30 a.m., in the vicinity of the disaster, the heat was intense. The fire was being tackled by throwing sand and stone dust at it and also by using fire extinguishers. At around the same time, Parry Davies, captain of the Llay No. 2 team, was alerted. In those days, members of rescue teams had a blue disc attached to their houses so that they could be called out if needed. Bearing in mind the urgency of the situation, it was likely that the No. 2 team would be made up of men already on night shift at Llay and that the captains of Llay Nos. 1 and 3 teams would have been alerted to put their teams on standby.

By 5 a.m., the No. 2 team was assembled at the Ambulance Room at Llay Main and shortly afterwards the men went by lorry to Gresford. Apart from one or two unattached rescue men employed at Gresford, they found themselves to be the only rescue team present at the pit head as the Gresford Team was already below ground.

Daylight came and with it bad weather – rain and cold. In the confusion, the Llay No. 2 team were moved around various rooms, including an old cabin, and during the process Parry Davies expressed concern that their equipment might become damaged. He appealed to Mottram, the Llay Main colliery manager, who appeared on site, and they were moved to better facilities in the Gresford general office.[61] They could not stay there long and once again were asked to move as the office was needed for conferences.[62]

William Bonsall, the Gresford manager, had sent instructions to have a six-yard 'dirt stopping' broken down in order to get direct access to 20s return from the Dennis Main, his object being to 'ascertain the state of the return airway.'[63] He thought that the return would be charged with carbon dioxide, and if so did not want anyone to go into it because no-one could be brought out that way. At around 7 a.m., the manager was told that the stopping had been broken into. He

Llay N°. 1 Rescue Team, c.1933. This photograph was taken outside the mines rescue training station in Wrexham. The trainer, Superintendent H. Herbert of the Wrexham Mines Rescue training team is standing. Sitting second from the left is Daniel Hughes who was killed in the failed rescue attempt at Gresford in 1934. Next to him third from the left is the N°. 1 team captain – John Charles Williams. [Wrexham Archives]

sent word to the two deputies he had appointed to be in charge, the Thomas brothers, that rescue men would be needed but that they were not to enter the return without permission from himself.

By 8.20 a.m., the Llay N°. 2 team had been relocated to the joiners' shop and had been joined at Gresford by the other two Llay teams (N°. 1 and N°. 3). N°. 1 team went to the general office. The Llay contingent was now a full complement of 18 men. Llay men had been on site for three hours, but there was still no call for any to descend the pit, despite the fact that they were desperate to go down to rescue their colleagues.

At 8.30 a.m., a man came into the general office and asked for two rescue men, a request that a minute or two later was altered to one for a whole team of six men. John Charles Williams (called Jack Lanc), captain of the Llay Main Colliery N°. 1 Rescue Team, got his men ready, 'with the exception of one whose apparatus was out of order'.[64] William Hughes, one of the unattached Gresford rescue men team, also prepared to go down, possibly as a substitute for the Llay man. At 8.45 a.m., the team went down the Dennis Shaft, then travelled inbye (into the mine) to where the stopping had been broached to give direct access to 20s airway. At 9 a.m., Jack Williams was told by the Gresford fireman, Harold Thomas, to go on to assess the conditions in the airway. The Llay captain then asked for a plan, but none was available. William Hughes, offered to act as guide. At this point we are told that there were five men in the team[65] so possibly another of the Llay team must have been found to have been issued with faulty apparatus.

Yet another breathing set was found to have lost oxygen, possibly that of Price Beard, so that left Jack Williams, Bill Hughes, Danny Hughes and Jack Lewis to carry on. A cage containing a canary was handed to the Llay captain by Harold Thomas, who accompanied him and William Hughes into the airway. They had only travelled some 40 or 50 yards when the unfortunate bird dropped dead. Williams said, 'I got the men together and told them the conditions we were in … that the atmosphere was dangerous … 'that the bird was killed.'[66] Williams then handed the cage back to Thomas and told him to go back. Williams, Bill Hughes, Danny Hughes and Jack Lewis then went a further 50 or 60 yards down the airway, the men walking about 20 yards from each other. At approximately 200 yards from the stopping through which they had gone into the airway, the Llay captain met a body of hot air. He continued in until it became impossible for him to get any further as the passage had become constricted due to the collapse of the ceiling and walls of the tunnel. Signalling for a halt, and unable to turn around, he came out backwards. At around 9.30 a.m. Williams came upon Bill Hughes and the two men went back to Jack Lewis and these three then came to Dan Hughes. By this time, they had cleared the narrow section and Williams told his men that they could go no further and, on account of the heat, they must return. He later recalled that they 'got well ahead of me and I thought they were going much too fast'.[67] He then came upon the body of Jack Lewis.

> He appeared to be dead. I examined his apparatus and couldn't find anything wrong with it. I proceeded to walk slowly out and came upon Bill Hughes who was down on his left side with the nose clip displaced. I replaced the nose clip and opened the valve of his apparatus wider – but to all appearances he was dead. I left him and came upon Dan Hughes who seemed to be in difficulty I helped him out for 40 yards and we both fell. I then found out that the feed pipe of my apparatus had become detached through struggling with Dan and I was getting no air from the bag. I tried to couple the pipe up but it took too long so I pushed the pipe into my mouth. Afterwards signaling for help to a party who's lights I could see about 30 or 40 yards away – top end of the airway. I proceeded out by … [unreadable] and was met by Beard and Povah at about 4 or 5 yards from fresh air. Assistance was then going in for Dan Hughes.[68]

On the surface, at around 9 a.m., there was a request for Parry Davies to supply two men to go down. He thought this was an unusual request as rescue teams were of five men (plus the captain), each with a distinctive role to play. In response to this request, Tom Price Jones and Richard Harrison were sent down. Then, at around 9.30 a.m., a call came for all available rescue men to descend and the rest of the Llay N° 2 team (Parry Davies, the captain, with Harold Povah, Emlyn Jones and Peter Hughes) descended the shaft.

Once at the pit bottom, the team made its way to the return airway. At this point the air was perfectly clear and they had not yet used their breathing apparatus, the road they were in being a cross connection between the intake and return airways. They then travelled along this road to a point within a few yards of the return airway and found an official (Thomas?) who asked them to go into the stricken section. Parry Davies questioned the man's reasoning in wanting them to go into what he considered to be 'a death trap fully loaded with carbon monoxide'. On entering the section, they encountered 'unbearable heat and fumes'. They were told that other men of the

Llay No. 1 team were in this area and in difficulty. Parry Davies's team coupled up their breathing apparatus and went into the foul atmosphere of the 20s return airway. Tom Price Jones and Richard Harrison, together with Parry Davies and Price Beard, helped to get Jack Williams and Dan Hughes, who had both been gassed, to safety but Hughes was already dead. They had not gone more than 20 yards down when they came across Danny Hughes's lamp. A further 150 yards down they found the body of Bill Hughes of Rhosrobin, the Gresford man, lying face downwards with his head towards the pit bottom. Despite trying artificial respiration, they were unable to get any response. They could then see a light further down the roadway, probably from Jack Lewis, but the No. 2 team decided that there was a possibility that a doctor could help Bill Hughes and they decided to carry him back for treatment. Then, as Parry Davies later recalled:

> We volunteered to fetch John Lewis of Cefn-y-bedd. We could see his lamp burning 100 yards ahead but he was certainly dead because he was further in than the other rescuers' bodies we had recovered. The heat was terrific and some of our men were feeling the effects of it and Mr Boydell, the Mines Inspector, refused to allow us to go for Lewis.[69]

The bodies of two of the ill-fated rescue men were recovered the same day, that of John Lewis was not retrieved until the recovery team, led by Parry Davies re-entered the colliery on 18 May, 1935. All three men had been poisoned by carbon monoxide which they had inhaled either directly through moving their mouthpieces to one side, as Jack Williams said he had done, or because the breathing sets were faulty.

Jack (John) Lewis of Llay No. 1 Rescue Team, who died in the rescue attempt at Gresford on 22 September 1934. [Wrexham Archives]

Thus ended a brave attempt by the Llay Main rescue teams to come to the aid of stricken colleagues under circumstances which were weighted against them from the start. Even if they had known beforehand the full extent of the difficulties they would face, of extremes of heat, gas and roof falls, and the poor chances of success, it is more than likely that they would still have made the effort.

In the aftermath, blame was apportioned to Harold Thomas for allowing the Llay teams into the airway. Sir Henry Walker (Chief Inspector of Mines) concluded that:

> Harold Thomas sent the Brigade forward without a life line, and without a reserve brigade in attendance. It is therefore difficult to escape the conclusion that Harold Thomas was guilty of manslaughter.[70]

The funeral of Daniel Hughes was possibly the largest ever held in the village of Llay.

> **Llay Honours her Hero**
>
> Llay Main honoured her own hero, and not since the disaster there about nine years ago have similar scenes been witnessed. Miners rushed form the pit to do homage to Daniel Hughes, the member of the Llay Main Rescue Team who lost his life. Every window had its blinds down, and fully five hundred

men and women followed the coffin from the house to St Martin's church, Llay. Hughes, as an old soldier was accorded military honours, six Royal Welch Fusiliers acting as bearers with another military contingent forming an escort. Immediately behind came the banner of the British Legion, followed by a hundred Legionaries. Outside the church the village schoolchildren were marshalled but once onside they could not be seated and stood to take a reverent part in the impressive service. One could almost feel the tension and poignancy when the following verse of a favourite hymn was sung:

> Think O Lord, in mercy
> On the souls of those
> Who, in faith gone from us,
> Now in death repose
> Here mid stress and conflict
> Toils can never cease
> There the warfare ended
> Bid them rest in peace.

The service was conducted by the Rev. Edward Jones, vicar of Gresford, who was assisted by the Rev. Eaton Lloyd, vicar of Esclusham and the Rev. Gore Rees, priest in charge of St Martin's. Two nonconformist ministers, the Rev. J. Rowlands (Presbyterian) and the Rev. J. Pickering (Methodist) took seats behind the choir. The Rev. Gore Rees read out the names of twelve men, all men of Llay, entombed, and he and his congregation prayed for their souls. The organist (Mr E. Harding) played the Dead March in 'Saul', the service was over and the mourners proceeded to Broughton, another colliery village four miles distant for the internment. Here another big crowd awaited the dead hero, and soldiers fired a salute as the coffin was lowered into the grave. Thus was Daniel Hughes, one of many gallant men honoured by his own folk.[71]

A tribute to Bill Hughes of Gresford and to Daniel Hughes and Jack Lewis of the Llay No. 1 rescue team was subsequently given by Parry Davies: 'All three had died heroes, and their names will never be forgotten in the mining world, we raise our hats to their memory.' Of Jack (Lanc) Williams he said:

Shone's Lane September 1934. In the background are new colliery houses and on the right Stone Cottages, which were occupied by Mrs Chesters and 'Auntie Sid' Crewe. The Llay Colliery band is part of the cortége for the funeral of Daniel Hughes, the Llay rescuer killed in the Gresford Disaster. [Catherine Williams]

By a mere thread was his life saved. He was helped from the pit in an exhausted condition. I saw him that morning, his eyes appeared to be coming out of his head and practically helpless. As Captain of the team he had lost three men, all except himself. He had struggled with each one of these mates, trying to pull them back to fresh air and he exhausts himself. Only 20 more yards and he knows there is a chance of life, but the struggle is too much for him and he has to leave them one by one and he himself staggers back to the fresh air. His unselfish attempt to save his mates whilst endangering his own life is worthy of highest recognition.[72]

It was not until March 1935, nearly six months after the tragedy, that attempts were made to re-enter the Gresford pit. Volunteer rescuers from the local area were put through a rigorous training programme and sent to Hafod or Llay Main to practise repair work underground using breathing apparatus. On Monday, 4 March, the Llay No. 2 Rescue Team, led by Parry Davies, was the first to descend the Martin shaft, not to the pit bottom, but just 200 yards down to inspect the Pump House, and then another 150 yards to check that, at their meeting point, the ascending and descending cages would pass each other. Parry Davies's story of the recovery operation is recorded in the *Transactions of the Denbighshire Historical Society, Volume 22 (1973).*

The teams had only enough air for two hours and took turns to carry out the work during that first day of recovery operations. By the end of the day, the rescuers reported on a scene of destruction at the pit bottom where even men familiar with the place could not recognise it, '… the floor of the roadway was lifted up … heavy girders bent and broken pointing in all directions … the landing and scaffolding all blown to pieces.'[73]

For the first month of the recovery operation, five rescue teams made up of six men drawn, from all the local collieries, were used. A variety of animals were taken down to check the air at this time, but they sadly all soon expired. Before any restoration could be attempted, it was necessary to make the affected areas of the pits air-tight and 'stoppings' were built by the recovery teams who were encumbered by their breathing apparatus. On 8 April 1935, the seal on the Dennis Pit was removed and, by dismantling the air lock at the top of the Martin shaft, ventilation was restored to the pit. This was the signal for all kinds of visitors to be taken to see the wreckage for themselves. Reporters from the press accompanied officials underground and one took the following photograph. The reverse side of a copy of this photograph states, in Parry Davies's handwriting,

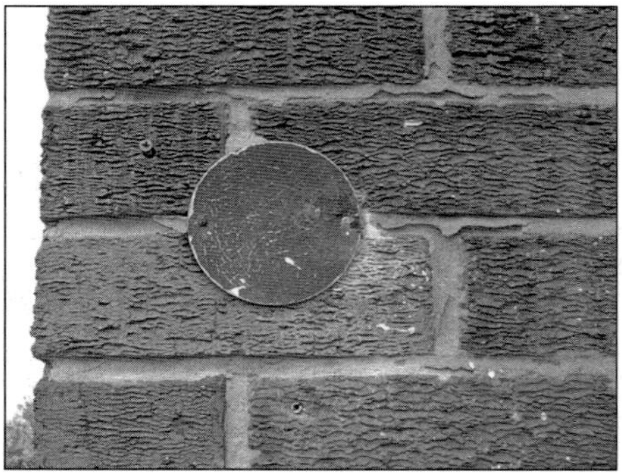

Blue rescue team disc on 122 Bryn Place in 2010. These discs were placed on the houses of trained rescuers.This is the last remaining disc in the village and is at the former home of Malcolm Williams.

Not everybody had 'phones in those days. The policeman would come around if there was an accident and they wanted mines rescue people out. At night, instead of knocking all the street up to see where I lived he'd shine his torch on this blue disc and the reflection would tell that policeman that it was a mines rescue house and he'd knock you up and we'd go to the incident wherever it was. [Malcolm Williams, 5 November 2010]

> I wrote the message on the tub, being unable to speak to my team they stood not far away shining the torches on the tubs which I had climbed to see for a way through. When some weeks after the pit was ventilated, the Chief Inspector came down with photographers and spotted the tub and photographed it.[74]

Gresford Colliery reopened in January 1936, but the Dennis section was sealed off and never worked again and still contains the remains of 255 men and boys.

At the same time that the Gresford recovery operation was underway, Llay Main's parent company, the Carlton Main Company, reported on a

Gresford Colliery, 3 April 1935 – scene at The 'Big Junction'. Photograph of fallen tubs. Chalked on tub is the message – 'Can't go this way. Same way back. P. Davies 11.3.35' [Muriel Davies]

Gresford Colliery, 4 March 1935 – Llay N°. 2 Rescue Team. Peter Hughes, Richard Harrison, unknown official, Parry Davies, Harold Povah, Tom Price Jones, Emlyn Jones. [Muriel Davies]

handsome profit for the year to 31 March 1935 of £238,670. This equated to around £9 million in 2010. The figure included a 19% dividend from Llay Main Collieries Ltd.[75]

Around 900,000 tons of coal were coming out of the colliery annually and with it large amounts of waste. The colliery chemist, R. G. Evans, delivered a paper for the annual conference of the Institute of Fuel in 1936 about the operation of the Rheolaver coal washing plant which had been installed in 1924. This, he said, was very efficient in recycling much of the coal waste to be used in the colliery boilers. However, he added a word of caution about the effect of coal waste on the environment:

> It is becoming increasingly apparent that coal cleaning, at any rate in a preliminary manner, must be carried out underground, and the refuse deposited direct to waste. I think that developments in this direction will be carried out in the future unless we continue to be prepared to pay haulage ... and are content to put up with the disfigurement of the countryside through the accumulation of tremendous amounts of waste material.[76]

By the mid 1930s, a large number of community organisations had been set up in the village of Llay. These reflected the interests and concerns of the of villagers and many were well supported by the colliery company.

Senior colliery officials often acted as president or chairman of these institutions and societies. In addition to those groups mentioned in the previous chapter, the following were set up before the advent of the Second World War.[77]

Llay Welsh Society (1926)[78]
Glanaber Welsh Presbyterian Church opened 29 November 1925
Llay Trinity Presbyterian Sisterhood
Llay Mothers Union (1925)[79]
Llay Tabernacle (Welsh) Wesleyan church – believed to have been a hut near the entrance to the caravan park on Gresford Road

Bill Rogers (right) and Llay Juvenile Jazz band, c.1935. *(Photograph was taken at Belle Vue Park, Wrexham). [Greville Williams]*

Llay Primitive Methodists Christian Endeavour[80]
Llay Male Voice Choir[81]
Llay Juvenile Choir[82]
Llay Juvenile Jazz Band
Llay St Martins' Gymnastic Club[83]
The Industrial Christian Fellowship
Llay Peace Pledge Union
Llay branch of the North Wales Womens' Temperance League
Llay Babies' Band of Temperance
The Temple of Light Spiritualist Church, Cefn-y-Bedd Road
Llay Angling Society
Llay Amateur Gardening Society (1926)
Llay Amateur Gardening Society Pantomime Company
1st Llay Scouts, Guides and Ranger Guides
Llay Women's Co-operative Guild
Llay Unemployed Association
The Lex Lodge of the Royal Antediluvian Order of Buffaloes (the Buffs)
Llay Tontine Society (Sick and Burial Club)
The Pride of Llay Lodge of the Manchester Unity of Oddfellows
The Star Lodge of the International Order of Good Templars
Llay St Martins' Boys Club
Llay St Martins' Girls Club
Llay St Martins' Clarion Cycle Club
Llay Liberal Party
Llay Labour Party
Llay Conservative Association

This was a village life then, everybody was here most, all of the time. We used to have these fetes. The processions used to go round the Ring and down the village. And the Rose Show and all that business, and people used to look forward to that in those days ... everybody was taking part. And we used to have a pantomime as well, my wife was one of the chorus girls in one of those. [Mr A][84]

The colliery company supported the Llay Amateur Gardening Society and its annual show which started in 1926 and became known as 'The Rose Show'. The company provided prizes and some competitions were reserved for gardeners from the village. The Miners' Welfare Institute became a popular venue for events of all kinds including the Rose Show. A Rose Queen was chosen by the senior girls at Llay School, a procedure which excluded all those who attended Grove Park Girl's Grammar School in Wrexham. Pre-Second World War queens that we know of are:

1928	Betty Mickleburgh	1930	Claudia Jones
1931	Nora Rogers	1934	Rose Jones
1935	Marjorie Williams	1936	Irene Rogers
1938	Rose Bolton		

Large numbers of men and boys travelled to Llay Main by bus from as far away as Chirk,

Glynceiriog, Cefn and Ruabon in the south and Buckley, Treuddyn and Mold in the north.[85] Various local bus companies were involved and when they put their fares up a round of management / union negotiations ensued.

> Fri, 16 Oct 1931 Meeting Mr Ball re increase in boys and workmen's bus fares to the colliery yard
> Fri, 23 Oct 1931 Meeting Mr Ball re Cefn & Ruabon Bus owners & fares of workmen[86]

Deductions of 2d for 'Hospital' and 3d for 'Doctor' went to two private schemes to cover what in time would be provided by the National Health Service (NHS). The Llay Main Colliery Medical & Hospital Fund was intended to ensure that miners and their families could receive the services of a doctor and, if necessary, be transported to hospital in the colliery ambulance. In 1924, an agreement was reached between the Llay fund and the Wrexham & District Medical Association to provide these services to Llay miners and their families. In the days before a 'rapid response' system, rule 9 stated that if an accident occurred to a miner at the colliery, then the doctor would decide 'which was the most available doctor to call upon to render first aid'.[87] As has been previously mentioned, the colliery soon established an efficient first aid system of its own and the colliery first-aiders, 'ambulance men' as they were called, were eventually required to go from house to house collecting the small subscriptions. Not everyone subscribed, but when an emergency occurred and a trip to hospital was required, no distinction was made between those who paid and those did not – the colliery's Sunbeam ambulance turned up.

Looking on the bright side, villagers perked up when in 1936, the colliery football team, Llay Welfare FC, won the Welsh Amateur Cup. Welfare beat Treharris of South Wales 3–1 in a replay at Oswestry, after the first game at Newtown was a 1–1 draw. The team had been formed when the Welfare and the recreation grounds were completed in 1931. Llay Welfare joined the Wrexham & District Amateur League in the 1932–3 season, it is likely that the team was the successor of the 'Llay Main' team. In the Welsh Cup of the 1936–7 season, after beating Llay United 2–1 in the second round, Welfare went on to beat Hereford United 4–3 in the fourth round, before falling to the eventual winners, Crewe Alexandra, 2–9 in the sixth round.

Llay Welfare FC were always regarded as being the colliery's team, whereas their rivals, Llay United FC, were thought of as the village team. They were set up in the southern end of the village and played on Miss Blackley's field on Pentre Lane. There was keen rivalry

THE LLAY AMATEUR GARDENING SOCIETY

AFFILIATED WITH THE ROYAL HORTICULTURAL SOCIETY — FOUNDED 1804 — ROYAL CHARTER 1809

9th Annual Show

Saturday, Aug. 3rd, 1935.

SPECIAL
FIRST PRIZE

Won by GORDON McDONALD

for Best Collection of WOOD WORK

No. MODELS Class KINDLY GIVEN by Mr CORF

Llay Rose Show 1935 – Gordon MacDonald won several prizes for woodwork in that year. He later worked as a wagon mender at the colliery and like many other colliery employees did work for the village which was sanctioned by the colliery management. Among many tasks he made the flagpole for the Welfare, a tombola drum for the Rose Show and fixed new seats into the cinema.
[Gordon MacDonald]

Llay United FC, winners of the Cheshire and District League Cup, and their supporters, 1933. Miss Blackley, the small lady seated to the left of the, owned the football field. The team members are (top row) Dick Thomas, Wilf Davies, Bill Gough (third row) Tom Williams. Harold (Llan) Williams, Matt Davies (second row) Harry Davies, Horace Jones, Joe Parry, Richard Weston (kneeling) Tommy Davies. Supporters include - Tom Hughes, Isaac Williams, Alf Ashfield, Doug Larkin, Bertha Ash, Sarah Ellen Davies [on the left holding baby], Geoffrey Davies, Nain Davies, Jack Chorley [with pipe],. Ivor Jones, Elsie Alsop, Jim Owens, Joe Wynne, Isaac Parry, Bill Payne, George Gaunt, Gwilym Evans, Gordon Davies, Tom Davies, Evelyn Thomas, Thomas Griffiths, Gwilym Williams, Fred Jones, Charles Sutherton, Haydn MacDonald. [Haydn MacDonald]

Llay United FC 1936–7. Winners of the St Martins Charity Cup and the Chester League Champions. Back row: Albert Williams, David Davies, Jack (Bala) Evans, Bill Hughes. Middle row: Jack Thomas, Gibson (?), –?–, Bill Gough, Wilf Davies, Joe Parry, Matt Davies, Felix Griffiths, Norman Williams (?) Front row: Albert Owen, Emrys Jones. Bill Roberts (Gresford), Tom Davies, –?–, Harold Williams, Harold Rogers, Arthur Davies. [Brenda Davies]

between the two teams. Llay Welfare FC were still playing in 2010, but Llay United folded when their ground was sold for a housing development in 1957.

By this time Llay Council School was having difficulty in accommodating all its pupils. The roll for this all-age elementary school had reached over 600 in 1931. At the age of 11, some pupils passed the scholarship examination for Grove Park Grammar Schools in Wrexham, but most of them stayed on until leaving at the age of 14. In September 1936, a secondary school was opened in Llay, known as Llay Central School.

> This school was opened today when 198 scholars were received from the Junior School. I Benjamin Williams have been appointed Headmaster. The school was erected at a cost of £1500 and was formally opened on Monday 21 Sept by Miss Kathleen Allington Hughes JP of Gresford and performed with a presentation golden key. Mr H.

Wagon menders, c.1936. Back row: Ernie Jones, Wilf Davies, Wilf Challoner. Front row: Stan Humphries, Gordon MacDonald, George Marsh, Bob Ashley. The wagon menders worked outside in all weathers

> *When the locos were out we used the loco shed to repair the wagons. They were a ten ton wagon or a twelve ton, that was the weight. Wagons had oak frames but the planks were softwood. There was an end door and two bottom doors and two side doors. They used to load the coal on to boats, still in the wagons – they'd open the side doors and bottom doors so that would empty into the hold of the ship. Len Rogers – he repaired wagons too and Don Smith was in charge of painting them.*[88]
> *[Gordon MacDonald]*

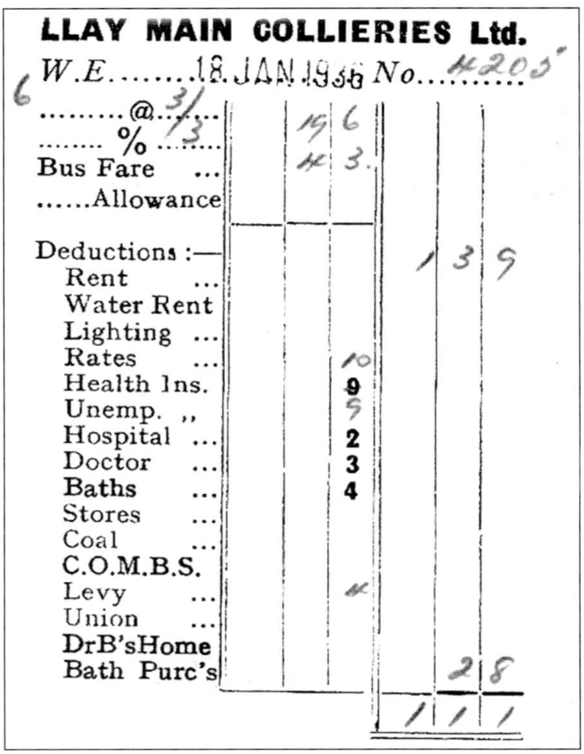

LLAY MAIN COLLIERIES Ltd.

6 W.E. 18 JAN 1936 No. 4205

@ 3/-		19	6		
% 1/3					
Bus Fare ...		4	3		
......Allowance					
Deductions :—					
Rent ...				1	3	9
Water Rent					
Lighting ...					
Rates ...			10		
Health Ins.			9		
Unemp. „			9		
Hospital ...			2		
Doctor ...			3		
Baths ...			4		
Stores ...					
Coal ...					
C.O.M.B.S.					
Levy ...			4		
Union ...					
DrB'sHome					
Bath Purc's					2	8
				1	1	1

Wage slip, January 1936. This wage slip is probably that of a boy worker. He was left with just over £1 for a week's work after deductions and out of that had to pay 4s 3d bus fare for which he received an allowance. [Herbert Gaskin]

Llay Central School opening ceremony – 21 September 1936. Left to right – Dick Harrison, Peter Hughes, Major W. P. Wheldon DSO, MA, Charles Jones (the Crown), H. Carleton Walker (Chairman of Llay Main Colliery), Ben Williams (Headmaster), Rev. John Charles Rowlands (Minister of Llay Presbyterian Church), Alderman Edward Williams JP (Secretary of the Welsh Department of the Board of Education), Kathleen Allington Hughes JP, Charles Williams JP, County Councillor Tom Jones (Denbighshire Education Committee representative), Thomas Henry Gaskin and an unknown schoolmistress. [Herbert Gaskin]

> Carleton-Walker, Chairman of the Directors of Llay Main Collieries Ltd remarked that everything that happened in this community was of vital interest to his colleagues and himself. Built to accommodate 280 pupils it was erected by Messrs Alun Edwards Ltd, of Cefn-y-Bedd to plans prepared by the County architect Mr G. D. Wiles. The site was presented by Llay Main Collieries Ltd.[89]

The first three pupils to be entered on the register were: Kenneth Cupit of 2, Second Avenue; Phyllis Ellis of Stone Cottage, Shone's Lane and Eirwen Jones of 61, Eighth Avenue.

The colliery's output in 1938 was 819,724 tons of saleable coal, an overall rate of 23.9 tons per 'man shift'.[90] From 1929, the annual figure had been around 900,000 tons per annum and the years between 1928 and 1938 proved to be the most productive for Llay Main and these results were never equalled. Moy Jones gives us a glimpse of the miners' work at this time:

> I came to start at Llay Main at the end of 1938 ... as a haulage hand on a day-wage. I could not get a start as a collier – they had a seniority system of promotion going where you had to serve a period on lasher haulage then on to timber haulage on to the face. The Long-wall system was just beginning to creep in – doing away with the old stall and plate system (men haulers). Production leaped up of course. I served my time on the haulages and eventually got a job as a ripper-repairer. We opened and drove out

Llay Junior School Teachers, 1938.
Back row: Albert Evans, Idwal Roberts, Aubrey Roberts (Headteacher), John William Hughes, Robert John Roberts, Ronald Hadlington.
Front Row: Winifred Lloyd Evans, Katie Samuels, Mary Jane Allen, Lottie Williams Parry, Morfydd Jones.

Mary Jane Allen was a pupil at Llay school from 1923 and went to Grove Park Grammar School Wrexham in September 1930. She appears to have been a teacher in the junior department for one month only, and thereafter spent her entire teaching career in the infants department where she was headteacher for many years.

Lottie Williams Parry of Rhos taught at Llay Council School between 1932 and 1939. She was a renowned pianist and piano teacher and was accompanist at the Llangollen International Music Eisteddfod. On 14 June 1947 she accompanied the opera diva Joan Hammond (soprano).[91] Many of Lottie's pupils took part in the village pantomimes. These were started at the Miners Welfare Institute and were produced by Llay Amateur Gardening Society with much support from the colliery.

Ronald Hadlington left the school to go into the Army and was appointed headteacher of Acton Park School in Wrexham in 1947. [Eryl Jones]

the East 'Quaker' seam at Llay Main – 90 yards of a drift down hill then opened both right and left hand sides to make a coal face 280 yards in length.[92]

By the end of 1938, both the colliery and the village could be said to be in their prime. Production at the pit was at a high level and, under the manager Thomas Mottram, many improvements had been brought about, not least that of improved mine safety. Village organisations were well established and supported, used by both miners and their families, and the Miners' Welfare Institute became the centre of activity for many popular events. A community had developed from difficult beginnings, finally characterised by friendliness towards one's neighbours and colliery workmates. These qualities would serve the village and colliery of Llay Main well in the years of war which lay ahead. In 1939, at the beginning of the war, some 2,500 men were employed at the pit,[93] but the armed services would take many of them far away from Llay.

Pay day at Llay Main Colliery offices, 1930s [Neville Rogers]

Llay Pantomime Company – Aladdin*, 1938. Back row: left Bill Rogers, Frank Crewe in soldier's uniform, left of 'Britannia'. Second row: –?–, –?–, –?–, –?–, –?–, Elsie Owen, Olwen Davies, Muriel Davies, Jack (Bala) Evans, Norman Hilton, Johnny Parsonage-Davies, Frank Lloyd, ?, Bill Crewe, saluting – Chrissie Lewis, Dorothy Price. Girls chorus: –?–,–?–, –?–, Joan Davies, –?–, –?–, –?–, Phyllis Vaughan, Betty Valentine, –?–. Orchestra: Bill Roberts, Jack Roberts (6th Avenue), Tom Dodd, Gladys Dunnico, Jack Donlan,–?–, Lew Moulsdale, –?– . These were lavish affairs and involved large numbers of villagers old and young as may be seen in the photograph below. Shows were usually staged for three nights and were always a sell-out. They were produced by either Harold Dunnico or 'Auntie' Gwen Blackshaw Jones. [Eleanor Bradshaw]*

4: Llay Main in the Second World War (1939–45)

On 30 September 1938, the British Prime Minister, Neville Chamberlain, returned from Munich claiming he had an understanding with *Herr* Hitler. His policy of appeasement failed but did at least provide a short breathing space, allowing vital preparations for war to be made. As the prospect of war became more imminent, the importance of the coal industry became clear – it was needed to power shipping and railways and to provide energy for the many industrial processes essential for the production of armaments, aeroplanes, ships, tanks and other vehicles of war. Llay coal fitted all of these purposes.

In April 1939, preparations for war had escalated when the government introduced the Military Training Act which called for all men between the ages of 20 and 21 to register for six months military training. Simultaneously, a list of reserved occupations nominated those jobs essential to the war effort and whose workers were exempt from military duties. Those not eligible for conscription were miners, farmers, dock workers, scientists, merchant seamen, railway workers and workers in the water, gas and electricity industries. This did not prevent many miners from Llay and elsewhere from joining the services.

On 3 September 1939, Britain declared war on Germany but the first six months became known as the Phoney War when nothing much seemed to be happening and work at Llay carried on as

Wagon shunting at Llay Main c.1939. [Peter Chadwick]

normal. During this period, perhaps the most noticeable change occurred with the arrival in the village of evacuees, the first of which arrived on 29 August 1939, two days before the official government instruction to carry out the evacuation scheme.[1] One evacuee, John Jacques, recorded his feelings.

> I left Durham two months ago to live with my aunt. I did not mind leaving Durham as I was eager to see Wales. After I had spent a few days touring Wales, I started at Llay Central School, and I thought it better than the school at Durham. The only thing I do not like is Algebra, but I will have to learn it, because I must do my best to uphold the honour of Durham. School at Durham was pleasant, but it is more pleasant at Llay. I like gym and arithmetic best of all. That I did not like at Llay was all the pit smoke and grime. I used to enjoy watching ships in harbour and aeroplanes at the aerodrome. I see no ships or aerodrome at Llay. The saddest part of my evacuation was that my dog got lost soon after I brought him to Llay.[2]

In 1939, the community of Llay was made up of 838 houses and with a population of 3,100 it was one of the largest villages in the Wrexham area. As such, it was expected to take its fair share of evacuees. The Llay billeting officers were Mrs E. J. MacKnight, Mrs R. J. Evans, Mrs H. Holmes, Mrs S. A. Foster, Mrs J. J. Sides and Mrs Tom Jones[3] whose task was to find homes for the evacuees. Billeting was compulsory and an allowance of 10s 6d was paid at the post office for each child under 10 years of age and for subsequent children, 8s 6d. An allowance of 10s 6d was paid for all children aged between 10 and 14. For those between 14 and 16 years, the allowance was 12s 6d, and for youths aged over 16, 15s. The allowances did not include the cost of boots and clothing, which remained the responsibility of their parents.

Throughout the country people who took children into their homes complained about the state of their health:

> Research suggests that around half of the evacuated children had fleas or headlice. Others suffered from impetigo and scabies. Billetors were sometimes appalled by the behaviour of the evacuees. It is estimated that about 5 per cent of the evacuees lacked proper toilet training. One billetor reported about how, when one six-year-old boy went to the toilet in the front room, his mother shouted. 'You dirty thing, messing up the lady's carpet. Go and do it in the corner.'[4]

Between 1939 and 1945, around 113 infant evacuees and 188 children of junior-school age were admitted to people's homes and the schools in Llay. To this number it is necessary to add approximately 100 pupils of secondary-school age. They were mostly given a warm welcome and some still return to the village from time to time. They came mainly from Liverpool or London, but some were from Manchester, Birmingham, the east coast towns of Essex and the Swansea area.

Year	*Infants*	*Juniors*
1939	8	18
1940	8	21
1941	49	65

1942	24	24
1943	8	15
1944	15	40
1945	1	5
Totals	113	188

Evacuees admitted to Llay Infants and Junior Schools

During the war, approximately 34% of admissions to the junior school were evacuees and infant evacuees accounted for around 25% of the total intake which must have made significant demands upon the ability of the schools to manage classes and to teach children of different backgrounds and capabilities. Some children stayed for only a short time – one family of four attended in the morning but left that afternoon. Such disruption must have had a adverse effect upon the education of all children at the schools. During this time, school life included fire-fighting drills with stirrup pumps and buckets of water, and air-raid drills with gas masks.

From the school yard at break times came the sound of the childrens' games of the day:

> Skipping to rhymes like 'north, south, east, and west. Who's the one I love the best? Capital A, B, C etc …' were played mostly in the Spring. This was the way you found your future husband's name. Another action rhyme that I remember well was 'I am a Girl Guide dressed in blue. These are the actions I must do. Salute to the King, Bow to the Queen. And turn my back on the German submarine.' I guess it is quite usual that schoolyard rhymes reflect the community state of affairs. It is not unusual that a child would adapt a known rhyme and make it topical. The item on which one 'turned one's back' could just as easily be a hated teacher or local politician. This one was relevant during the war years and I think demonstrates how much our lives were governed by war, even at that young age. We also had a singing game which the boys and girls did separately. Two girls (or two boys) would link arms and walk around the schoolyard saying 'Who'll join up in the ATS' The boys would say 'Who'll join up in the RAF' Anyone who wanted to play the game, joined in the line and took up the chant.[5]

In April 1940, with the German attacks on Norway, Denmark, Belgium and France, the French and Belgian coalfields were lost and Llay coal became all the more important. Before going underground at the start of his shift, the collier's first task was to pick up his cap lamp which was being charged up in the lamp room. Each lamp had a unique number and next to it, hanging on a cup hook, was a brass tally with the same number stamped on it. The number was also the collier's pay number. The battery pack attached to the cap lamp was then strapped onto the miner's trouser belt and worn at the back. From the lamp room, the collier would make his way to the pithead taking his tally with him. Before entering the cage to descend, the banksman collected the tallies. He was in charge of loading and unloading the cages and he searched the miners for 'contraband' – matches, lighters or cigarettes as these constituted a fire risk. Miners could not enter the cage unless they had handed in the tally.

After the last man had descended the mine, the tallies would be sent up to the Wages Office for the clerks to record who was down the mine and the time each of the colliers had started their shift. Once recorded, the tallies would be taken back to the pithead and hung on a large board.

At the end of the shift, the miner would collect his tally from the board, return his lamp to the charging racks in the lamp room and hang his tally next to it. As long as both lamp and tally were in place in the lamp room, it was known that the miner had safely come up from the pit. If neither were present then the miner was clearly working overtime and the Wages Office would record this. It had been known for a miner to forget to place his tally alongside his lamp before going home and, after checks had been made underground, someone would be sent to the miner's home to see if he was there, and if so, he would be brought back to the colliery to retrieve his tally from his working clothes in the pithead baths and place it in its correct position in the Lamp Room. Over the years, there were variations of this system and in the shape of the tallies.[6]

The supply of food to Britain was being cut off as German U-boats in the North Atlantic sank merchant ships and the rationing of scarce items was introduced on 8 January 1940. In Llay, ration books were distributed from the Llay Miners' Welfare Institute and the allowances per person per week were 4 ounces of butter, 4 ounces of bacon or ham and 10 ounces of sugar. Two months later, meat was rationed on the basis of 1s 10d per week, with children under six years on half rations. Food coupons were exchanged for goods at the Co-op or Meredith's Stores. Owing to the restriction of fat and sugar people generally ate healthily.

Llay Main Colliery Company Ltd lamp tally pre-1947.

We used to go to Bill Wynne's dad's farm during the war to get greengroceries. Lizzie was his favourite. He used to say 'Come on now Mrs Larkin, you can have just what you want.' She couldn't bear Bill Wynne's dad but we used to say 'Go on, get some stuff for us.'[7]

By this time, the Ministry of Agriculture's 'Dig for Victory' campaign was pressing people to grow their own food and by 1943, over a million tons of food were being produced in this way. In Llay, allotments were opened up on the Gresford Road.

Walter Holt's 'chip vans' were a boon to hungry villagers during the war. Mr and Mrs Holt each had a fish and chip cart. The two carts would be pulled by one horse and were parked in Third Avenue and Eighth Avenue. Walter's house was just below the waste banks, alongside the Cefn-y-Bedd Road, across from the entrance to Llay Hall Farm. An aerial ropeway carried buckets of waste which were tipped up as they rounded a stanchion at the end of the line. Now and then, a bucket was full of coal, not mine waste. The rope would be stopped when this bucket had reached the rear of Walter's house so that the contents could be tipped into his back garden for use in his fryers.

Government programmes encouraged people to be thrifty and to 'make do and mend'.

Woollen garments were recycled by unpicking the stitches washed dried and re-knitted again. Coats were unpicked, turned inside out and made into smaller coats for children. Ashes in the fire grate were raked out in the morning and put back on the fire when it was lit.[8]

MINISTRY OF AGRICULTURE AND FISHERIES

WAR-TIME
GROW MORE FOOD
CAMPAIGN

Certificate
of
Merit

Awarded to

Mr. H. Gaskin.

who cultivated a plot of land to the best advantage and so made a valuable contribution towards the Nation's effort to grow more food in time of war

1945

T. Williams
MINISTER OF AGRICULTURE AND FISHERIES

OMNIA VINCIT LABOR

Certificate for growing food. [Herbert Gaskin]

During the war, many Llay women worked at the large Royal Ordnance Factory at Marchwiel on the site of the present-day Wrexham Industrial Estate. Started in 1939, the factory made cordite, a propellant for shells. Some Llay women made munitions closer to home and could walk to a small factory which was set up in the grounds of Gresford Lodge in the Singret.

In 1940, Mrs Peggy McAlpine responded to a call for more munitions and contacted friends of her family to organise a factory for women who, because of family ties, could not work far from home. Together with Mrs McAlpine, Mrs R. M. Duckworth and her daughter Miss Josephine Duckworth of Gresford Lodge and Mrs K. Nicholson of Marford, set up as the Elliott Engineering Company to produce small engineering parts for the government, including the L-delay fuse. This secret factory was staffed by women from Llay, Gresford and the surrounding area and had 35 employees at its peak. Blodwen Griffiths, Eirwen Jones, Mona Preston, Lizzie Robinson and Emily Walker were some of the Llay women who worked there. Mrs and Miss Duckworth worked alongside others in the team in this enterprise, not knowing the full reason for their endeavours at the time.

The 'L-delay' was a delayed action fuse favoured by the Special Operations Executive and was dropped to Resistance units throughout Europe.

> [It was] timed to go off at intervals from an hour to a month, was no bigger than a fountain pen, inside which was a striker, attached to a spring that, in turn, was fixed to a small piece of black metal. The principle of its working was the time taken for the metal to break when stretched by the spring. The metal had to be ground to one ten-thousandth part of an inch.[9]

At the colliery, preparations for war included air-raid precautions (ARP). The colliery had its own air-raid wardens under the control of R. G. Evans, the colliery chemist. Each warden was

"BACK-ROOM GIRLS" OF GRESFORD

HOW PEN-SIZED SECRET WEAPON WAS MADE

("Chronicle" Special)

North Wales Chronicle, *Saturday, 24 November 1945. [North Wales Media Ltd]*

given a copy of the *ARP Practical Guide* and training was arranged to cover gas attacks, incendiaries and high explosives. The blackout was strictly enforced and during the build-up to war, the Defence Regulations of 1939 required that all artificial lighting at collieries should be extinguished as a permanent condition from the outbreak of hostilities. At the power house, shaded lamps were to be provided only to illuminate switchgear and winding-engine controls and winding-engine indicator markings were to be treated with fluorescent paint, activated by ultra-violet light. There was no exterior lighting.[10]

The village saw little enemy action but on the night of 19 August 1940, a bomb fell on land at the rear of the cemetery and sadly a horse belonging to Ted Jarvis (who used to deliver coal to the local houses) was killed when it was blown into a tree.[11] A goalpost on the Llay United football field was shattered at the same time. Another of Jarvis's horses was hit by shrapnel in a field alongside the New Road, between Sixth Avenue and Pentre Lane. This horse had wounds, but fortunately they were not too serious and for many years it could be seen pulling Jarvis's coal cart around the village with the quite visible scars on its rump.

There was a serious threat to the colliery that German bombers returning from raids on Liverpool would jettison any remaining bombs over the village. On 30 September 1940, the colliery had a near miss when in mid-afternoon two bombs were dropped near to the colliery reservoir. Part of the baths' roof was blown off, leaving some miners running for 'essential cover'. The Heinkel aeroplane was seen by pupils as they came out of school and bombs were seen leaving the aircraft. A whole shift could have been trapped underground if the bombs had exploded a short distance to the west of their impact point.

> I'll tell you where he dropped it: right behind the bike shed at the colliery. It was daylight and there was a chap we called big Tom in the locker room of the baths. We had top lockers and bottom lockers for dirty and clean clothes and like a ridge, about two foot high you could put your feet on to lace your shoes up. The bomb dropped, made a hole in the roof of the baths, made a hole in the roof of the canteen. And Big Tom tried to scramble underneath these lockers! And Peter George that kept the bike shed, he run across the road and he landed flat on his back in the baths! And the chap that kept the barber shop by the Ring, he was always a bighead. He said 'I could see it was a German,' he said 'So I run in to get the rifle … ' [laughs] He never had a rifle! [Mr S][12]

In 1940, two units of the Local Defence Volunteers (LDV) – known everywhere as 'Look, Duck and Vanish' were formed in Llay, one at the colliery, the other in the village. The LDV was renamed the Home Guard on 22 July 1940.

> I was in the Home Guard from the first time it started as LDV. We did our training in the Drill Hall. We did shooting on the shooting range - it belonged to the Territorials at sometime. When the LDV started we only had one gun between us . We had a lamp, a lantern, oil or paraffin. Sand Hole Farm on Higher Lane was used for training for the Llay Home Guard. We used to stop the buses and everything and ask for their identity cards. When challenging vehicles there'd be two on the road waving lanterns for you to stop. One Home Guard would go to either side with colleagues waiting in the bushes with guns. You could be on duty at night and have to go to work on the 6 a.m. shift. Boredom was rife and ceramic insulators on power wires were used as target practice.

The shadows of two bomb craters were still visible in a field near the reservoir entrance on Rackery Lane in 1999. [Graham Hughes]

Llay Main Colliery Air Raid Wardens 1939–40. The sign reads 'Calling all ARP – get in touch with Mr R. G. Evans' Back row: Arthur Folwell, I. Jenkins, E. Griffiths, Sam Dingley, H. E. Bray, Lewis, –?–, Harold Dunnico. Middle Row: –?–, H.Smith, Tom Love, Jack Probert, –?–, Harry Goss, I. B. Evans, –?–,–?–, Stan Jones, –?–, Leslie Crewe. Front row: T. J. Roberts (instructor) Rowlands, Robinson, Jack Hammerton, R. G. Evans, Harold E. Dudley, Abrahams, Archie Parkin, –?–. [Henry Bray]

You'd go home from work, have your dinner and change into the LDV uniform, a blouse it was, thick – same as the soldiers had. The trousers – we used to put these on and go up to the Drill Hall. We had a sergeant, came to train us – Bill Salisbury – a sergeant major. Ted Griffiths, the farm on the back road – he's standing just in front of me in the photo, and 'Johnny Bash 'Em' – Johnnie Davies.'[13]

Llay Drill Hall in 2006. Built in 1934 on the New Road next to the children's recreation ground, this was the HQ for the wartime Llay Home Guard and had an indoor rifle range at the rear. It was demolished in 2006. [Graham Hughes]

In addition to his efforts with the Home Guard, Gordon also volunteered for duty as a carpenter in Wrexham in case repairs were needed to bombed buildings.

Wartime duties of the Home Guard included guarding the viaduct over the River Alyn to protect the colliery rail link with the main line. Doug Foulkes was an engineer in the colliery power house and he was detailed to guard this point. Tommy Jones (Yorkie) also spent time there on Saturday nights, guarding with his mates Tom Parry and Jackie (Bala) Evans.[14]

Llay Village Home Guard 'A' Company, A4 Platoon, 1944. Back row. Norman Fidler, Harold Ellis, Noel Williams, Dennis Turner, John E. Davies. Third row: Jim Worthington, D. Jones, Ted Levey, R. Williams, Walter Thomas, Ben Griffiths, –?–, John Knight?, Glyn Hodgkinson, Jack Humphreys, Gordon Macdonald, Ted Lloyd. Second row: Jim Langford, Ben Williams, Dan Hodgkinson, Graham Forsyth, –?–, John Mulvaney, Wilfred Williams, Albert Cummings. Front row: Ralph Lush, Ivor Jones, Kevin Loughran (The Chemist), Jack Worthington, Ronald T. Hughes, Bill Salisbury, Glyn Hughes, Ted Griffiths, –?–. [Gwilym Owen]

Air-raid precautions were serious matters and Llay folk needed to know where to shelter, how to comply with blackout restrictions, extinguish fires and how to put on gas masks. Morrison shelters were provided by the District Council at key locations, but many dug their own in their back gardens.

Gordon MacDonald with his Defence Medal in February 2009. As far as we know, he is the only Llay man to receive this award solely for Home Guard duties, although many were entitled to it.

I lived at the top of Pentre Hill and my brother-in-law emptied the brick coal place and filled sacks with sand and placed them all around it, cleaned it out and we all sheltered in there when the air-raid siren went off. There was a communal shelter off Platts corner and one on the end house in Tenth Avenue where Mr Taylor used to live. I worked for a time in the munitions factory in Marchwiel, occasionally we had 'Workers' Playtime' concerts which we all enjoyed.[15]

The air-raid siren was quite loud. On hearing it my mother used to take me through a gate in the wicker fence between the church and Seventh Avenue and into the boiler house under the church. There was an air raid shelter at the top of the road but we never used it. I remember the drone of the aircraft above.[16]

A large brown box was delivered, it contained baby brother Colin's gas mask. Mum had to practice putting him in it and squeezing a bellows-like handle to get air to him. It frightened her to death and she said she didn't know if she could ever actually put Colin in it if there was a gas attack.[17]

Llay Home Guard set up a gun emplacement on top of the waste banks facing the Miners' Welfare Institute and a steel post marks another defensive position.

The villagers were determined to pull together to ensure that as far as possible there was an air of normality in spite of the desperate situation they were facing. The annual Rose Shows continued, and village clubs and societies were as popular as ever, many of them meeting at the Miners' Welfare Institute. Night classes were held there

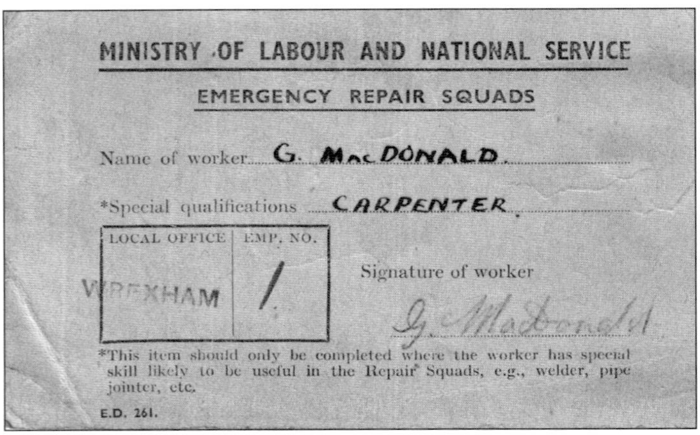

MINISTRY OF LABOUR AND NATIONAL SERVICE

EMERGENCY REPAIR SQUADS

Name of worker G. MacDONALD

*Special qualifications CARPENTER

LOCAL OFFICE	EMP. NO.
WREXHAM	1

Signature of worker G. Macdonald

*This item should only be completed where the worker has special skill likely to be useful in the Repair Squads, e.g., welder, pipe jointer, etc.

E.D. 261.

Air Raids – Emergency Repair Squad I.D card. [Gordon MacDonald]

to teach people how to deal with poultry. Dances and concerts took place, there was a local choir and pantomimes were produced.

> During the war, the Welfare hosted ENSA concerts, one a month. The Hallé Orchestra performed there, conducted by John Barbirolli. His wife was an oboeist in the orchestra. There was also a visit by Dame Edith Evans.[18]

The church hut was home to the Wolf Cubs, Scouts and Girl Guides, the scout-master being Tom Gaskin from First Avenue. Alf Jones (Little Alf), from Fourth Avenue, taught the drum and bugle band.[19] St Martin's Boys Club had a dance band and the cinema was a major attraction. Films were shown there and children would try to persuade the American soldiers to get them into the cinema, 'When we attended 'the flicks' we took our Mickey Mouse gas marks just in case'.[20]

In May 1941, a report by T. H. Gaskin, who was clerk of works for the Llay Housing Association, provided an insight into the extent of air-raid shelters in Llay at that time:

> We have now built 92 blast walls which makes 55 shelters between houses. I have 34 walls to build to complete all the passages – 73 shelters. Each one will take 18 persons. We have completed one 48-person shelter in the square of Third Avenue and we have started to build another in New House Avenue which will be completed in three weeks. There are about ten of these surface shelters to build in our part of the village at present.[21]

Air-raid precautions sometimes extended to the protection of musical instruments:

> After Dr Hennessy left for Gresford, Dr Mitchell, from Wem, took over in Llay and was there when war broke out. He liked a pint and would spend an hour in the kitchen in the evening in the Crown. He had an expensive baby grand piano which he thought very highly of. One morning after a bombing raid a small crater or hole was discovered in his garden. It was thought that it might be an unexploded bomb and Dr Mitchell offered a reward if a few men would remove the piano, but there were no takers. It was later decided that a dog had buried a bone.[22]

Sometimes air raids were a source of fascination:

> The nights were more exciting when we were allowed to watch the fingers of lights made by searchlights darting across the sky trying to pick up the source of the drone of aircraft engines.[23]

Home Guard barrier post 2009. This is still standing near the old colliery entrance. A wire rope was stretched across Hope Road at this point so that vehicles could be stopped.

The turmoil of the war brought about the dislocation of many families throughout the country. Husbands joined the armed services and wives went out to work and they were left to muster what help they could to look after their children. For large families this might mean that children were shared between relatives, a long-standing practice and necessity among the poorer working people. Llay families also housed the children of relatives from the areas of the country more at risk from bombing and even from local places such as Penycae, Wrexham and Llandudno.[24]

Llay Carnival. Ken Jones and Beryl Mathews c.1940.

> After one heavy air raid on Birkenhead, Mum hired Mr Manktelow (the colliery chauffeur) to go to look for her parents. The taxi wove up and down the streets and people were lined up at temporary soup kitchens. Bodies covered with tarpaulins were lying on the road. Eventually Mum spotted Gran and Grandad, all their possessions were gone, and they came back to Llay with us. At various times during the war Mum's sisters, Aunie Jo and Aunie Kit, came to live with us, plus all their children. Their husbands were fighting in Africa or Europe. My cousins Joan, Georgie and Philip Kneen stayed for a long time, but they returned home from time to time.[25]

During the war, Llay Miners' Welfare Institute was a reception centre for evacuees arriving from Liverpool, London and other towns subjected to bombing. Some left home in such a hurry that they arrived at the Welfare without identity cards and ration books. Llay Parish Council asked Wrexham Rural District Council to provide an officer to deal with this problem.[26] After arriving at the Welfare the evacuees were given a hot meal by Llay Women's Voluntary Service (WVS) and reassurance that all

Blast wall between 'entry' houses. The blast wall between numbers 17 and 19 Seventh Avenue can be seen on the left. This made the passage between the houses, or 'entry' as it was known, into a rudimentary air-raid shelter. In this photograph, taken in 1944, Bertha Hughes, a member of the WVS, is holding her daughter, Maureen, who was six months old. The Hughes family has been 'digging for victory' by planting vegetables in their front garden, normally a lawn. [Graham Hughes]

Evacuees – the Hesketh children at 31 Eighth Avenue in 1941. William Edward aged 5, Jean aged 8 and an older sister came to stay with the Lloyds (Randal Lloyd on the right). Their home was at 15 Maggie Street, Liverpool 5. [Randal Lloyd]

would well whilst they waited to be taken to billets by the billeting officers. The WVS were part of the country's civil defence structure and the local chairman between 1941 and 1945 was Miss Kathleen Allington Hughes, MBE, JP, so often the benefactress of the village.

By 1941, food was in short supply and a civil defence plan for the local distribution of foodstuffs was drawn up. It would only be put into operation in a dire emergency and parish councillors, Charles Jones and Jim Sides, were placed in charge of it. They would have had an estimated population of 3,852 to cater for.[27] At the same time, Ernest Ankers was installed as Food Production Officer for Llay. Ernest had won the Military Medal in the 1914–18 war for carrying a wounded officer off the battlefield, and was therefore considered to be an ideal choice for the post.[28] More agricultural workers were needed and Marjorie Hughes, Phyllis Holmes and Rhona Evans joined the Womens' Land Army unit based in Gresford to work on local farms. These were joined by Italian and later German prisoners of war.

> I remember seeing prisoners of war working on Moore's farm on 'the Ring'. They wore boiler suits which had a large yellow circle sewn into the back. We watched one of them planting a row of poplar trees along the left hand side of the farm drive. Two of these survive and can be seen across the road from the bus shelter by the Ring.[29]

LLAY COMFORTS AND WELCOME HOME FUND

(Registered under the War Charities Act, 1940)

Chairman: Rev. T. D. C. Williams, St. Martin's Vicarage, Llay
Treasurer: Mr. W. T. Parrott, 4 Fourth Avenue, Llay
Secretary: Mr. F. Owen

33 Shones Lane,
Llay,
Nr. Wrexham

Dear Neville,

It is with extreme pleasure that we enclose a gift of cheque from the Welcome Home Fund, and we are asked to express to you our very sincere admiration of the services you rendered your country in the late war, 1939—1945.

The men and women of Llay played their part nobly and saw service in every theatre of war and always distinguished themselves.

If you have returned to "civvy street," we wish you good health and good luck in the future; if still serving, we look forward to your early return to your home and family.

In conclusion, we would like you to know the debt we owe to the people of Llay for their support of our efforts during the last seven years. They have readily responded to all calls made upon them.

With renewed appreciation and gratitude,

On behalf of the Committee,
T. D. C. Williams, Chairman
W. T. Parrott, Treasurer
F. Owen, Secretary

Llay Comforts and Welcome Home Fund – letter to Neville Rogers, 1946. [Neville Rogers]

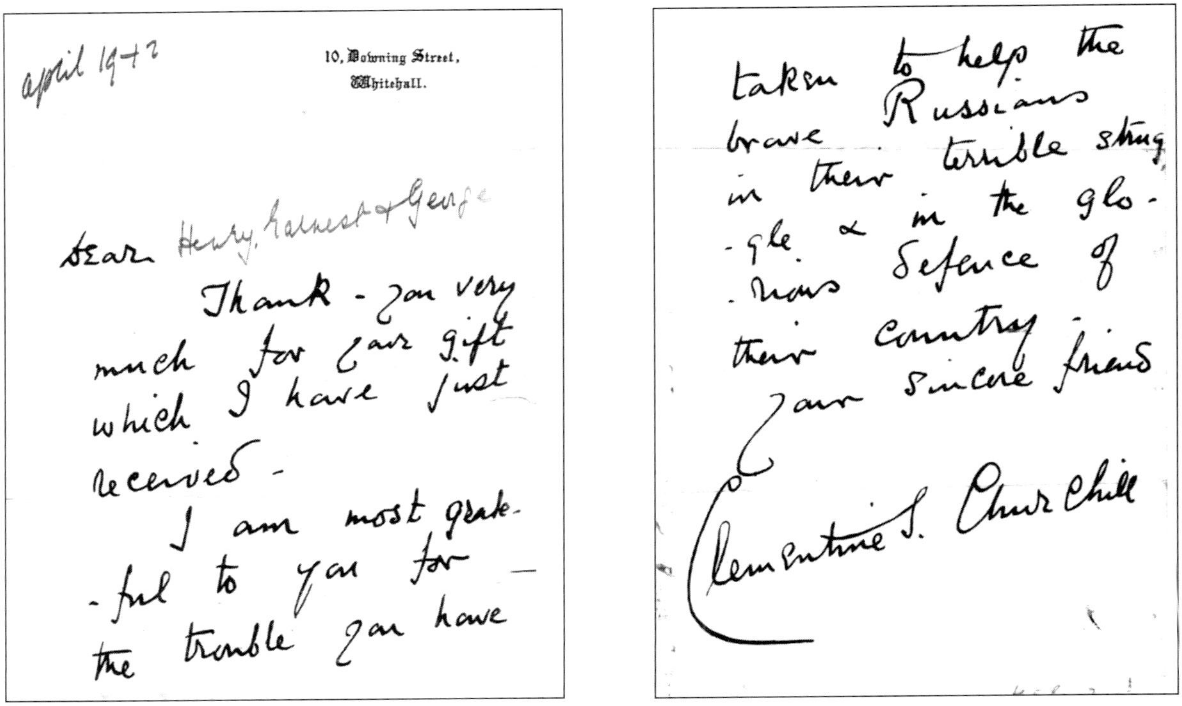
april 1942

10, Downing Street,
Whitehall.

Dear Henry, Earnest & George

Thank - you very much for your gift which I have just received -

I am most grate-ful to you for the trouble you have taken to help the brave Russians in their terrible struggle & in the glorious defence of their country.

Your sincere friend

Clementine S. Churchill

Letter to Henry Bray from Clementine Churchill, 1942. [Henry Bray]

People were asked to support the war effort by contributing to various causes. Local areas were asked to fund the cost of building ships and aeroplanes. The Wrexham area had a Warship Week in early December 1941 with the objective of raising £210,000 to buy a destroyer. Earlier in the year, a dance was organised by the Womens' Institute at the Welfare in aid of 'Prisoners of War Funds and Distressed Areas'.[30] The Llay Comforts and Welcome Home Fund was set up to provide extras for the Llay servicemen who were on active duty and for those retuning home after the war had ended. The following letter was sent to Neville Rogers on his return from duty in the Royal Navy:

In 1941–2, toy making was banned and toy manufacturing companies, such as the London-based Lines Brothers (Tri-ang toys), turned to munitions work; their 7,000 workers being employed to make over 1,000,000 machine guns, shell cases and aircraft identification books.[31] In the winter of 1941, three Llay schoolboys, Henry Bray, Ernest Dunnico and George Vaughan decided to make wooden toys which they sold in aid of Clementine Churchill's Red Cross 'Aid to Russia' appeal. Germany had invaded the Soviet Union in June 1941 and the fund was set up to alleviate the suffering of the Russian people. The boys raised £10 and had a letter of thanks from Mrs Churchill who chaired the Fund committee.

We had to amuse ourselves a best we could. There was no tele and not many had anything in the way of toys only what you made yourself – an old bike frame with pram wheels on, a catapult, a kite made out of brown paper and bits of string scrounged form Irene in the Co-op drapery. Maybe a fishing rod made out of a cane from the greenhouse, with a penny hook and two-penny cork float bought from

Tommy Yorkie. It was then down to Walter Holt's pond or the twenty-two-acre pond. While we fished at Walter Holt's, we could see the buckets on the aerial system tipping the waste, and the bulldozer driven by Jack Tryddyn levelling it out at the top of the tip. We even stocked out the bomb crater by the colliery with fish when it had filled with water and fished there. We made rope swings down in the School Wood with ropes found in the colliery tips.[32]

Working conditions underground at the colliery had been steadily improving over the years but one health problem persisted. Miner's nystagmus was one of the first medical conditions to be classified as an industrial disease and is characterised by quick involuntary movements of the eyes, usually from side to side and the miners version was thought to be caused by working for long periods in poorly lit mines. In 1925, it was estimated that 25% of miners suffered from it.[33] Glyndŵr Cooper of 125, Pentre Lane was certified as suffering from this condition in January 1942 and was on full compensation until 1 December 1942 when he was examined by a doctor at Rodney Street in Liverpool. The doctor's prognosis included his view that in considering what sort of future employment might be offered to Glyndŵr, the effects of war should be taken into account. In particular his patient would '… not be able to be out in the blackout. In peacetime I do not think he would be employable but during the war the colliery company might be able to offer some light work on the surface'.[34] Glyndŵr did return to light work at the colliery but his claim for compensation dragged on until November 1944. Miners' nystagmus is no longer recognised as an occupational disease as the conditions that led to it are believed to no longer occur in today's industry.[35]

In March 1942, a series of lectures was given by the Food Advice organisation for Llay Womens' Institute at the Miners' Welfare Institute. These meetings were well attended as housewives sought to make the most of what little food stocks they had. A British Restaurant was opened by Wrexham Rural District Council on 27 April 1942 at the church hut next to St Martins church where a three-course meal cost only 9d.[36] It was closed on 25 September 1943 when the school canteen was opened.

Mum and Dad were more interested in feeding my brother and myself than in feeding themselves. Colin and I would share a fried egg and Mum would insist that Dad had the other one as 'after all he was a working man'. Dad would pick mushrooms for us on his way home from work when he was on 'days' and that would be a special treat for us.[37]

I remember being presented with my first banana after the war. I had only seen pictures of them before.[38]

When I was abroad, I got a letter off the churchwarden saying that I was in arrears with my subscription. I was little bit upset about it because at the time you didn't know whether you were going to be alive the next day! We were making a quick dash back from Gibraltar to Liverpool, so I thought one way of appeasing the Churchwarden was to bring something back and I brought a great big bunch of bananas, green they were. And they'd just installed the new Church pipe organ and they raffled these bananas because bananas weren't heard of during the war. So it got me out of bad books. [Mr R][39]

Almost every house in our street kept chickens to supply eggs and meat, especially at Christmas. Along with the chickens were roosters and the mornings were a cacophony of cock-a-doodle-dos.[40]

Evacuees continued to arrive. In 1943, William and Harriet Phillips came to Llay from Liverpool and were billeted with Mr and Mrs Meadows at 9, Sixth Avenue. William, aged 9, was admitted to the Junior School on 27 September 1943. Harriet, who was 14, was admitted to Llay Central Secondary School on the same day. Theirs was a particularly sad story as their mother Maria had died in 1937, aged 42, leaving father Robert to look after his five children. The family home was in Islington Row at the back of Higson's brewery. Robert was an air-raid warden and during the night of 7/8 May 1941 (which turned out to be the last of the major blitzes on Liverpool) was checking on his family at the Wilton Street air-raid shelter, not far from the family home, when the shelter took a direct hit. All inside were buried under the rubble and it was discovered that amongst the dead were Robert, aged 45, and his daughter Jane, aged 22. The other children, Rose, Harriet and William were rescued and taken to Whiston hospital. Rose remained in Liverpool.

Harriet and William were both homesick in Llay and returned to Liverpool in October 1944 to be looked after by Rose and their brother, Robert. In later life, William became an artist in Basle, Switzerland whilst Harriet had a post in the Cunard shipping company.[41]

> We had four evacuees living with us, a brother and sister, Dorothy and Roy Hughes, from Gainsborough Road in Liverpool, Dorothy Jones who lived across the road from them and Leonard Chipchase from Waterloo. I remember going with them to the Church Hut which at that time was a canteen serving meals at lunch time for the evacuees.[42]

St Martin's Boys' Club football team, 1943–4. Back row: Frank Tarran, Arthur Mellard (club leader), Les Jones, Ivor Davies, Harold Rogers, Gwilym Powell (County Youth organiser), Ken Jones, Morgan Yemm, Ray Jenkins, Ron Fisher, John Griffiths Front row: Jack Love, Ben Jones, Ronnie Hughes, Arthur Powell, Cyril (Alec) Davies, Gwyn Thomas, Bill Jackson. [Greville Williams]

In June 1943, the second edition of the St Martin's Boys' Club magazine, *The Ace of Clubs*, was published. It reported that a three-day conference was to be held at Llay for the North Wales Federation of Boys' Clubs and that the main issue under discussion was to be post-war reconstruction. One hundred and twenty former club members were serving in the forces. The magazine indicated that a very full programme of activities was keeping Llay boys busy: speakers at the club included Lieutenant Nagorski of the Polish Army and there were numerous sporting activities, summer camps, a choir, chess competitions, day trips and an ATC detachment. A drama group had been formed in 1941 in collaboration with the Girls' Club, but their last performance, *Scrooge*, was marred by inadequate stage management which 'almost ruined the whole performance'.[43]

In 1943, the colliery hosted a visit by Canadian bomber pilots, arranged by the British Council. This took place on Thursday, 9 December when the pilots were taken on a conducted tour of the underground workings of the mine. The airmen were accompanied by Flt Lt T. W. Thomas (liaison officer to the British Council and the Royal Canadian Air Force), Harold Tudor (representing The British Council) and J. M. Pearson (director of The British Council). H. G. Davies, the chief surveyor of the colliery, and his assistant, Jim Worthington, took the pilots down to the pit bottom and to the coal face.[44] A few weeks later, on 24 January 1944, David Holmes, colliery under-manager, and Jack Rogerson, the secretary/manager of Llay Miners' Welfare Institute, made a radio broadcast on the BBC in support of Llay servicemen stationed in the Middle East, India and the Far East. Mr Rogerson sent his greetings to those stationed in India and said:

> I am speaking to you from the Main Hall where some of you have danced many happy hours. The Hall is full to capacity. Your mothers, fathers, wives, sisters, brothers, aye and your sweethearts on whose behalf I am speaking to you are all here … Boys of Llay! We extend to you our best wishes and look forward to the day when you will be able to return home to those you love.

David Holmes' message was for those in the Middle and Far East. He wished the Llay lads:

> God speed and a rapid victory in 1944. We will endeavour to do all at home to hurry this day forward and to make the old country a better place than it was before you left.

Afterwards, the evening's entertainment included a concert by Llay Welfare Prize Band

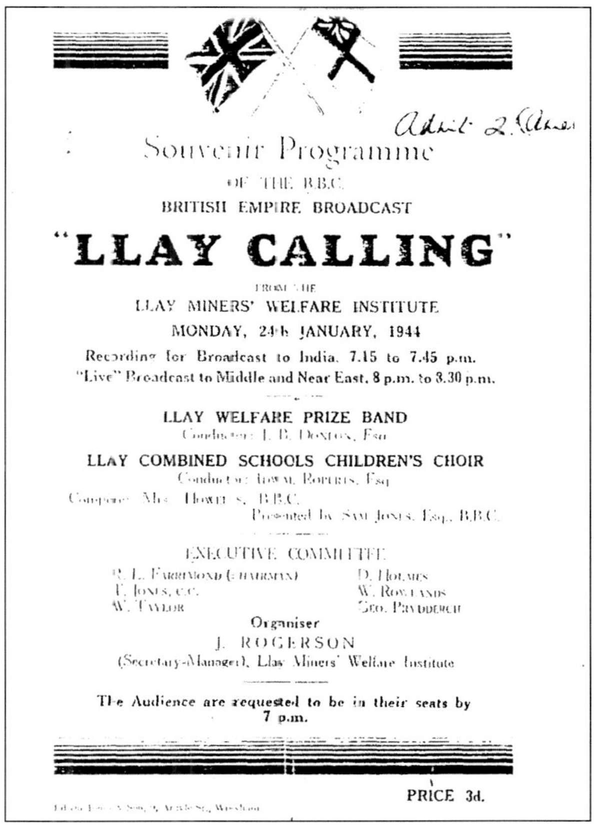
Souvenir Programme
OF THE B.B.C.
BRITISH EMPIRE BROADCAST
"LLAY CALLING"
FROM THE
LLAY MINERS' WELFARE INSTITUTE
MONDAY, 24th JANUARY, 1944
Recording for Broadcast to India. 7.15 to 7.45 p.m.
"Live" Broadcast to Middle and Near East. 8 p.m. to 8.30 p.m.

LLAY WELFARE PRIZE BAND

LLAY COMBINED SCHOOLS CHILDREN'S CHOIR

EXECUTIVE COMMITTEE

Organiser
J. ROGERSON
(Secretary-Manager), Llay Miners' Welfare Institute

The Audience are requested to be in their seats by 7 p.m.

PRICE 3d.

Programme for the Radio Broadcast from Llay in 1944. [Beryl Baigent]

(conducted by J. B. Donlan) and the Llay Combined Schools Children's Choir (conducted by Idwal Roberts).[45]

Nationally, coal production had slumped to alarmingly low levels and by the end of 1943, it was estimated that Britain had only three weeks supply of coal in reserve. The nation needed another 40,000 more coal miners. In December 1943, Ernest Bevin introduced a scheme whereby a ballot took place to put a proportion of conscripted men into the mines instead of the armed services. In this way 48,000 Bevin Boys were conscripted for National Service employment in the mines. Any refusal to comply with this direction resulted in a heavy fine or imprisonment under the wartime Emergency Powers Act.[46] In September 1943, a call went out for 700 extra miners for the north Wales pits.[47] Haydn Macdonald, living at Nant-y-Gaer Road, was a Bevin Boy at Llay Main. He was recruited on 14 August 1944 and told to report for training to Swinton Rugby League ground in Manchester. His first experience of colliery life was in Pendlebury:

> This colliery ... Newton colliery it was ... in Pendlebury ... ooh it was a hot colliery and you know that ... it was very low ... like that ... you'd have to go on your belly in certain parts like ... and all you had on was a pair of shorts and a pair of boots ... it was too hot ... and you'd see these men there ... the sweat was pouring off them and that's what we did was more or less ... help them and learning different jobs like with the trucks and the coal bringing them down from the face to go to pit bottom to go up.[48]

Haydn described his work at Llay Main:

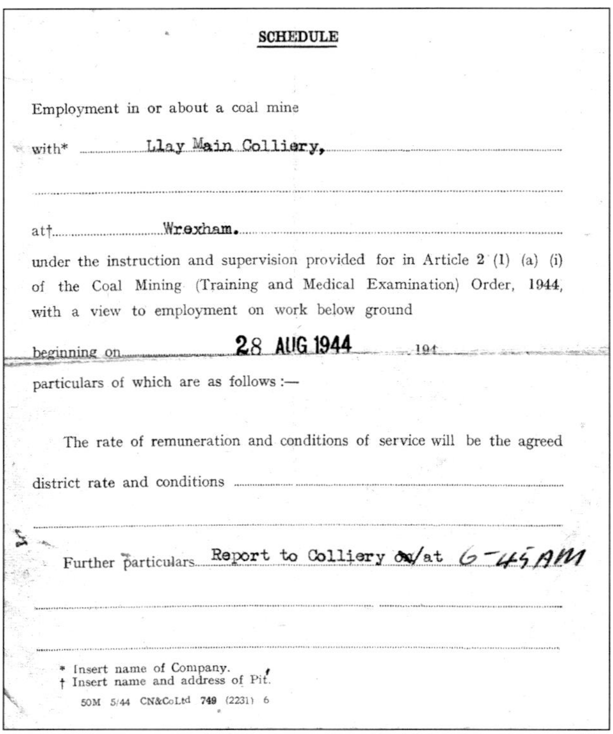

SCHEDULE

Employment in or about a coal mine

with* Llay Main Colliery,

at† Wrexham.

under the instruction and supervision provided for in Article 2 (1) (a) (i) of the Coal Mining (Training and Medical Examination) Order, 1944, with a view to employment on work below ground

beginning on 28 AUG 1944 19†

particulars of which are as follows :—

The rate of remuneration and conditions of service will be the agreed district rate and conditions

Further particulars Report to Colliery on/at 6-45 AM

* Insert name of Company.
† Insert name and address of Pit.

50M 5/44 CN&Co.Ltd 749 (2231) 6

Bevin Boy letter of 1944. [Haydn MacDonald]

March 2010. Haydn MacDonald – Bevin Boy at Llay Main Colliery wearing his Bevin Boy veterans badge and holding his certificate of appreciation from the Secretary of State for Energy.

After all this training they could send you anywhere ... Scotland ... south of England ... wherever they were short ... so I put Llay Main, Gresford, Hafod.

At Llay we had to report to Ernie Garston he was in charge of the Bevin Boys. We were on land when we first started. We had a boiler suit and helmet and a pair of boots ... the miners just wore their ordinary clothes shirts and trousers.

Say we were on the morning shift you had to be down by six ... I used to leave home on my bike. I used to leave home about twenty past five I think it was ... the half past five hooter would go, then the ten to six would go and finally at six o'clock that would be it ... no more rides. If you were there after you wouldn't go down ... because once they'd started that was it.

I went with a fireman like you know a qualified fireman they used to have stick ... a long stick, Gordon used to make them ... just a knob on the end like a policeman's stick and they used to tap like you know ... and they could tell if the roof was sound and all that ...

The miners were great to work with ... the mining community down the pit was a community of their own ... mind you I must say this ... they had a language of their own as well ... but forgetting all the language that they used ... it was something you got used to of course ... because at home you never used bad language or anything like that you know.[49]

By April 1944, 58 Bevin Boys had been allocated to work at the mine with a further 17 employed at Llay Hall.[50]

My Dad, Colin Adams, was born at Caer Estyn. He was one of the Bevin Boys, being conscripted to work at Llay Main Colliery in the early '40s. He had moved to Saltney and used his motorcycle when it was going and his pushbike when it wasn't. He always spoke fondly of his time there, and of his workmates with whom he shared a close camaraderie. Most of them were known by nicknames, e.g. Dai Rhondda, Percy Pigeon.[51]

In anticipation of casualties after the D-Day landings, the US Army set up hospitals in the Penley area, south-east of Wrexham, and in Coedpoeth. The US Army General Hospital billeted some medical staff at Llay. Some stayed at Llay Place Hall and nissen huts were erected in the grounds for accommodation. Many others were allocated to houses in the village, and the Llay hosts now had to contend with people of a different nationality and culture.

One day, the billeting officer knocked on our door. He had an American officer with him and he asked how many people lived at this address. Billy told him and he said that we could take in two soldiers. Billy said 'Over my dead body! The only pair of boots going up them stairs are mine!' He was lucky to get away with that because they could force them on you. The Americans left quite a few children behind in the village when they left and quite a few girls who they promised to return and marry. [Mrs W][52]

The Americans brought chewing gum, peanuts, cigarettes, chocolate, sweets and nylons for the girls, and were allowed to use the pithead baths.

We lived at No. 26 Second Avenue, myself, my mum and dad, Louie and Bill, my two brothers and a young lady named Edie Madison who had come from Liverpool to work at the Broughton factory helping to build Wellington bombers. In the later years of the war, Edie started going out with an American soldier, Danny Stakowski, who was stationed in Llay. [53]

In 1944, Llay became a separate parish from Gresford with the Revd Charles Williams as its first vicar. Reginald Foort, the 'most famous theatre organist of all time', was invited to give a recital on the new organ which was installed in St Martin's Church.

In the spring of 1931, Norman Wilbraham Williams had married Violet Mabel Mathews at St Martin's Church and went to live in First Avenue. Norman had been born in Welshampton, near Ellesmere, in February 1906. His father was a butcher from Hope, but Norman was an overman at Llay Main Colliery. During the later part of the war he joined the RAF and qualified as an air gunner on 30 June 1944 at the air-gunners' school at Bishop's Court in County Down, Northern Ireland, flying in Avro Ansons. He trained on B-17 Flying Fortresses in the first part of September 1944 and on 22 September, was transferred to No. 214 (Federated Malay States) Squadron at RAF Oulton in Norfolk. His unit was the only RAF outfit to fly the large American Flying Fortress bombers. The B-17s were chosen because of their ability to fly particularly high since the unit was involved with deploying top secret radio counter-measures over Germany.

After completing his training, Norman flew his first operational mission over Holland on 29 September in aircraft HB 801. Most of his missions were Window patrols – dropping small metal strips in advance of bombing raids which created confusing signals on German radar screens and concealed the position of the bombers. On the night of 14/15 February 1945, his crew were on a 'Jostle' jamming raid to Chemnitz near the Czech border. The town's oil refinery was a key target and on this night, 717 RAF bombers attacked it. During the attack, German fighter aircraft were disabled by 'Jostle' radio transmis-sions from the B-17s. These drowned out radio communi-cations between the fighters and their controllers. The crew of Flying Fortress HB819 BU-U on that night were:[54]

Flight Sergeant Angus L. Cameron, wireless operator, Royal Australian Air Force
Flying Officer Basil P. Coates, navigator, Royal Australian Air Force
Sergeant D. T. Hatch, rear gunner, Royal Air Force
Sergeant J. M. Lando, flight engineer, Royal Air Force
Pilot Officer Charles Miflin, special operator, Royal Australian Air Force

Audrey Washington Jones' wedding, 1945. In the summer of 1945 Audrey married Leonard Valukevich of the US Medical Corps. This photograph was taken in Fourth Avenue. [Glenys Price]

Sergeant J. S. Scott, mid-upper gunner, Royal Air Force
Flying Officer Marc C. J. 'Marc Mark' Stainier (Belgian), pilot, Royal Air Force
Warrant Officer Phil N. R. Troutbeck, bomb aimer, Royal Australian Air Force
Sergeant W. Walsh, air gunner, Royal Air Force
Sergeant Norman W, Williams, air gunner, Royal Air Force

Sgt Norman Williams, 214 Squadron, RAF. [LLHSA]

Norman flew his last mission on 13 April 1945, a 5½-hour flight over Hamburg on a Window mission. His tour of duty was completed, having flown 36 operational missions, all of them night flying. He was awarded a commendation from the Air Officer Commanding 100 Group and finally handed in all his kit on 24 April 1946.

Hitler's death was announced on 1 May 1945 and in Llay there were big celebrations on VE Day, 8 May which was floowed by street parties, bonfires and dancing.

> We placed the wireless in the open window with the volume turned up for dancing around the bonfire which was on the square in front of the house [in Second Avenue].[55]

Afterwards, the annual round of village events proceeded as usual. Llay Amateur Gardening Society decided to add an *eisteddfod* to the calendar and the first of these took place on Friday, 27 July and Saturday, 28 July 1945. The event was sponsored by Crane & Son of Wrexham who donated a special prize of a sheet music case valued at £5 5s for the best piano-forté solo. Friday was given over to drama groups whilst the programme on Saturday comprised children's and adults' solos, piano, violin, mixed and male voice choirs and recitations. The 19th Annual Rose Show and Gala day took place on 4 August.[56]

Further celebrations took place on 15 and 16 August, when a two-day national holiday was declared to mark the Japanese surrender. The *Wrexham Leader* recorded the events in Llay:

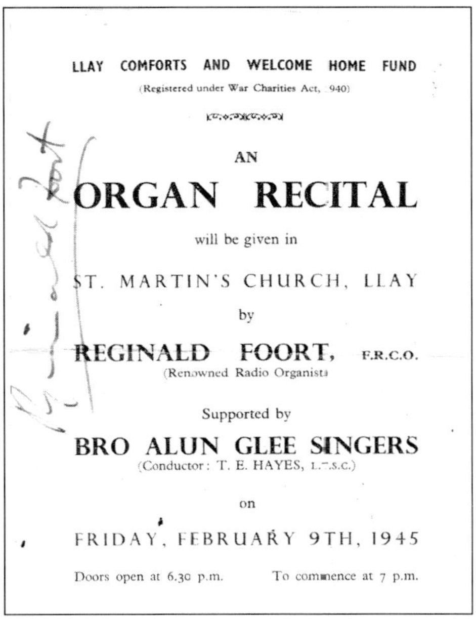

LLAY COMFORTS AND WELCOME HOME FUND
(Registered under War Charities Act, 940)

AN
ORGAN RECITAL
will be given in
ST. MARTIN'S CHURCH, LLAY
by
REGINALD FOORT, F.R.C.O.
(Renowned Radio Organist)
Supported by
BRO ALUN GLEE SINGERS
(Conductor: T. E. HAYES, L.T.S.C.)
on
FRIDAY, FEBRUARY 9TH, 1945
Doors open at 6.30 p.m. To commence at 7 p.m.

Programme for organ recital at St Martin's Church. [Henry Bray]

> VJ CELEBRATIONS. – Celebrations were held on similar lines to VE-Day three months ago, and are continuing. On Thursday VJ–Day 2, the Seventh and Eighth Avenues joined in celebrating the occasion with tea for the children and adults at the Church Hut. Races and other amuse-ments were provided for the children with old time dancing for the elders. The illuminations were attractive, and a VJ bonfire was set ablaze by Mrs Ruth Walker. The party broke up at 2 a.m., after a sing-song around the fire. Pentre Lane celebrated, with gusto on Wednesday and Thursday, with dancing to the strains of a jazz band. On Thursday, tea was provided for about 50 children and a similar number of adults. A feature of Thursday's event was the crowning of the VJ Queen (Miss Jean Lawrence) on a field adjoining. She was crowned by Miss Mary Allen (head-mistress). The Queen had a retinue and four train bearers, the crown bearer being Paddy Lloyd, with Miss Barbara Roberts lady-in-waiting. Sports were arranged.
> VJ DAY – Following the midnight news of the BBC on Tuesday, week, the whole village became active with rejoicings of a vociferous nature, which was continued for the rest of the night. But the more serious-minded section of the village took a different view of the situation by offering thanksgiving. The vicar of the parish, the Revd Charles Williams, who had already retired for the night, was called up by a messenger. Arriving at St Martin's Church, the vicar was pleasantly surprised to find his organist at the organ, and a congregation of about 300 waiting to offer thanksgiving for final victory. Many had arrived straight from their beds clad only in pyjamas, and a covering. Greatly encouraged by the concourse, the vicar readily joined in and an impressive service ensued, with suitable hymns to suit the occasion. On Wednesday another service of thanksgiving was conducted in the presence of a large congregation. Sunday, in accordance with the Royal Command, was observed as a National Day of Thanksgiving.[57]

The colliery had a difficult time during the war. Its productivity in terms of output of saleable coal did not match that which had been previously achieved. Moy Jones, treasurer of the Llay Main Lodge of the NUM, said that in 1939:

> I used to go to work every Sunday – ripping on the Main roads and dips with mate called Jack Dodd. We used to clear a yard of ripping away and set up a steel girder every Sunday for the princely sum of £1 1s. of the old money. We had to see to it that the cench (place of work) was all cleared and safe for the haulage to start off on the Monday morning.
>
> After opening out 23s set on the Quaker seam we had the option to have first claim as to whether we wanted to stay on the face as colliers and this Gore Edwards and myself did. I had got back on to the face after all these years. We had a fine run on this first face we did not lose a turn-over on 2$^{1}/_{2}$ years.[58]

By the end of the war, the total tonnage was 41% down on the 1938 figure. There was a steady decline in output per man shift. The Two Yard (Diamond) seam was closed down in 1940 and from then until 1944 the output was obtained solely from the Main seam. Having been closed in 1938 the Quaker (Brassey) seam was re-opened in 1944.

By 1943, the number of men employed at the colliery had fallen to 2,000 from its earlier complement of 2,500. Five hundred workers having been lost to the services.[59] By the end of the war, the number of workers at Llay Main had recovered and in 1945, the manager, T. W. Mottram, and his under-managers, David Holmes and Raymond Robinson, supervised the activities of 2,401 employees, but of these only 1,840 worked underground.[60] The loss of men was a problem and led to shortcomings in coal getting. A later view claimed that bad mining practices had crept in and concluded that 'Over the war years there was a serious decline in discipline and a custom became established which reduced the amount of labour employed on waste coal recovery, and it became the practice to use coal for the strip and roadside packs'.[61] The blame for poor practices was being laid at the feet of Mottram, the colliery manager since 1928, but the lack of manpower and the design of the pit underground were major causes of low output.[62]

The people of the village were relieved that the war had ended and hoped that the world would be a better place afterwards. During this war, the village had contributed to the war effort at home and abroad and the community of Llay had tried to maintain a semblance of normality by continuing the round of annual village events. The sounds of the wartime village are still remembered:

> I remember the sounds of the village as the day progressed, best heard lying in bed with a so-called stomach ache to get off school. Clogged feet making their way to and from the pit in answer to the wailing sirens of both Llay and the more distant Gresford Collieries. Shod horses pulling the carts of Jarvis the coal, Walter Holt's fish and chip vans, Arthur Owens the mid-day milkman, Lunt's milk cart which was much earlier or perhaps the sounds of the rag and bone men. There were also the horses and carts of the fruit and veg men – Billy Wynne or the veg lorry of Ernie Lloyd. Along would come Albert 'the Co-op' Evans in the Bedford van with the horrible honking horn, collecting tallies for the four pence halfpenny loaf. Morris's little Morris eight meat van from Caergwrle or the rumble of the cockle man's handcart while he should out his special call. On wet days, you could hear the double banked steam locos pulling a load up Gresford Bank. Then quietness … the few village cars were laid up because of petrol rationing [63]

The end of the war was viewed with mixed feelings in Llay, gratitude that it was over and a sense that Llay had been fortunate, the village and colliery had suffered no bomb damage. Villagers had made outstanding contributions to the country's war effort both at home and abroad. Community life had been maintained throughout the period and the people of Llay had accepted and looked after many strangers – evacuees, foreign soldiers and Bevin Boys. On the other hand, there was great sadness in the families and friends of the 18 Llay service men who had lost their lives in the conflict.

The amount of coal coming from the colliery had almost halved from the pre-war figure and something had to be done to put this right. On 26 July 1945, the Labour Party won a landslide election and later announced its intention to nationalise the coal industry.

Llay Main Colliery, c.1950. Baths building on the left; General Office in the centre and the Ambulance Room on the right. [via Ithel Kelly]

Year	*Annual output tons saleable*	*OMS overall*	*Proceeds*	*Wages Cost*	*Total Cost*	*Profit/Loss*
			£ s d	*£ s d*	*£ s d*	*£ s d*
1938	819,724	23.9	15-11-05	09-00-04	13-04-05	+02-07-00
1939	791,849	23.3	16-01-04	09-04-00	13-08-02	+02-05-02
1940	701,430	22.4	18-07-08	11-01-01	16-04-05	+01-08-06
1941	553,542	18.1	21-10-01	14-01-06	20-01-04	+02-01-05
1942	565,727	19.8	24-02-06	16-06-01	22-01-01	-00-03-03
1943	502,397	17.4	26-09-06	20-04-03	27-00-02	-01-09-04
1944	500,291	17.0	30-09-02	24-04-00	32-06-06	-00-04-04
1945	483,114	16.7	34-09-05	26-02-09	35-01-09	

Llay Main Colliery – output figures for the war years[64]

5: Coal for the Nation (1946–54)

A period of austerity which affected Llay people after the war years was followed in the mid-fifties by a growing ability to buy consumer items such as television sets and refrigerators. At the same time, at the colliery a major reorganisation caused optimism about its long-term future. The government took the mines into public ownership and introduced free secondary education and the Welfare State, changes welcomed by all.

In 1946, Llay's ex-servicemen began to return to their old jobs at the pit. This was not as easy as it might seem. Ron Berry, a fireman at the colliery, had joined the Royal Navy during the war as a stoker on the Russian convoys. In order to get into the navy, he had needed the Llay doctor to certify him unfit for pit work and the colliery manager told him that if he left, he would not be able to get his old job back when the war ended.

> When I came back I went for a job and the manager said, 'There you are … you know what I told you … you'll never work here again'. So I went to the doctor and he gave me a lift. He said you're fit for working down the pit … and I had a thing from the navy to say I could claim my old job back, so he had to take me on.[1]

Returning service men were given a warm welcome and the end-of-war celebrations spilled over into 1946. In Llay, the Miners' Welfare Institute was the centre of activities – dances were held each Wednesday and Saturday. That of 23 January 1946 included a waltz competition, dancing to:

> Al Morris and his Dance Band. M[aster of]C[eremonies] Eric Edwards. Late buses to Cefn-y-bedd, Gwersyllt, Bradley, Summerhill and Wrexham. 7.30–11 – Admission 3s. HM Forces in uniform 2s.[2]

On Thursday and Friday, 2 and 3 May 1946, the Welfare played host to the Llay Players' production of *Hay Fever*. Proceeds went to the Llay Nursing Association and Llay Welcome Home Fund.[3] This was followed at the Welfare by the second annual Llay Eisteddfod on 4 and 11 May. A play *The Sanctuary*, produced by Mrs Hughes of Mill House and performed by the Mill House Company, won first prize in the English section. The Eisteddfod drew performers from a wide area of north-east Wales.[4] The Welfare was the centre of village life, a position it retains to this day. Other events held there at this time included:

> Llay's first annual dance band competition on Thursday, 2 April 1946
> The Horticultural Show (Rose Show) on Saturday, 3 August 1946

Youth Drama Festival on Thursday, 25 February 1947
Llay Carnival on Saturday, 4 October 1947
Llay Tennis Club Annual Dance on 29 October 1947[5]

Jack Davies of Eighth Avenue worked at the colliery in the time office and for a while in the lamp room. He devoted most of his spare time to the organisation and administration of Llay Amateur Gardening Society and its annual Rose Show, one of the highlights of the village year. The one in 1946 was the last to be subsidised by the colliery owners before nationalisation. Harry Ball, the colliery secretary, was president of the society. The directors of the Llay Main Collieries gave £40 in prize money for the colliery tenants with the best-kept gardens. Year after year there was fierce competition for the top prize between two neighbours, George Smith of 75 Shone's Lane and Bill Rowland of 77 Shone's Lane.

The post-war period brought shortages in many raw materials required by industry and rationing was still in force, but with this came the promise of a brighter future. The nation was urged to work hard and industry was expected to modernise. For collieries, this meant increasing mechanisation in the pits, and men from Llay Main were sent on training courses to absorb the latest methodologies.

On 12 July 1946, the National Coal Board (NCB) was established and 1 January 1947 was designated as the 'vesting' date for the mining industry. Coal-mines were nationalised and the assets of Llay Main Colliery – its employees, buildings, underground workings and coal deposits – were transferred from the Carlton Main Company to HM Government in the form of the NCB.[6] Carlton Main, which had a capital of £2,846,400 and a yield of 8.4%, received a pay off of £2,649,700 for its pits, the equivalent of about £65 million today.[7] 'Shinwell celebrates with 1,000 guests' ran the headline in the Tory *Sunday Graphic*, but the Minister for Fuel denied this and said

Sheffield Mines Mechanisation Training Course 1946/7. Ken Salisbury – (second row sitting, second from left) a power house electrician, with course colleagues. [Lisa Jones]

there was only room for 50 guests in the unheated Ministry HQ. On Vesting Day, miners and their families marched in their thousands behind banners and colliery bands to the pit heads. They cheered and some openly wept, as the blue and white flag of the National Coal Board was unfurled above them. They crowded round the unveiled plaques which proclaimed that 'This colliery is now managed by the National Coal Board on behalf of the people.'[8] At Llay Main, the celebrations were muted, the NCB flag was unfurled on the headgear on Saturday, 3 January and a similar flag was hoisted on the flagpole at the Miners' Institute.[9]

The summer of 1947 was particularly hot and dry and as a result, a large crowd attended the Rose Show in August. Two large marquees held the horticultural exhibits and the Welfare's grounds were packed with people who had travelled from near and far.

The colliery continued to be a generous sponsor of the Rose Show and of Llay Amateur Gardening Society. Gordon Nicholls, the area general manager of the NCB, became the society's president in 1947. On Rose Show day, the new Rose Queen and and her predecessor would be paraded around the village. Each queen had her attendants and all had to be squeezed onto the highly-decorated floats. The parade began and ended at the Welfare, with the Llay Colliery Band at the head of the procession. The crowning of the Rose Queen usually took place at the bandstand on the Welfare's grounds. The queen would be crowned by a local dignitary and handed her sceptre by the retiring queen. In September, Llay Colliery Band went to London to take part in The *Miner comes to Town,* a celebration to commemorate the nationalisation of the coal industry.

The end of the 1947 autumn school term was marked in the Llay by a school party and a visit to the cinema. Until 1947, all children received a shilling from Harry Ball, the colliery secretary, with an admonition to make sure it was saved. The winter months were eagerly anticipated by children for, in addition to the promise of snow and sledging, it usually heralded the village pantomimes which were lavish productions at either the Welfare or at Llay Cinema. Many of those held at the Welfare were produced by 'Auntie' Gwen Blackshaw Jones and a large cast of children and juveniles was the order of the day. Many mining families were involved,

Wrexham Leader *advertisement for the Rose Show of 1947.*[10] *This poor quality image gives some idea of the large number of activities held at these events. [North Wales Media Ltd]*

Llay Miners' Welfare Silver Prize Band at Marble Arch, 23 September 1947. Back row: –?–, Tom Cash, J. Daniels, Ern Jones, Bob Davies, George Abrams, Bert Young, Dai Thomas, J. Lawlor, –?–, Jack Pritchard. Second row: Ern Denson-Williams, –?– , Morgan Kelly, –?– , Martin Caveney, Idwal Williams, Bill Touch, Bill Simpson, Dan Hughes. Front row: Bill Bowering, Les Hughes, Roy Huckeridge, Bandmaster J. B. Donlan, Geoff. Griffiths, Lew Moulsdale, Dai Williams, –?–. [Tony Williams]

the children treading the boards, and mothers, fathers, aunts and uncles often worked as background staff or in the orchestra. The beautiful costumes made an impression on an audience used to the austerity of wartime. Each performance was a sell-out, the throng being augmented by many people from outside the village. At that time, the Welfare walls were adorned with murals of north Wales castles and climbing the stairs to each show set the scene for the magical evening ahead. *Snow White, Cinderella* and *Goldilocks and the Three Bears* were three of the post-war productions at the Welfare before 1950.

The Llay Colliery Band members received a commemorative medal for their London endeavours in March 1948. In stark contrast to this came news that Llay Hall Colliery, a mile away from Llay Main, was likely to close in 1949. The NCB said that output was unsatisfactory as was the surface preparation of the coal. The colliery management and unions disagreed and said that the pit produced first-class house coal and that they were meeting their production targets.[11] The return of Llay's servicemen led to an increase in the number of babies born in the village. Ninety were recorded in the Infants School's register as having been born in 1946. This figure was up by 22% on those born in 1945 and extra accommodation was needed. Wrexham Rural District Council erected single- and two-storey pre-fabricated steel houses in Shone's Lane.[12]

The cast of Snow White c.1949. *Back row: –?–, Marion Hughes, Jean Davies, Jean Oliver, Iris Lloyd, Brenda Griffiths, Brenda Howells, Jean Randles, Wilfred Ankers. Third row: Gwen Blackshaw-Jones (producer), –?–, –?–, –?–, Pat Challinor, Maureen Larkin, Muriel Edwards, Eileen Jones, –?–, Alethea Jones, Jimmy Larkin; Granville Evanes. Second row: -?-, Gloria Rawlings, –?–, –?–, Gweneira Griffiths, Marie Davies, Jimmy Robinson, Kathleen Evans, Lilian Rowlands, Elsie Larkin, Sheila Tilston, Neil Davies, Mary Worthington, Olwen Davies, Audrey Evans, Anita Churchill, –?–, –?–, –?–. Sitting: Vivien Davies, Maureen Howells, Jean Roberts, Beryl Rowland, Elsie Owens, Wendy Davies, Olga Churchill, Bernice Walker, Pat Owens, Marjorie Ankers, Ann Larkin, Jean Davies. [Jean Edwards]*

The North Western Division Area of the NCB included the coalfields of north Wales, Lancashire and Cumberland. Nº 5 (North Wales) Area had two sub-areas – Nº 1 comprised of the collieries of Gresford, Llay Main, Llay Hall and Point of Ayr. Nº 2 was Bersham, Hafod, Ifton and Black Park.

> The manpower [of the north Wales area] numbered about 9,000, and the annual output was around 27 million tons. By comparison, in 1929 there were 14,000 men with an output of 32 million tons. Office accommodation was a problem and the Llay Main colliery offices also became the Area Office for the Area officials as well as for colliery personnel.[13]

Llay Main wages and survey staff continued to use the colliery office building. The following table lists managers based at Llay at this time:[14]

The 'Steel Houses' on Llay New Road, c.1949. Back row: Tony West, Valerie West, Bertie West. Front row: Alan Hughes, Janet Hughes, John Price.

NCB North Western Division Area Nº 5 (North Wales) Area Offices at Llay

	1948	*1949*
Area General Manager	G. Nicholls	G. Nicholls
Mechanical Engineer	H. E. Dudley	H. E. Dudley
Electrical Engineer	R. Street	R. Street
Safety Engineer	T. W. Mottram	T. W. Mottram
Planning Engineer	R. Foster	R. Foster
Chief Planning Surveyor	H. G. Davies	H. G. Davies
Chief Buyer	E. Hughes	E. Hughes
Estates Manager	S. E. Hayes	S. E. Hayes
Coal Preparation Officer	R. G. Evans	R. G. Evans
Chief Accountant	R. W. Callin	R. W. Callin
Finance Accountant	T. Hughes	T. Hughes
Accountant	T. A. Ellis	T.A. Ellis
Administrative Officer	G. Bellis	G. Bellis
Labour Officer	T. Rogers	T. Rogers
Welfare Officer	R. Williams	R. Williams
Chief Scientist	–	C. F. Myers

Llay Main Colliery, Wrexham

	1948	*1949*
Agent	R. Gill	R. Gill
Assistant Agent	–	S. J. Young
Manager	G. Crowther	H. B. Lewis
Assistant manager	–	D. Holmes
Under manager	D. Holmes	G. A. Folwell

Under manager	R. Robinson	R. Robinson
Under manager	–	J. T Hesketh
Employees	1,889 below, 489 above	1,900 below, 500 above

Perhaps the first noticeable change at Llay Main after nationalisation was the abolition of the charge of 6d a week for using the pit head baths. Soon a malpractice affecting the underground workmen was abolished:

> The deputy had permission to make contracts with workmen. They'd have their price list fixing certain jobs for them. There might be some work outside that contract work, doing perhaps a fault hole in the ground. The deputy could negotiate with the unit head – a price to do that job. So when it came to the end of the month all those negotiated contracts went to the manager and he'd cross the buggers off or reduce them, which was illegal of course. When it came to nationalisation that was stopped completely. Any contracts made had to remain untouched.[15]

Despite the euphoria in the first months after nationalisation, some small disputes still occurred at Llay Main. On one shift, the surface workers withdrew their labour due to poor working conditions. Area union leaders were called to arbitrate but according to one observer 'worked to break the unity of the men'. By a majority of one vote the men agreed to return to work.[16] By September, the surface workers had reached an agreement on their pay for tasks below the ground – they would work a 7$^{1}/_{2}$-hour shift at an agreed minimum rate of 17s 11d per shift for tradesmen such as plumbers and joiners.[17]

When the colliery was in private hands, the colliery managers had adopted an unofficial policy of allowing colliery resources to be used for village purposes. This practice continued after nationalisation. The notebook of Herbert Gaskin, foreman of the Building Department, reveals that in 1947/48, as a part of their normal work at Llay Main, he and his men constructed a stores office and the lamp room was given a major re-vamp. At the area depot on the Llay Hall site, they erected a large 'Robin' hangar, a recycled RAF shed. The building team also addressed the upkeep of village amenities and a fence around the Welfare FC football field was completed on 18 September 1947 at a cost of £32 11s 1d. The breakdown of costs was:

12cwts cement	£2 8s 0d
carting 1 day	£1 5s 0d
gravel & sand	£4 10s 0d
labour costs	£24 8s 1d

Carting prices were 7s 6d per hour for a motor lorry and driver, but a horse and cart could be hired for only 25 shillings for 8 hours. The team also put a new roof of galvanised sheets on the church hut and Gaskin was asked to look at a problem with a roof at the Welfare.

> Llay Miners Welfare Institute
>
> Beam across centre of refreshment room upstairs. Inspected same on 5.5.48 … owing to faulty workmanship any excess rainfall overflows lead gutter and follows course of vent pipe (which has never been enclosed properly) and so finds its way into wall surrounding timber principal.[18]

In August 1948, the colliery manager, Geoffrey Crowther, resigned to take up an appointment as an industrial consultant. He had overseen the change from private to public ownership and viewed his previous job with disdain. He was quoted in the local newspaper as saying that he could not see much future in the colliery manager's job. According to Crowther there were too many meetings and he contended that 'everything could not be run by consultation'.[19]

The year 1949 started badly for H. B. Lewis, the new manager at Llay Main, as the entire colliery workforce stopped work on 11 January in protest at the pay level for fixing the new hydraulic pit props.[20] The colliery was one of the first to use the Dowty pit prop which miners were wary of using and wanted extra money to use what they considered to be dangerous experimental equipment.[21] Moy Jones, the Llay Lodge NUM treasurer, remarked:

> I remember the introduction of the Dowty props into the pits. I used to work on the Road end where a 12 ft steel girder had to be set after clearing the coal. The orders were to use these props under the girders, three of them, one on each end and one in the middle.
>
> I refused to use them after the first day and insisted that I have two rigid steel props for the ends and I'd put one Dowty prop in the middle. I had to go and see Mr Crowther the manager before I left the surface. I explained to him my reason for not using these hydraulic props on the ends – 'it is hidden power', I said and should the pump on the prop fail, down would come the girder on the men working on the Road coal. He agreed with my sentiments and instructed the deputy and overmen to always to see that rigid steel props be laid under the ends of all girders.[22]

By 1949, all of the Llay churches had become well-established and Sunday congregations were substantial in number. Colliery employees and their families supported the annual church events. On Monday, 3 January 1949, 240 'juvenile members' of the Methodist Church were given a party treat when Father Christmas (L. Crewe) gave out gifts from the tree.[23] Numbers of pupils at all Sunday Schools were high at this time. Scholars at Trinity Presbyterian church were expected to volunteer for an annual examination in their knowledge of the Bible.

In 1949, the closure of Llay Hall Colliery led to the transfer of its railway engine, *The Welshman*, to Llay Main. This had been built in 1890 by Manning Wardle of Leeds, one of only two long-boiler locomotives ever built. It moved to Gresford colliery when Llay Main closed in 1966 and from there to Bersham colliery. Today, *The Welshman* is owned by the National Mining Museum for England and is at Chesterfield where it is in danger of being scrapped.

Trinity Presbyterian Church Exam certificate. [Beryl Baigent]

(Above left): The Welshman *after its transfer to Gresford colliery in 1967. [Ann Jones]* (Above right) *John Price on* The Welshman. *He drove all the engines at the colliery. In his leisure time, he was goalkeeper for several local football teams including Llay Welfare FC. [Edith Price]*

The Welshman – they stripped it, refurbished the boiler at Llay Main. The two drivers, at the time I started work, were Fred Jones's dad, Jack Jones – they lived in Caer Estyn. The other driver – he lived in Caer Estyn too – on the road over the Rhyddyn Hill. We had a man who used to wash them down and oil them on night's regular. Tom Owens worked with Johnny Price driving the engines.[24]

The locality of Llay provided the opportunity for many recreational activities for 'off-duty' miners.

> One of the chief hobbies of a miner is gardening. Some of the vegetable gardens and flower gardens created by miners are often a sight for sore eyes. I know too, scores of miners who produce lovely chrysanthemums, beautiful tomatoes and luscious grapes. Other hobbies are fishing, tennis, cricket, bowls, pigeons, football, singing and I have worked with men who would spend their last bob to hear a philharmonic concert. Do they drink? Of course they do, but the miners are not responsible for the beer shortage. They like a 'flutter' too but the miner's money is only in the bucket that goes to make up the million taken by the pools, dogs and racehorses. Smoking: a miner often does not smoke for ten or twelve hours on end. I don't think the miner has made the cigs scarce and today the miner is as well-dressed as any other workman and generally takes great pride in his attire. Often a miner's only luxury is to take his wife to the cinema, theatre, concert or whist drive and dance. Then their sons and daughters. Well, in Llay at any rate there are well-organised youth clubs. The young men can play billiards, table tennis, chess, draughts. They can learn boxing, drama, art and handicrafts, join discussion groups or read. For the girls, we cut out billiards, introduce domestic science, mothercraft or dancing classes. The outside recreations mainly consist of soccer, hockey, cricket, netball, tennis, swimming, cycling, hiking. Many of them go to night school, perhaps to grasp and master theoretical details or maybe to ambulance classes.[25]

Soccer was the winter sport of choice for the young men of the village and the two village teams were very popular. Llay Welfare FC, the colliery-sponsored team, were supported by villagers from the northern part of Llay. Their bitter rivals were Llay United FC, who played on a pitch at Pentre Lane. Formed in around 1931, Llay United joined the Welsh National League in 1946 and made an immediate impact, winning the league title at their first attempt. In the same year, they reached the final of the Welsh Amateur Cup, the first final to be held after the Second World War. A crowd of 3,500 saw them lose 5–1 to Caerau United at Machynlleth. In 1947, they again reached the final of the Welsh Amateur Cup, but sadly there was a similar outcome to the previous year as they lost 5–0 to Troedyrhiw at Llanidloes. Apparently not disheartened by their losses, United came back strongly to win the Welsh Amateur Cup on Saturday, 23 April 1949, beating Hanwood Welfare 2–0 at Wrexham Racecourse. The score line is said to have flattered the opposition. According to the report of the game in the local paper, 'If United's forwards had realised the goal was on the ground and not on top of the stand, they may have put on a glut of goals.'[26] As it was, goals from Stan Valentine and Cyril Davies within the first half-hour proved enough to win the match. A large contingent of the crowd of 6,859 went happily back to Llay. United's final season was 1956, their last match being against Cefn Druids. Their pitch on Pentre Lane was then sold for house building.

On Saturday, 6 August 1949, a record crowd of over 4,000 passed through the turnstiles for the Rose Show. The following description gives us an impression of the lavishness of these events:

> The ceremony of crowning the Rose Queen was performed by Mrs Nicholls of Llwyn Onn, wife of Mr G. Nicholls, area general manager of the National Coal Board, and president of the Gardening Society. The queen-elect was Marion Hughes, the thirteen-year-old daughter of Mr and Mrs T. G. Hughes, of Eighth Avenue, Llay. She wore an elegant gown of peach satin, cut Victorian style, with overlay of pink net, a train of turquoise quilted satin trimmed with rosebuds, and wearing a string of pearls, the gift of Madame Blackshaw Jones. Sequins and rosebuds formed her crown. Her sceptre was made by Mr

Llay United FC, Welsh Amateur Cup winners, 1949. Back row: John B. Griffiths, Edward Jones, Albert Williams (senior) Albert Pleavin, Bill Holden, Jack Roberts (6th Avenue). Second row: Richard Weston, Cecil Davies, Ivor Davies, Harold Rogers, Dennis Povah, Trevor Roberts, Matt Davies, Arthur Davies. Front row: Tom Jones, John Edwards, Estyn Griffiths, Stan Valentine, Cyril (Alec) Davies, Gwilym Williams, Walter Taylor. [Brenda Davies]

Rose Queen, Marion Hughes, and her entourage in 1949. (The children in the photograph are described in the text below.) [LLHSA]

Llay Welfare Bowls Team, 1949. Back row: Jack Evans, Dan Hughes, Glyn Roberts, Vince Bannister, Humphrey Richards, Harold Povah, –?–, Mr Ankers?, Bill Mulvaney. Middle row: Herb Williams, Mr Humphreys (Hope), Tom Davies, –?–, Billy Thomas, Jack Love, Richard Williams, Herb Hughes, –?–, Mr Prydderch, Bob Roberts, Ernest Ankers (groundsman), Herb Davies, –?–. Front row: Dan Hodgkinson, Bill Williams, Lloyd Challoner, Tom Jones, –?–, Jack Matthews (club captain), Ben Reed, Ern Jones (Buckley), Horace Jackson, George Povah, Jack T. Davies . By October 1949, Llay Welfare Bowls team had won four major trophies – the Burton Cup, the Conway Shield, the Garden Society Cup and the Owen Phillips Cup.[27] [Llay Miners' Welfare Institute]

St Martin's Boys' Club Senior Football, 1949. Back row: Jack Love, Gilbert Hughes, Raymond Rogerson, Terry Fisher, Noel Lloyd, Noel Ralphs, Gerald Shaughnessy, Peter Davies. Front row: Gordon Griffiths, Walter Phennah, Glyn Hughes, Keith Mathews, Glyn Davies, Mr Newell (club leader). [Noel Ralphs]

George Rimmer, while her bouquet consisted of rosebuds and maidenhair fern.

Train-bearers were Peter Hughes (brother) and David Ankers in white satin suits with red bows, white shoes and hose, Margaret Lloyd and Jean Roberts; wearing white crinoline dresses, white bonnets trimmed with red rosettes. Jimmy Larkin, in a green and lemon suit, was crown bearer, while Bryan Jones, attired in a green and lemon suit, was the sceptre bearer. A pink and red suit was worn by the courier, Granville Evans. The flower girls were Maureen Hughes. Allison Lloyd, Janet Jones, Kathleen Wynyard, Joyce Hughes and Roselyn Jones. They wore pink and blue dresses, and carried Dorothy bags and posies. Averil Harrison. Sheila Rogers, Diana Wynyard, Pat Roberts, Olwen Davies, Dorothy Davies and Gillian Randles were attendants, all in green and lemon crinoline dresses and bonnets, each carrying a Dorothy bag and a posy. The lady-in-waiting was Violet Morris, in a green crinoline dress, with a picture hat and carrying a basket of flowers. Presents were showered upon the Queen. All the dresses and suits were artistically made by Mrs Percy Lloyd, Eighth Avenue. Mrs Gwen Blackshaw Jones took charge of the dancing.[28]

St Martin's Boys' Club and St Martin's Girls' Club were well established by 1949 and membership was over 100. Arthur Mellard, the charismatic wartime leader of the Boys' Club, moved out of the area and was eventually replaced by Jim Margison , 'Major' Margison as he was known. Most of the boys in the 1949 team worked at the colliery.

In 1949, there were considerable reserves of coal at Llay lying in fifteen seams but only six seams were assumed to be workable.

Seam	*Thickness*	*Available Tonnage*	*Workable Tonnage*
Top Droughy	4 feet 6ins	11,880,000	Nil
Lower Droughy	4 feet 6ins	11,880,000	Nil
Smith's	2 feet 3ins	5,940,000	Nil
Drowsell	2 feet 6ins to 2 feet 10ins	6,600,000	Nil
Powell	3 feet 6ins	9,239,000	Nil
Two Yard (Diamond)	4 feet 4ins to 5 feet 7	10,444,000	7,423,000
Quaker (Brassey)	5 feet 0ins to 7 feet 2	10,095,000	7,704,000
Main	10 feet 0 ins to 13 ft	6,931,000	3,583,000
Crown (Prince)	3 feet 3ins to 5 feet 2ins	9,753,000	8,511,000
Fireclay seams	3 feet 9ins to 8 feet 6ins	9,695,000	Nil

Stone	2 feet 3ins to 4 feet 9ins	5,784,000	Nil
Lower Stone	3 feet 9ins to 7 feet 0ins	9,582,000	Nil
Ruabon Yard	2 feet 9ins to 3 feet 0ins	6,330,000	6,330,000
Queen	2 feet 9ins to 3 feet 0ins	6, 345,000	6,345,000
Lower Yard	1 foot 10ins to 3 feet11ins	?	?
TOTAL		121,925,000	39,896,000

Llay Main Colliery – Coal reserves[29]

After three years of nationalisation, the pit managers and their superiors at NCB North Western Division were familiar with the strengths and weakness at Llay Main. On the plus side, there was coal of superior quality lying in thick seams, but this was outweighed by an inefficient system of getting coal up the pit and with over-manning on the surface. The first move to reduce surface over-manning came on 1 January 1950 when the Llay Main workshops became the official area workshops as a consequence of which 104 men were transferred to the new team and only a small staff was retained on the Llay Main books.

In 1949, the Dennis shaft at Gresford colliery had been equipped with two aluminium alloy cages manufactured by Allens of Tipton which were the first of their kind in the country and formed part of the design study for a major underground redevelopment at Llay Main.[30] In July 1950, a scheme of mine re-organisation was submitted by F. G. Glossop, NCB Divisional Production Director, to NCB Headquarters in London for their approval. Plans to make the underground workings more efficient had been drawn up pre-war but not implemented. The aim was simple, to produce more coal with less manpower.[31] The scheme estimated that there would be a saleable output of 750,000 tons a year for a capital expenditure of £360,000. The improvements in terms of output per man shift were expected to be as follows:

	1949	*1950 (half year)*	*After reorganisation*
Face	61.1 cwts	63.5 cwts	64 cwts
Overall	20.0 cwts	21.8 cwts	28.4 cwts

Output figures during the post-war period up to this time were:

Year	*Annual output tons saleable*	*OMS * overall*	*Proceeds*	*Wages Cost*	*Total Cost*	*Profit/ Loss*
			£ s d	*£ s d*	*£ s d*	*£ s d*
1945	483,114	16.7	34-09-05	26-02-09	35-01-09	–
1946	526,812	17.9	35-06-06	26-03-09	35-04-07	+00-01-09
1947	556,173	19.4	40-11-05	26-06-04	44-10-06	-03-11-01
1948	626,566	21.1	46-10-07	27-10-09	47-07-03	-00-08-06
1949	566,766	20.0	48-10-08	29-08-01	50-05-09	-01-07-01
1950 (6mths)	204,408	21.9	49-09-05	28-00-02	48-08-04	+01-01-01

(* output per man shift in hundredweights)

Llay Main Colliery, output figures 1945–50[32]

The main problem in the pit was that of inefficient haulages. It had been an issue which was getting worse over the years as coal from the more remote parts of the mine had to be extracted up steep inclines with increasing difficulty. The preamble of Glossop's 1950 reorganisation scheme pointed an accusing finger at the colliery's founders, blaming them for their focus on maximising profit at the expense of sound engineering principles for, as many Llay miners of the 1950s suspected:

> The shafts were sunk in the worst possible position from a mining point of view. The pit bottom was constructed between the Main and Two Yard seams and practically the whole of the take lies to the dip. The pit bottom layout itself has resulted in excessive tub handling costs, but in addition the steepness of the seams and the distance to be traversed have produced anextremely inefficient and expensive haulage system. Generally speaking, the main roads were driven to the full dip until the haulage gears were working at the limit of their capacity. A level was then made to the right or left and another main road dip was driven, the process sometimes being repeated a third time. Many of the existing levels, leading finally to the loading points are narrow, crooked, and have variable gradients so that after tubs have left the ends of the gate conveyors they may be hauled by as many as seven different ropes before they reach the shafts.
>
> In the early days of Llay Main Colliery, before the system had become so complicated, some very big tonnages were wound and the colliery made some handsome profits; but conditions have vastly deteriorated as the faces neared the boundaries and for many years the colliery results have been extremely poor – in spite of the thickness and good quality of the seams.[33]

The report went on to explain how this situation came about:

> At first sight it is surprising that the shafts were sunk in the north western corner of the available area as the gradients are much steeper there than further east … as a result … the main haulages were necessarily short, culminating in steep gradients near the shafts. The provision of connecting levels to other dip haulages was required and this side-stepping has been repeated until an intricate and very expensive haulage system has developed. The main reasons why the shafts were so places are as follows:
>
> a) A connection could be have been made either to the LNE or GW railway. The former requiring a cheaper viaduct across the Alyn Valley was adopted. To suit this connection it was desirable to have the shafts in the north west corner of the take.

Coal tub being pulled up a steep incline in 1950. Getting coal up from many deep levels was both inefficient and costly. This supply road joining N°2 dip was made redundant when the new tunnel was finished. [LLHSA]

b) The site chosen could conveniently received an adequate water supply from the River Alyn through mains alongside the railway connection.

c) Probably another factor … was its position in relation to the estate of the Clark trustees. They had borne the cost of two boreholes. It is therefore clear that they had a legitimate claim for reimbursement. Llay Main Colliery Company Ltd were reluctant to make restitution in the form of a capital sum, but as a compromise agreed to take out a lease of the Clark minerals on highly favourable terms to the lessees. The benefit of these would have been nullified unless coal was worked from the Clark estate at the earliest possible time and in such quantities as to guarantee an annual income in excess of the minimum rent. To make this possible the shaft pillar was sited to avoid sterilising coal in the Clark estate.[34]

The main elements proposed in the re-organisation scheme were:

1. The deepening of No. 1 shaft to a depth of 1000 yards from the surface.
2. The need to drive a locomotive tunnel for a mile from the pit bottoms to eliminate the steep gradients of the old roadways.
3. The installation of two Martin stoker boilers which burnt inferior fuels thus releasing better quality fuels for the market.[35]

The old mine cars were of heavy gauge in order to withstand 'the heavy rope load at the bank heads of the over-rope endless haulages'.[36] Their capacity was only 12 cwts, whereas the new aluminium mine cars could hold 30 cwts.

In 1950, before the advent of television, the children and young people of Llay made their own entertainment. Youth groups and sports organisations prospered. From an early age, village children would play street games outside their houses. 'Tick' was a favourite game involving lots of chasing around trying to touch (tick) someone who would then be told 'You're on it'. They would then have to pass on the tick. Many pavements had the chalk marks of a hopscotch grid and, if there were only two players for skipping, girls tied clothes lines to gate posts.

Ball games were popular too. Playing double-ball against a wall, or tossing a ball from one partner to another while the one in the middle tried to intercept. If you played alone with a bouncing ball you could do 'One, two, three, Elera.' On 'Elera' you lifted a leg and bounced the ball under it.

Llay Main – 12-cwt pit tubs in 1950. These are seen having gone through the air lock ready to descend No. 2 (upcast) shaft. The tubs had a high tare (empty) weight of 7 cwts. [LLHSA]

Llay Central School play, c.1950. Back Row: Jim Chorley, Menna Hughes, Roy Richards, Dalony Lush, Haydn Baker. Kneeling: Phyllis Vaughan. [LLHSA]

> 'Queenio, Queenio who's got the ball' was also a nice sedate game played when the one who was 'dipped in' began by throwing the ball over her head. Whoever caught it hid the ball behind her back. If the thrower guessed correctly she had another throw. If not, the ball holder became the thrower. This is how we learned to have poker faces![37]

For boys, the main games were football and cricket, unlike the south Wales coalfields, there was no tradition of rugby in Llay. Street lamp-posts became goals, as two-a-side teams tried to hit the post. Occasionally, football matches were arranged between avenues and these could be quite rough affairs. Children were free to wander around the village and the surrounding countryside, including the area around the colliery, although you were meant to be accompanied by an adult in the latter. The colliery waste tips were particularly attractive for boys and the one near the Crown Inn was occasionally lit up at night by blue flames flickering on its surface as a result of spontaneous combustion. The tip at this location was always hot, strikingly so if you disturbed the surface climbing up it. Steel helmets belonging to Home Guard and ARP were dumped on this tip after the war and these were greatly prized.

In 1951, John Henry (Jack) Hammerton was the day engine wright at Llay Main with responsibility for the 430 surface workers at the pit. In June of that year, his life story and portrait appeared in the monthly issue of *Coal* magazine. H. Andrew Freeth (1912–86) an exhibitor at the Royal Academy, had been commissioned in 1947, by the newly-formed NCB, to undertake a series of portraits of its mineworkers. Between 1947 and 1952, these portraits were reproduced each month by *Coal* magazine in a series called 'Pit Profiles'. Jack was born in Sheffield on 17 May 1888, son of a colliery engine driver. For sixteen years, he was foreman at Grimethorpe Colliery which, like Llay Main, was one of the Carlton group of pits. He became assistant engineer at Llay in 1930 and engineer eight years later. He was a well-known village character and his pastimes included fishing, bowls, snooker and gardening. He lived at 1A Colliery Villas, across the road

Llay Welfare Cricket Club First XI, 1950. Back row: Syd Horton (umpire), Charlie McDonald, Glyn Evans, Noel Rogers, Herb Jones, Joe Parry, Walter Thomas, Charlie Beattie, R. Joseph Roberts (president), umpire. Front row: –?–, Bill Jones, Les Speed, Dick McDonald, Glyn Hughes, Neville Rogers, Ernest Jones (treasurer). [Llay Miners' Welfare Institute]

Llay Youth Club Choir in 1950. Back Row: Ron James, Ossie Morris, Peter Davies, Eric Davies, Glyn Ralphs, Malcolm Jones, Haydn Thomas, Ron Jones?, Bob Evans, Gren Downing, Eddie Jones, Llew Morris, John Davies. Second Row: Bobby Love, Jimmy Churchill, June Trevor, Margaret Jones, Jean Ash, Jean Adams, Joan Valentine, Hazel Roberts, Edith Jones, Josie Baker, Megan Wynne, May Bellis, Margaret Owen, Joanne Peters, Pat Holden, Beryl Jones, Joey Challoner. Front Row: Ted Davies, Christine Trevor, Marion Jones, Maureen Jenkins, Mary Richards, Jillian Gaskin, Elsie Heath, Ken Trevor, Beryl Lewis, Una Williams, Rose Pritchard, Valerie Edwards, Beryl Jones, John?, Major Margison, Islwyn Evans. [Greville Williams]

Jack Hammerton in 1951 by H. A. Freeth.[39] *[Rod Challoner]*

from his place of work, and the colliery reservoir was a few yards up the road where he regularly caught 'Albert' – a perch, which he always put back. Across the road from Jack's home was the officials' club, where he could be found playing snooker most evenings. At around 5 ft 2 ins, Jack was quite short and had a prominent nose:

> One day in the workshop Jack Hammerton was demonstrating to some young apprentices how to use a file. As was usual Jack had a bead on the end of his nose. One of the apprentices could not contain himself and spoke out saying 'Mr Hammerton you've got a drip on the end of your nose'. Mr Hammerton quickly replied, 'Well thee wipe it lad, thar's nearer to it than me'.[38]

> 'Jack might be sixteen stone and as big as Carnera',* commented the manager, 'the way he throws his weight about. I was in my office one day when Jack came in with a list of things he wanted done'. When he had gone, Mr Gill turned to me and said, 'By gum Lewis I thought he was going to sack you'.[40]

In 1951, the NCB bought the interest of Llay Housing Association, the latter having been responsible for building the first 200 houses in the village. The houses had not changed much in the 30 years of their existence as can be seen below.

In 1951, approval for the reorganisation scheme at the colliery was delayed for a while but, after pressure from the Area Office, work began. The intention was to 'restore the pit to the place it once held as one of the most productive in Britain.'[41] The new tunnel, called 388s, was started. When finished, this would enable coal from the faces to the east to be brought directly to N°. 1 shaft and would eliminate the need for steep haulages. 388s would connect with a new pit bottom at N°. 1 shaft. One section of the tunnel was made from the workings towards the pit bottom and the other from the pit bottom outwards. The colliery surface buildings were also being redeveloped at this time. Clive Holt, an electrician at the colliery explained:

> The whole of the surface coal handling and screening plant was replaced with a modern sequence controlled system. A new specially constructed motor control room was built, and an ultra modern control panel installed. All installed and commissioned by Llay Main electricians.
>
> Another new conception was a telescopically constructed galvanized steel lighting mast which was about 35 ft high. On the top of the mast was a large platform, with several high wattage spotlights fitted. This lit up large areas of the railway sidings. I can remember working will Billy Lewis on this mast which swayed in the wind or when you stood towards the end of the platform, bill was reluctant to go up the mast, so Abby Bray had come and help. Abby an ex paratrooper as you can imagine had no fear of heights, or nothing much else as far as that goes. Abby said to me one very foggy morning,

* Primo Carnera, World Heavyweight Boxing Champion, 1933.

Houses in First Avenue, 1951. Llay Cenotaph was dedicated in 1951 and Raymond Ash the Llay Scouts' leader takes the salute as part of a parade headed by the colliery band. Teddy Taylor to the right looks on. The houses had not altered from when they were built in 1920 as can be seen in the photograph. Scouts include Richard Platt, Derrick Williams and David Ash. [Greville Williams]

> 'I want you to come with me to get some pigeons'. We went to the two wooden cooling towers, when Abby said, 'Here hold this hessian bag, I'll throw the pigeons down to you'. Much to my astonishment Abby went inside the cooling tower, climbed to the top and started to walk along the narrow wooden parapet picking up the pigeons, killing them and then threw them down for me to put in the sack He was quite a dare devil, but a really great chap. If Big Allan was on the winding engine, and he knew Abby Bray was in the cage, he would send the cage down at coal speed, stop in the middle of the shaft, it was quite hair-raising, I was always hoping that Big Alan was not aware of Abby being on board.[42]

1952 marked the 30th anniversary of the founding of the Llay branch of the Women's' Institute. The WI was set up to 'revitalise rural communities and to encourage women to become more involved in food production in the First World War'[43] The first UK meeting was at Llanfairpwll in Anglesey in 1915. Over the years, the WI had become a well-respected village organisation and had helped Llay women to share good practice in developing the skills associated with their many roles.

On 25 June 1952, the roof at the coal face fell in and George Williams of Old Rhosrobin was trapped, pinned down by an iron roof support held fast by falling stones and debris from the roof. Luckily for George, Bill Partington, a pit deputy, and Joe Parry, a shot firer, were close at hand and began the dangerous work to free him. They worked for over 45 minutes with stones and debris still falling on and around them from the roof and using their bare hands. Eventually, they

Llay WI members with their banner c.1952. Back row: Dora Roberts, Mair Ankers, Lilian Evans, –?–, –?– Jones, Jane Dingley. Second row: Florence Lawrence, Helen Holmes, Marjorie Parrott, Violet Williams. Front row: Mrs Jones, Mrs Stott, Elsie Owens, Mrs Hughes, –?–, Amy Challoner. [Eleanor Bradshaw]

released George and pulled him clear. Immediately after the three men had managed to scramble clear of the fall area, a very large stone which had hung over the men's heads during the rescue fell, bringing with it another massive roof collapse. This would have killed all of them had they remained a second longer. George escaped with abrasions and injuries to his hand and face, and his rescuers also damaged their hands in the process of removing the debris. On 16 December, William Partington and Joseph Parry received the Queen's Commendation for Brave Conduct and their names were listed in the honours list in the *London Gazette*. Both were presented with silver laurel-leaf emblems which remain treasured family possessions.[44]

On 2 May 1953, a dramatic FA Cup Final at Wembley was televised and Blackpool beat Bolton 4–3. Those with television sets opened their doors to friends and neighbours so that they could get a glimpse of the action. 2 June 1953 marked the Coronation of Queen Elizabeth II and the Government had given thought as to whether it would be 'right and proper' to televise the event.

Colliery workers outside the old workshops c.1952. Back row:Tom Williams (labourer), Ernie Lewis (labourer), Billy Lewis (electrician). Front row: Clem Mumford, Clive Holt (electrician), Percy Davies (ambulance man). [Clive Holt]

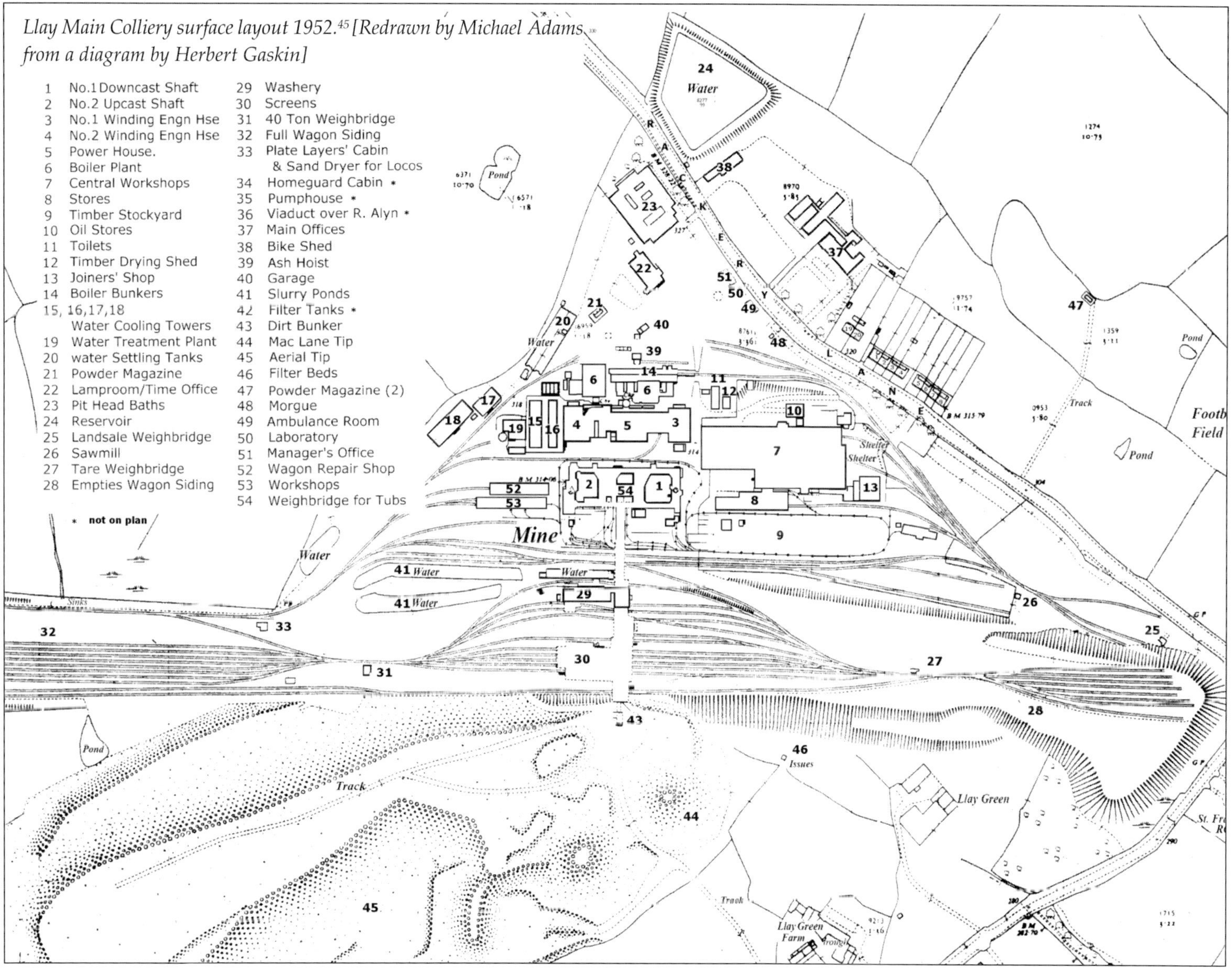

Llay Main Colliery surface layout 1952.[45] [Redrawn by Michael Adams from a diagram by Herbert Gaskin]

The heroes of Llay Main, 25 June 1952.
Joe Parry. [John Parry] *Bill Partington. [Tony Partington]*

The Queen insisted that the people should share in the occasion. The day itself was rainy but this did not stop thousands of street parties. Llay celebrations included its own Coronation Queen, Maureen Larkin, and the Central School records relate how the day unfolded:

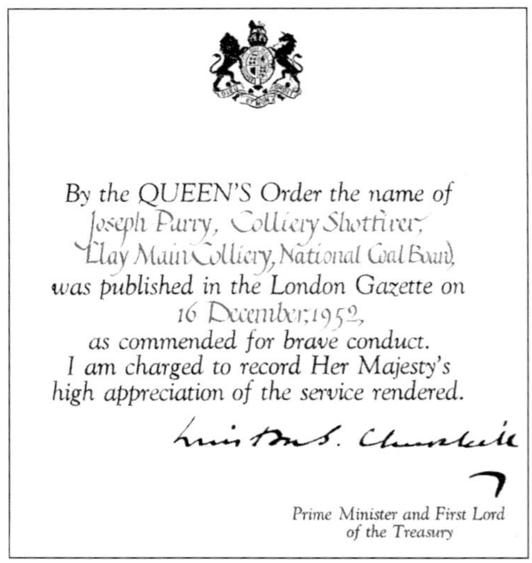

By the QUEEN'S Order the name of
Joseph Parry, Colliery Shotfirer,
Llay Main Colliery, National Coal Board,
was published in the London Gazette on
16 December, 1952,
as commended for brave conduct.
I am charged to record Her Majesty's
high appreciation of the service rendered.

Winston S. Churchill

Prime Minister and First Lord
of the Treasury

Joe Parry's letter from Winston Churchill. [John Parry]

> While some villages are spreading their celebrations over a period of two or three days, Llay has decided to have one big celebration on Coronation day. Each child was presented with a souvenir Coronation mug, the gift of the Education Committee. In order to avoid clashing with the televising of the Coronation ceremonies from London, activities did not commence until 3 p.m. when tea was provided for our children in the School Hall.
>
> At 4 p.m. a procession of school children, members of youth organisations, together with the Coronation Queen proceeded to the Welfare Grounds led by the village band. Then followed a programme of singing, sports and dancing. Highlight of the attractions was reached at 10 p.m. with the lighting of a huge bonfire and a brilliant display of fireworks. The coronation spirit has been evident in the school for the past few weeks … pupils and staff have been busy for several days, making models, dresses and drawings to illustrate the homes, customs and religious influences of the first Elizabethan age. An exhibition of their work was held on the Welfare Grounds on coronation day and was much appreciated by the public. Later it is hoped to give public performances of three one act plays and part of the proceeds will be given to the coronation committee and for expenses for the magazine. We are much indebted to Mr Gwilym Prytherch and to Mr and Mrs Baldwin who were responsible for typing and binding of the copies.
>
> 'God bless the Queen may her reign be long and glorious'[46]

The 1944 Education Act had introduced the 11-plus examination system. Children aged 5–11

Llay Coronation car, 1953. Eddie Crewe is the chauffeur with Maureen Larkin the Coronation Queen beside him. The attendants Bernard Crewe on the left and Geoffrey Crewe on the right are ready to walk behind in the procession from the car's garage in Sixth Avenue. [Vernon Crewe]

would attend a primary school and children aged 11–15 would attend a secondary school. At this time, there were three types of secondary schools – grammar schools, technical schools or colleges and secondary modern schools. Each school was designed to fit in with the child's abilities, so a grammar school would suit those who were academic and wanted to go onto university or teacher training, a technical school suited those who wished to pursue a trade, while a secondary modern delivered a vocational curriculum notionally for those of more limited academic ability. At this time in Llay Junior School the two classes in each year were streamed into 'A' and 'B' forms.

As the dreaded 11-plus examination approached, not all of the 'A' class were selected to sit the exam, and those that were considered likely to

Llay Junior School trip to Cardiff, 1953. From left: Catherine Humphries, David Humphries (above), Mildred Bannister (above with hair bow), Lillian Griffiths (above), Janice Jones, Beryl Anyon (above), Gillian Mathews, Ann Harrison, Jean Hughes, Rosalind Jones (above), Ann Bannister, Kathleen Hayes (above), Marjorie Parrott, Miss Elaine Johnson (above), Kathleen Davies, Miss Jones (above), Barbara Davies, Ruth Williams, Mr John Charles, Billy Taylor, Alan Davies, Gwyn Downing, –?–, –?–. [Ruth Blacknell]

Llay Rose Show, 18 July 1953. Parry Davies, vice-chairman of Llay Amateur Gardening Society with the Lord Lieutenant of Denbighshire, Colonel J. C. Wynne-Finch and Mrs Alice Wynne-Finch, admiring the roses grown at the NCB Area Office gardens at Llay. [Muriel Davies]

pass were given extra tuition from the headmaster. Sitting a life-changing test at the age of 10 in strange and unfamiliar surroundings was difficult. Children had to attend Grove Park Grammar Schools in Wrexham for a day's worth of tests based upon the IQ test. This test has now been discredited by some education professionals. If you passed the exam, you left some of your friends behind and lost touch with them.

The 27th annual Llay Horticultural Show (Rose Show) took place in July 1953.

> We had loose tops, benches and trestles. They folded and you opened them and put the tops on them to make tables. We kept all the stuff in Parry Davies's (Llay Green House). Used to store them there 'til the following year. They put the marquees up, (after) they had a show in Rossett ... big ones and they were filled with tables, built up in tiers for showing the flowers.[47]

The Rose Shows made a small loss or small profit each year, the one in 1958 produced a loss of £33, but the previous year had made a £23 profit. Expenses included £12 12s for the Llay Band and presents to the value of £1 11s 10s for the Rose Queen. Her parents had a grant of £4 4s which equates to a value of about £70 in 2010.[48] The 35th and last Rose Show was in 1961 when the Rose Queen was Janet Evans. A major factor in the demise of the Rose Show was the retirement of its main organiser.

> My wife's dad, Jack Davies ..., he was in charge of the flower show ... lived for it ... he didn't drink ... he did it until he was sixty ... his wife was getting fed up with it and he packed it in and the show packed in. He'd be in the sitting room writing to different firms getting it all ready – he'd be twelve months there.[49]

In the summer of 1953, as part of

Packing up the show, 1953. Benches and trestles being loaded on the NCB lorry are bound for storage at Llay Green House barns. John Williams stands on top of the NCB lorry as it is loaded by Dai Jones, Arthur Lloyd and Syd Horton. [Muriel Davies]

the colliery redevelopment scheme, Ron Berry was engaged in driving 388s tunnel. John Kerr was the colliery manager by this time and the deputy manager, David Holmes, was in charge of the development of 388s and of the shaft deepening operations. The project overman was Bob Adams, with Ron as one of three deputies overseeing the work of each shift.[50] The tunnel was already one mile long in the early autumn of 1953 the deepening of N°. 1 shaft was nearly complete A new pit bottom and landing level had to be built at the new depth – at over 3,096 feet the shaft was the deepest in the country.[51]

> The hoppit would just accommodate probably three ... four people at the very most ... So Danny, Bill Williams the under manager and myself got into this and we went straight down ... we were lowered down to the bottom ... ninety feet down or what have you ... and when you got to the very bottom we got out. There were a couple of guys working around there, I think they were bricking up around the bottom as they were finishing the job.
>
> I looked up and all I could see was this little tiny light and that feeling of claustrophobia ... for the first time ... got to me a little bit and I thought ... woof ... if something happens here we're goners there's no running this way or that way ... we had nowhere to go.[52]

Normal operations continued at N°. 1 shaft during the deepening procedure. The upcast shaft (N°. 2) dealt with man-riding and the transfer of stores underground.

By the end of 1953, the new pit bottom had been made and tunnelling from this point towards the section being driven from the faces began. On 1 April 1954, the two sections were joined. At the meeting point there was only a minute error of alignment and grading – a marvellous tribute to the surveying staff.

Sinkers of 1953. Danny Doherty was the foreman sinker in charge of this team which sank N°. 1 shaft a further 200 yards. The large bucket, or hoppit, was used to move waste, building materials and men up and down the shaft extension. [Herbert Gaskin]

The new N°. 1 pit bottom nearing completion in 1953. The horizontal 5 ton girder in the top of the photograph was set in place by the sinkers during an autumn weekend. The event was recorded in Coal *magazine as follows:*

> *... they manoeuvred the girder gently into the cage pit of N°. 1 shaft. It took two hours of patient work before the big girder was finally slung onto the end of the cage-rope. But that was only the beginning. The girder had to be dropped some 800 yards to the shaft-bottom-in this case a false bottom, below which the shaft had been re-sunk almost another 200 yards. Below, there was a safety scaffold erected to protect sinkers. Still farther down were headgear and detaching gear used in winding men and materials from the re-sinking, and the level and its instal-lations from which the sinking hoppits were discharged. The girder had to be coaxed past all this equipment until, finally, it reached the new pit-bottom, below the sinking scaffold. There Danny Docherty, the Galway -born foreman sinker, and the Llay Main team he had trained would take over. Using block and tackle-and patient ingenuity-they would place it in position on top of a two-ton 'cocker' girder. After a long week-end's work the super-structure of the new shaft-bottom would be ready.*[53] *[LLHSA]*

Winding engine 840 yards below ground in 1953. [LLHSA]

The winding engine was used to deepen the N° 1 shaft. A winding engine house was constructed adjacent to the shaft and a winding engine installed (shown in the photograph). A penthouse was constructed under the shaft in which the sinking deepening) headframe was constructed. The penthouse was a protective shield above the deepening shaft to protect the sinkers from falling debris.

A solid pillar of rock was left between the original shaft bottom and the penthouse. When the deepening was completed this pillar was broken through and the shaft lining coupled to the original shaft lining. 388s tunnel was then connected at the new hoisting level to the deepened shaft.[54]

Electric loco approaching the battery charging station in 1954. Three new electric battery locomotives joined one already in use – the first ever to be used underground in north Wales. The four locomotives hauled cut coal and took men to their working places. [LLHSA]

When N° 1 shaft was sunk to a new depth and a level drift was cut. battery operated Electric locomotives were installed. At the far end of the drift, a battery charging station and loco maintenance area was built. In it were installed several large Mercury Arc Rectifiers, which were fascinating to watch. They were constructed of large round glass containers about 2ft 6ins in diameter with a lake of mercury in the bottom, and several electrodes coming in from the side, the arc would strike between the electrodes the arc would then flash and dance across the mercury, for a few hours until the batteries were in a fully charge state. [55]

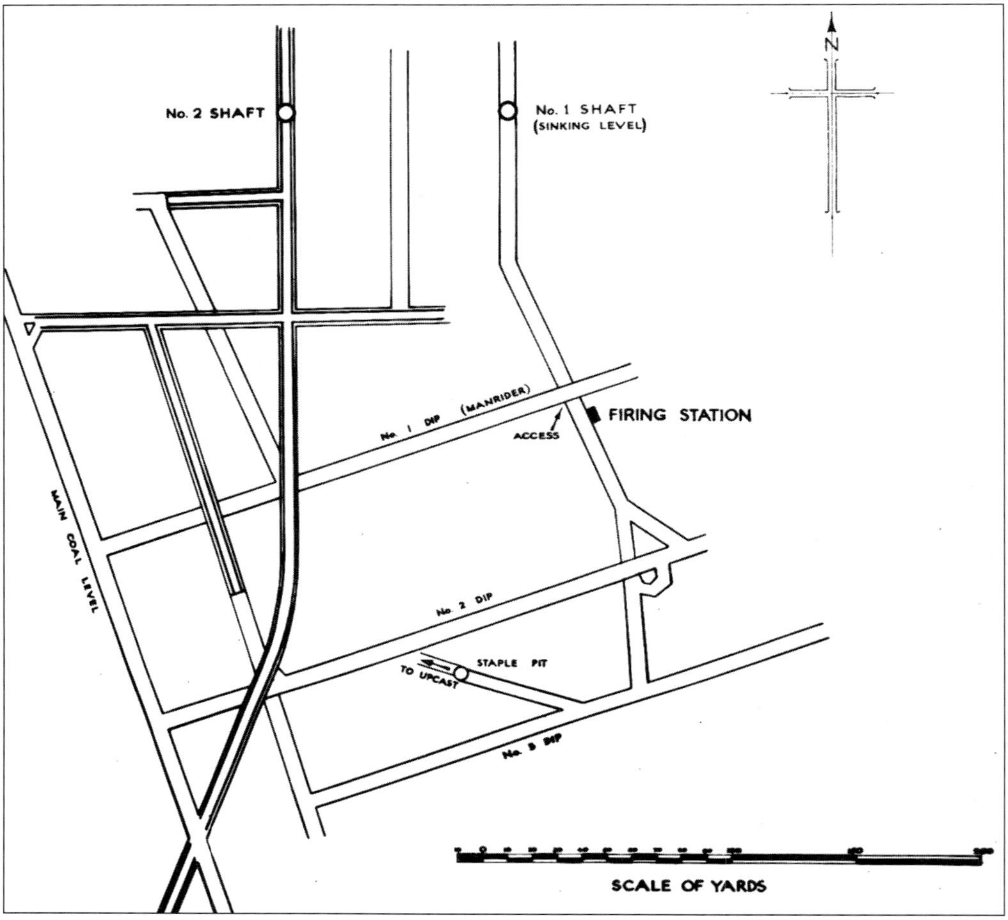

Mine Plan during re-organisation. 'This shows the roadways in the Main coal seam and the accesses to it from the pit bottom at N°. 2 shaft. The pit bottom was established above the 'Main' coal seam in the initial sinking. The roadways which are double delineated in the plan are roadways driven in rock rather than driven in a coal seam. Where they intersect a coal seam they continue as single lines. The sinking level was driven in the Main coal seam and under the N°. 1 shaft.' The deepening of the N°. 1 shaft was achieved was by driving roads (the sinking level in the plan) from the Main coal seam development, namely N°. 2 and N°. 3 dips, underneath and beyond the N°. 1 shaft. 388s tunnel was driven on the same horizon as the new pit bottom at N°. 1 shaft (apart from a slight gradient of 1:200 in favour of the full mine cars to ease the load on the locomotives).

The staple pit shown on the plan was developed many years before to facilitate the ventilation of the Main coal seam workings. The return air from the Main coal seam operations was directed up the staple pit and then coursed along a road to the N°. 2 (upcast) shaft and thence through the fan drift to the surface. The term 'staple pit' means a pit or shaft between two coal seams and in this case I think it was between the Main and Quaker coal seams. The firing station was used to fire the shots (explosives) during the shaft deepening and was a safe place from which to detonate the round of shots. N°. 1 Dip was driven in the Main coal seam and was one of the initial main haulages through which the coal was transported to the shaft bottom. In later years it was used to transport men to their place of work.[56] [LLHSA]

Llay Main – the new N°. 1 pit bottom, 1954. The new cage and equally new aluminium mine car and cage can be seen in the photograph. [Rod Challoner]

The Martin Stoker of 1954. A new water-tube boiler was installed by Daniel Adamson & Co. Ltd, the first of its kind in Britain, to burn slurry and other low-grade fuels. Its stoker, manufactured by Josef Martin of Munich was key to maintaining a flow of oxygen so that the slurry burned fully through. The boiler produced 50,000 lbs of steam per hour.[57]

Llay Main was the first colliery to have the new slurry burning steam boiler. It was of German manufacture, with moving hearth grate with screw feeders fed by a crane located half way up the construction. Slurry ponds were dugout for the slurry to lose some of the water content, it was then loaded into railway wagons by the old steam crane and brought up to the boiler by locomotive. It was then lifted by the crane on the boiler and dumped into screw feeder hopper of the boiler. It obviously had teething problems, but it relieved the boiler men who had to feed the old Lancashire boilers by hand. Included in the package was a new water softening plant.

The colliery was more or less self sufficient, it produced 75% of its own electricity with steam generators. This supplied electricity for surface and underground plant, including a large fan for ventilating the mine.[58]
[Lisa Jones]

The changeover to the new pit bottom was made during the annual holiday shutdown in 1954. After the reconstruction, coal continued to be hoisted up Nº. 2 shaft using 12-cwt tubs whilst at Nº. 1 shaft coal was hoisted in 30-cwt mine cars via 388s' tunnel.[59]

In the 1950s, St Martin's Youth Club staged several pantomimes at Llay Cinema. Its chairman was Mr Hesketh, undermanager at Llay Main Colliery, and the producer was Harold Dunnico. The smaller stage could not accommodate quite as many actors as the Welfare, but each performance was a sell-out just as those at the Welfare had been. Harold's productions included *Aladdin* (1952), *Babes in the Wood* (1952/3), *Red Riding Hood* (1953/4) and *Sleeping Beauty* (1955). *Red Riding Hood* was also staged at Coedpoeth Parish Hall on 22 February 1954 and the proceeds went to Coedpoeth OAPs outing fund. Bill Rogers was assistant producer for these shows and Reuben Cleverley was stage manager. George Rimmer and Percy Lloyd were props managers and Percy's wife, Eunice, was wardrobe mistress.

Harold Dunnico's family were strong supporters of the Methodist Church in Second Avenue. As in most other Llay churches, children attending Sunday School there were rewarded with an outing to the seaside once a year. Weekly attendance stamps were issued and if enough were saved, the scholar had a free trip. In theory, those who were not regular attenders had to pay the coach fare and so attendances rose sharply as the day of the outing approached. The excursions

Making 388s tunnel - anti-blast nets in position. Ready for firing a section of roof to enlarge the tunnel workings. [LLHSA]

Breakthrough point on 388s' tunnel in 1954. The chalk text on the girder says – 'break through point 5 feet'. The eastern end of the tunnel started at workings were beyond the old Wrexham to Chester Main Road at a distance of 2,200 yards from the shaft. This locomotive tunnel eliminated the need for inclined haulage roads which by that time were very much extended, inefficient and costly. [LLHSA]

Trinity Presbyterian Church – Sunday School outing, 1954. Among those present here are (left to right): Emily Walker, Doris Jones, Winifred Robinson, Megan MacDonald, Gwen Davies, Dora Roberts, Malcolm Braithwaite, Clive Lush, Iorwerth Roberts, Olga Churchill, Lilian Evans, Victor Jones, Clara Evans, Granville Evans, Olwen Davies, Bernice Walker, Ann Roberts, Clive Ankers, Elsie Larkin, Peter Davies, Mair Ankers, Brenda Hughes, Karen Hughes.

of two or three churches would sometimes coincide and a long line of coaches queued at the bottom of First Avenue and around the Market Square.

In the early 1920s, John de Seyfried, the colliery manager, had offered the use of one of the sinkers' huts as a Catholic Mass Centre. This hut was used until 1954 when the new Church of St Francis was erected on land near the Crown Inn given by the colliery. The church was built by J. W. Bostock of Gwersyllt and cost £6,933 2s 2d and was formally opened by Bishop Petit on Pentecost Sunday, 6 June, 1954. The last wedding in the old church was on 20 February 1954, when Phyllis Mary Lawlor and Leonard Thorne were married by Father Billington.[60]

In the early 1950s, Llay colliers began to take family holidays. 'Miners Fortnight' was the last week of July and first week in August. The week before the holiday was called a 'bull' week as the colliers

The Church of St Francis of Assisi, Llay, 2010.

collected holiday pay in addition to their normal wages. The village became a ghost town during this time as families were installed in holiday camps in Rhyl or in digs in Blackpool. Few had cars and many were transported to Rhyl and Blackpool by local coach firms or by train. All the Rhyl holiday camps were a substantial walking distance from the town as a result of which, Golden Sands camp was a particular favourite as it was the nearest. Even though there were hundreds of Llay people on holiday there, it was always felt to be a surprise to meet up with other Llay holidaymakers in Rhyl or Blackpool.

At the colliery, some of the workers resisted changes introduced by the redevelopment programme. The initial submission had stated that 'This re-organisation will mean that some 300 men and boys will be released for face and other work- including the reclamation of tons of steel from miles of disused roadways'.[61] The re-deployment of surface men and underground haulage hands did not go smoothly and there were a number of unofficial strikes. The new employers took a dim view of such stoppages. The NCB announced that it was going to sue 41 miners for breach of contract. Gildart stated:

Programme for a performance of Little Red Riding Hood *by St Martin's Youth Club at Coedpoeth on 22 February 1954. [Bob Gray]*

Characters

ROBIN HOOD (an Outlaw) ... Brenda Davies
MAID MARIAN ... ... Arlene Lloyd
BARON STONEYBROKE (her Father) ... Terry Griffiths
RED RIDING HOOD (his Niece) Phyllis Vaughan
GRANNIE DURDEN ... ... Dorothy Jones
JIMMIE GREEN } Two Bad Lads Noel Cleverley
JOHNNIE STOUT } Gerald Owens
FIDO (Red Riding Hood's Dog)... Grenville Griffiths
FRIAR TUCK... ... ... Grenville Williams
WILL SCARLETT (Robin Hood's Henchman) ... Geoff Davies
MR. WOOD the Woodcutter ... Geoffrey Davies
FAIRY BLUEBELL (Fairy of the Woods) ... Joan Richards
RED RIDING HOOD'S MOTHER June Humphreys
WOLF ... ... Randall Lloyd

Synopsis of Scenery

Scene 1 ... The Village of Sunny Dell
Scene 2 ... The Village Schoolroom
Scene 3 ... The Kitchen of Red Riding Hood's Home
Scene 4 ... The Woodland Path
Scene 5 ... The Fairy Dell
Scene 6 ... The Glade
Scene 7 ... Outside Grannie's Cottage
Scene 8 ... Inside Grannie's Cottage
Scene 9 ... Corridor of Stoneybroke Hall
Scene 10 ... The Palace

Dancing Troupes

Senior Chorus
Elizabeth Edwards, Elfreda Evans
Beryl Jones, Pam Williams
June Humphreys, Joyce Gregory
Sheila Tilston, Valerie Bannister
Olwen Williams, Muriel Griffiths

Junior Chorus
Jillian Gaskin, Eileen Edwards
Margaret Lloyd, Enis Gabrial
Kathleen Davies, Betty Cupit
Maureen Vaughan, Doreen Edwards
Sheila Rogers, Christine Jones

Children's Chorus
Christine Vaughan, Valerie Edwards
Jennifer Davies, Wendy Davies
Jean Davies, Pam Foster
Barbara Gaskin, Ann Evans

Specialties
Ernest Dunnico, Margaret Lloyd
Vic Cunnah, Betty Cupit
Michael Newing, Christine Vaughan

Orchestra

Mrs. D. H. DUNNICO ... ... Piano
Mr. E. EVANS ... ... Saxophone
Mr. A. DENSON WILLIAMS ... Percussion

Producer .... D. HAROLD DUNNICO
Asst. Producer .... W. ROGERS
Stage Manager .... R. CLEVERLEY
Property Managers ... GEORGE RIMMER & P. LLOYD
Wardrobe Mistress .... Mrs. P. LLOYD
Dances arranged & taught by Mrs. PEGGY GRIFFITH
Lighting Effects .... N. HOWELL, Coedpoeth

Llay holidaymakers in Blackpool, 1954. Back row: Bernice Walker, Greville Williams, –?–, Peter Davies, Jimmy Churchill. Front row: Gwen Davies, Emily Walker, Percy Davies, Olwen Davies, Megan MacDonald. Ron Walker.

The (Llay Main) Lodge did not pursue the disputes through the conciliation machinery agreed by management and with the union and this threatened the validity of agreed industrial relations practices. The men on strike lost their case and union support and ultimately had to pay damages. Between 1947 and 1955 the number of disputes had increased, mostly without the direction of lodge or area leadership. there had been two at Bersham, nine at Gresford, one at Hafod, six at Ifton, forty two at Llay Main.[62]

After nationalisation, miners' wages had improved so that by 1950 they were at the top of the industrial wages league in contrast to the 'starvation pay of pre-war private enterprise.'[63] One problem at Llay was the differential way in which the 'datallers', the day wage men, were paid. Tom Ellis, who was appointed assistant manager in 1954, was put in charge of sorting the wages out.

> The wages of pieceworkers in the two parts of the pit reflected the characters of their respective under-managers, the one tending to permit generous allowances and the other tending towards miserliness. The unfortunate consequence was that wages for the same job were higher in one part of the pit than

Jean Roberts – Llay Carnival Queen, autumn 1954. Dennis Wynne, Betty Tarran, Christine Williams, Jean Roberts, Wendy Davies, Maureen Howells, Valerie Rogerson, Barry Jones. Carnivals were held later in the year than the Rose Shows and involved a much longer procession around the village. [Jean Roberts]

Seventh Avenue – happy neighbours, 1954. Flooding has flushed out Bertha Hughes, Marge Gabriel, Lydia Lloyd and Mary Foulkes. [Vernon Crewe]

in the other. This, naturally, created a great deal of resentment among those who were less well paid and resulted in numerous minor strikes taking place.

Each Friday there were strikes and threats of strikes from various sets and on one or two occasions during the past year or two, all the pieceworkers in one half of the pit had been on strike for a day. It had been agreed at the time of the most recent strike just before the summer holidays that the average earnings in the two halves would be the same. And that was the task now falling on my plate. Unfortunately, of the nearly 1,000 daily paid workers, some 70 per cent were on too high a grade, 10 per cent were too low and 20 per cent were graded correctly.[64]

The issue of piecework and pay differences did not go away until the Ruabon Yard seam was opened up in 1960 when the manager changed the payment system. By the end of 1954, there was renewed optimism that, with the pit reorganisation completed, productivity at the colliery would improve. Surely a bright future lay ahead for Llay Main? Sadly this was not to be the case.

6: The Last Miners of Llay Main (1955–66)

The year 1955 marked a turning point in the fortunes of Llay Main Colliery. The amount of coal raised in the year, 652,493 tons, was the highest in the post-war period. Although manpower was also at a post-war high of 2,489 employees, productivity had not increased since before the reorganisation of 1951–4. John Kerr was promoted to group manager in 1955 and David Holmes, who had been deputy manager, was promoted to manager. Mrs Holmes was a prominent member of Llay Women's Institute.

All the village organisations had members working at the pit and the colliery offered guided tours to these groups. Llay Women's Institute, youth groups and church groups all went underground and witnessed the difficult working conditions the miners had to endure. According to Tom Ellis, who was later MP for Wrexham,

> The most striking physical difference between Llay Main and Bersham was the underground temperature. It was unbearably hot in the districts furthest from the pit bottom where temperatures over 90 degrees fahrenheit were not unusual, so that merely walking along the dusty roadways was a burden. One face, the furthest of all from the pit bottom, was being worked beyond Gresford parish church. A pillar of coal some 200-yards square had been left as a support beneath the church and the face was being worked along the fourth side of the pillar furthest from the pit bottom. Since the seam dipped in the direction of the church, the face was some 1200 yards below the surface, the deepest face in Wales I suspected and surely the hottest.[1]

Going underground – colliery visitors, 17 April 1955. Arfon Ellis, Pat Challinor, Mr Paul, Audrey Hughes, Marie Davies, Gwyn Hughes, Harry Hughes. [Gwyn Hughes]

NCB
National Coal Board
North Western Division
AREA FIRST AID CHALLENGE SHIELD COMPETITION

This Certificate is awarded to
N. Tyler Jones
a member of the Team from
Llay Main Colliery
winners of the No.5 Area Competition
held on 30th April 1955

Area General Manager

First Aid – Norman Tyler-Jones, 30 April 1955. From being a miner, Norman became an ambulance man and taught first-aid to miners at evening classes at Llay Central School. He regularly went down the pit to check the first-aid equipment and was probably reporting on this in the photograph.

After the nationalisation of the coal industry, the safety record at Llay Main improved and annual first -aid competitions between teams from the north Wales pits helped to prepare miners for emergency action.

The telephone system could be difficult to use:

> When Herbert Bray retired he worked in the telephone exchange, which was accessed by iron stairs above the Electrical workshop. We used to go upstairs and have a chat with old Herb, he was a very interesting character, and could tell a tale or two. When answering or making a call you had to turn the old magneto, which all the mine telephones had, with a separate ear piece on a flexible cord and a mouthpiece on the phone unit itself. You had to practically put your mouth up to it, to speak into it.[2]

The 29th Rose Show was held on Saturday, 13 August 1955. A great deal of time and energy was spent in getting lorries dressed up as floats for the procession which started at 2 p.m. at St Martin's and led up First Avenue for the crowning ceremony at the Welfare bandstand at 2.30 p.m. Once again, it was Mrs Alice Wynne-Finch who crowned the Rose Queen, on this occasion Gillian Mathews. With the temperature in the mid-seventies, the programme included a gymkhana, a boxing competition, Morris dancing and show jumping. Colonel Wynne-Finch, the Lord Lieutenant of Denbighshire, said:

> It is in the right spirit that you people put on these shows for other people to enjoy. You miners have always had a taste for horticulture in general. I am glad that you will be encouraged by the number of people who have turned up.[3]

Prize winners included Mrs Denton Clark, widow of Henry Denton Clark, who won several

Rose Show First Aid, 1955. Harold Dunnico, Percy Davies, Jack Berry, Bill Roberts, Norman Tyler Jones, Stan Rogers, Herbert Henry Jones, Harry Gabriel, Walter Thomas. Harold was rewarded for his labours on this day by winning the raffle for a bottle of whisky.

prizes for her flower and fruit exhibits, while Mr T. Edwards won the Wrexham RDC Cup for the Best Kept Council House Garden in Llay. At the Rose Show, the immaculately kept colliery ambulance was driven on to the Welfare field by Stan Rogers. The front doors bore the title 'St John Ambulance Llay Division', and a full team of first-aiders were on duty.

On Sunday 25 September 1955, members of Llay Angling Club took part in the Welsh National Coarse Fishing Championships at Llandrindod Wells. The 'B' team comprised T. H. Jones, A. Cassidy, E. Hammerton, E. Parker, W. Holding and G. Kent. In low-water conditions on the River Ithon, the team beat over 40 other teams and T. H. Jones (Tommy Yorkie) won the Gibson Watt Cup for the heaviest individual 'bag'. Having been runners up in 1952 and 1953 and third in 1954, the Llay team won at long last. The headline in the *Wrexham Leader* read 'Welsh Angling Trophies come to Llay'.[4]

Around 1955, a new workshop was constructed at Llay Main, near No. 2 shaft, which housed a welding bay, fitter's workshop and electrical workshop. Further improvements took place at the

Llay Angling Club presentation evening c.1955. Tommy Jones (Yorkie) on the left and Bob Adams (second from right) and members display the many trophies won by the Club. [Michael Adams]

Quaker Loading Point – new lighting, 29 January 1957. [LLHSA]

Quaker loading point when new lighting was installed in 1957.

In the 1950s, the Cold War with the Soviet Union was at its height, the perceived threat being a hydrogen bomb attack on the country. Llay Main Colliery had its own unit of the Civil Defence Corps and the colliery played a major part in running industrial civil defence programmes dealing with the aftermath of a nuclear attack and had its own set of 'bombed' buildings used for rescue training.

On 29 September 1957, a large-scale civil defence exercise took place in Llay, called 'Exercise Jupiter', this involved local collieries, emergency services, voluntary agencies and local authorities.

Exercise Jupiter necessitated the setting up of a Wrexham Sub Area Control and Field Units. The scenario was that of fires at Llay, Gresford, Hafod and Bersham mines. Responders had to rescue trapped people and provide emergency feeding and accommodation for anyone moved from the danger area. The Sector Control Unit organised the various Civil Defence units from its HQ at Llay Main. The Regular and Auxiliary Fire Services set

Model of Llay Main Colliery, Exercise Jupiter, 1957. Made by Gordon MacDonald, this was used at the Control Room at Llay Main. [Phyllis Holmes]

Left: Exercise Jupiter rescuers climbing N°. 1 headgear. During the exercise the headgear provided a suitable location for a simulated rescue from a high building. Live casualties were used throughout and one brave person was lowered from the top on a stretcher. [Phyllis Holmes]

Above: Exercise Jupiter – making an alternative access road. In the centre of the photograph you can see heavy earth-moving equipment being used to build a roadway to the accident site. This view is of the colliery tip at the rear of Llay Green Farm. Adjudicators were sited here and at each of the rescue points. [Phyllis Holmes]

up bases at Llay Main Colliery and wardens operated from the police station. Llay Central School was used as a rest centre to provide food and shelter to people evacuated from the scene.[5]

Further exercises took place at Llay Main in 1962 and 1963, the last being in June 1966 when 'teams from Rossett and Denbigh operated with the Chester Food Flying Squad at Llay … the poor result of emergency feeding emergency was overcome by a hasty visit to a local grocer '. In October 1967, the Llay rescue set was demolished.[6]

In 1957, Tom Ellis moved from Llay to become the manager at Bersham. His experience of promoting mechanisation at Llay had not been a happy one. The Meco-Moore coal-cutting machine had been installed in 1955 and Tom given responsibility for overseeing its development. Unfortunately, the machine proved to be too fragile and in time was supplanted by the more robust Anderson Shearer.

The Meco-Moore was among the first machines to do both cutting and loading at the same time. Its introduction at Llay was treated with disdain by the older miners but, despite this, they worked hard to get it to function. Its failure highlighted a problem that would eventually contribute to the colliery's demise. Tom Ellis recorded that:

> … the main problems were … chiefly that of keeping the roof under control. The seam behaved as though it objected to the new method of working, so that the roof conditions deteriorated seriously

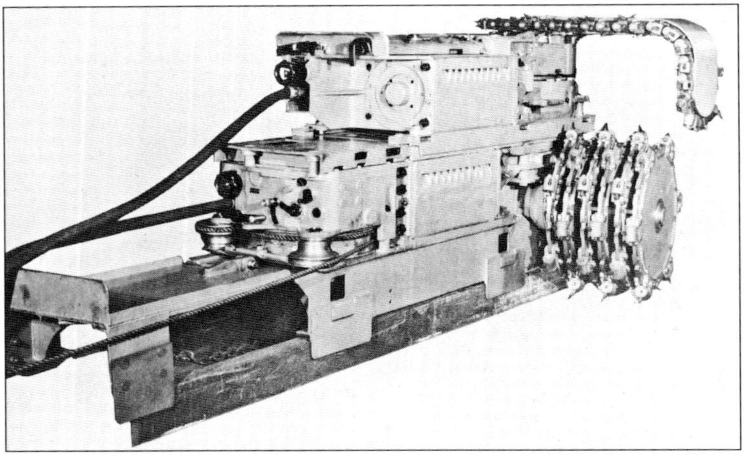

An Anderson Boyes disc shearer. This is an early possibly experimental, version with a curved jib over-cutter.[7] [LLHSA]

despite the greater density of support being applied. There was a plague of falls of roof, an interesting consequence of which was the division of opinion among the face workers, the younger ones in favour of the machine even with its difficulties and older ones against. The young contingent laid the blame for the falls of roof, without justification it has to be said, on poor craftsmanship by the older men, who in turn, although reluctant to accept the new system, seemed almost to welcome the opportunity of displaying their ability to secure the sometimes frightening cavities in the roof. They surpassed themselves in tackling large falls which at first sight seemed impossible to clear in less than a week, but which in fact were cleared in a matter of hours.[8]

A new colliery manager, Keith Folwell, was installed late in 1957. He came from a Llay family, his father Arthur being an undermanager. Moy Jones, the union official, warned him about dangerous working conditions in the Quaker seam.

We had large holes in the roof on the face side. You could put a double-decker bus up there and they would not reach the top. The place was treacherous and dangerous to life and limb. I had a chat with young Keith Folwell the manager … I said when I used to work at the old pits, Plas Power and Bersham, the old colliers used to teach and show us that if you want a good roof … if you leave a leave a little bind-coal up on the face you'll have a smashing roof … 23rd's set which hadn't lost a turnover in two and a half years became a dangerous place to work in.[9]

Floors also had their problems:

The ground used to swell … the floor would come up and you'd have the road going smaller so what they'd do … they'd cut into it … perhaps it would be a metre or something like that … and they would have the rails coming up and you'd have to drop the railwork again you see … to this new level … because the floor used to rise and you'd get very narrow until the tubs couldn't get through so then they'd have to dint to take it down again and that was called 'dinting'.[10]

In 1956, only the Main and Quaker seams were providing coal at Llay. Of the total output of 744,886 tons, 66% came from Quaker. Of this total, 644,540 tons was saleable coal.[11] The last of the

View of Llay Main Colliery from the south-west c.1957. A westerly wind blows steam from the cooling towers across the colliery. The baths and office block are in the left middle ground and, beyond No. 1 headgear on the right, are the new workshops. The latter are still there today. [Phyllis Holmes]

Main seam reserves was mined in 1958. By 1959, the down-dip Quaker seam roof conditions were deteriorating and the haulage system from the up-dip reserves was proving to be too expensive to retain. It was decided to develop the Ruabon Yard coal seam which averaged two feet six inches (0.75m) in thickness. This compared with the Main seam which was thirteen feet (4m) thick and the Quaker seam, four feet six inches (1.4m) thick. The Ruabon Yard seam was an extremely good quality coking coal and was highly sought after by steelworks for their blast furnaces. Access to the latter was off the cross-measure drift and was much nearer to the No. 1 shaft bottom than the Quaker workings. Production from the Ruabon Yard started around 1960 and the Quaker seam ceased in 1962.[12]

> During my time as manager the top floor of the main baths block was made into colliery offices and showers for the manager, undermanagers and colliery officials. The reorganisation scheme involved the closure of the Main and Quaker seams and development of the Ruabon Yard seam. The latter was the deepest seam mined at the colliery. Main and Quaker were sold as Steam and House coal and Ruabon Yard was a very high grade coking coal. During the time that we were producing from all three seams we used to wash the Ruabon Yard coal separately through the coal washing plant so that it did not get contaminated with either Quaker or Main coal. I know of no time when the Quaker or Main coal were washed separately from each other.[13]

In 1958, Llay Royal British Legion opened its new headquarters on Shone's Lane on 17 October. The Branch had been active since 1923.[14]

In 1950, the NCB had announced its divisional reconstruction plans. North Wales did not feature in these plans and no new collieries were envisaged. It was thought that between 1951 and 1965, the number of men employed in north Wales pits would reduce from 8,500 to 6,700.[15] It was perhaps inevitable then that at some stage, a programme of pit closures would follow. At Llay Main, investment in the latest technologies did not overcome the problems associated with extracting coal from remote coal faces and in 1959, the transfer of Llay miners to other pits began.

Jobs once eagerly sought by the miners were now being lost at Llay Main. At the end of the year, R. J. Roberts, the Area Industrial Relations Officer, wrote to the secretary of the Bersham Lodge of the NUM giving details of surface workers to be transferred from Llay Main to Bersham

Opening of new headquarters of Llay Royal British Legion, 1968. [Gwilym Owen]

Llay Royal British Legion Darts team, winners of eleven open competitions.
Back: Dave Hallett, Elwyn Salisbury, Emrys P. Jones, Albert Harrison, Stan Valentine.
Middle: Bill Gough, Billy Howard, Bill Lloyd, Ivor Salisbury, Viv Chettoe, Harry Ellis.
Front: Ron Fisher, Bill Gregory, Iorwerth Davies, Norman Tudor, Cliff Cunnah.
[Gwilym Owen]

Ken Trevor conducting Llay Mixed Choir, 1957. Back Row: Jack Monslow, Harold Ankers, Les Morris, Greville Williams, Frank Crewe, Bob Evans, Estyn Edwards, Bill Rogers, Jack Roberts. Third row: Marion Jones, Rose Pritchard, Rene Davies, Wyn Rogers, Peter Davies, Jimmy Churchill, Granville Evans, Nell Williams, Ann Worthington. Second row: Alma Lewis, Clara Evans, Doris Jones, Emily Walker, Gwen Davies, Kate Rogers, June Trevor, Ethel Trevor, 'Auntie Beet' Davies. First row: June Davies, Aubrey Abram, Pam Williams, Pat Roberts, Sheila Rogers, Olwen Davies, Valerie Tiler, Dorothy Lloyd, Barry Tilston.

on 4 January 1960. Their jobs: screens, waste remover, belts, wagon leveller, browman, brakesman, shunter, gave witness to the years of hard work undergone by the employees.[16]

Output dropped from 640,557 tons in 1957 to 277,970 tons in 1960 and manpower had been virtually halved from 2,473 to 1,298. Output per man shift plummeted to 18.7 cwts.[17] Coal mining operations ceased at N°. 2 shaft in 1960 and were then concentrated on the new 388s level which accessed coal at the far limit of the workable area, about 1½ miles east of the shafts.

With the outlook uncertain for the local pits, miners began to look for work elsewhere before closure overtook them. Doug Gregory started to develop a drift mine near the site of the old Ffos-y-go mine on the Minera road.

Around this time (early 1961), Llay Cinema closed.[18] It had occupied one half of the St Martin's Church Hall, the other half being used as the premises of the Boys' Club. The cinema hall was

Coal Board Calendar, 1959. Tom Blaze and Tony Hughes pictured in the NCB calendar. They were in the Llay Main Team that won the 1958 Divisional Fire-Fighting Competition. [Tony Blaze]

Before the afternoon shift, c.1960. Albert Thomas (2nd from right) and Trevor Roberts (extreme right) and their mates relax and enjoy a bottle of milk before descending. [Glenys Price]

equipped as a gymnasium for use during the day-time. When the building was being demolished in 2005 the 'D-rings' for attaching ropes could still be seen fastened to the roof joists. It had a sprung maple dance floor and a stage with dressing rooms at the rear. Although a couple of concerts were held in the hall in its early life, it did not stage any other live events until the 1950s when the Youth Club annual pantomimes were held there.

The cinema opened on Friday, 9 November 1928, and the first film shown was the Buster Keaton silent comedy *The General*. By January 1929, the cinema was so popular it had a first and second house every night. The first house started at 6.00 p.m., and the second house at 8.30 p.m. The programme was changed every Monday, Wednesday and Friday right up to the time the cinema closed. The cinema could seat 280 patrons downstairs and a further 72 in the balcony giving a total of a possible 352 paying customers.[19]

Church of the Nazarene baptisms c.1960. David Wynne, Trevor Gabriel, Gwyn Downing, Bessie Jenkins, Melvin Ellis, Esther Filer, Dilys Parry, Ruth Davies, Sarah Newton (Bradley), Pat Gregory, Rev. Clifford Filer, Doug Gregory. On the left is the farm house for New House Farm.

> The first time we went to the pictures in Llay they were silent, somebody was playing the piano throughout the film. Bob Thomas's dad was the caretaker. The cinema building belonged to the church, it was part of the church hall. Money from the cinema went back to the church. It used to be 2d, and upstairs a bit dearer. They were all black and white films. The first I saw was *The Lost Special,* a serial about a train, a bit each week. Then we had cowboys, Tom Mix, Roy Rogers, the singing cowboy, he had a horse called 'Trigger'.[20]

The building's internal walls and ceilings were covered in wooden cladding. This made it a huge fire risk by modern standards. Luckily in its lifetime no such calamity occurred. The sprung dance floor was covered with removable heavy timber planking for about four fifths of its length from the back towards the stage. Bolted to these planks were rows of plush seats, with aisles down each side of the auditorium.

> They had ordinary chairs and then they bought some from another cinema, maybe The Majestic [Wrexham], which had new ones. I put them in, screwed them to the floor, just downstairs. That was in my spare time.[21]

The balcony seats were upgraded at the same time to match the ones downstairs, but one of the original seats survived. This was a double seat, much sought after by young couples. The uncovered part of the dance floor was equipped with eight rows of hard wooden bench seats, which were not attached to the floor. These were believed to be some of the original seats; it is thought that they were situated around the walls of the hall. These bench seats were the cheapest seats in the house and in the 1950s cost 7d (3p) to sit in them, the downstairs 'plush seats' were 10d (4p) and the balcony seats cost 1/6d ($7^1/_2$p).

> Halfway down the passageway from the cinema entrance was a serving hatch, which opened into the counters inside the Boys' Club. At this hatch you bought ice cream and Revlon potato crisps. I remember these crisps as the best ones I have tasted. They were made in St George's Crescent in Wrexham and were so popular in the area that the giant Smith's Crisp Company was forced to buy the Revlon factory, just to close it down![22]

In the 1950s, the cinema opened at 7.00 p.m. Monday to Saturday, with an additional children's matinee at 2.00 p.m. on a Saturday afternoon for which they had to pay 2d (1p). This admission charge had only gone up to 3d ($1^1/2$p) by 1959. The matinee used to get extremely noisy with loud cheers when the cavalry arrived, accompanied by stamping of feet on the wooden floor, cheering and loud booing at times, especially when the film snapped causing a break in the performance. Order would be instantly restored by Mr Davies the Manager, going into his 'headmaster mode'. He would thump loudly on the wooden wall of the balcony and bellow at the top of his voice, 'QUIET OR I'LL THROW YOU ALL OUT'. This was guaranteed to keep the children quiet for at least 45 seconds.[23]

Ginny Ellis from Seventh Avenue was a wonderful old lady and a real character. She always sat in the front row of the bench seats because her eyesight was not good. Her favourite films were cowboy films. She would shout at the 'baddies' and throw her pumps at the screen.[24]

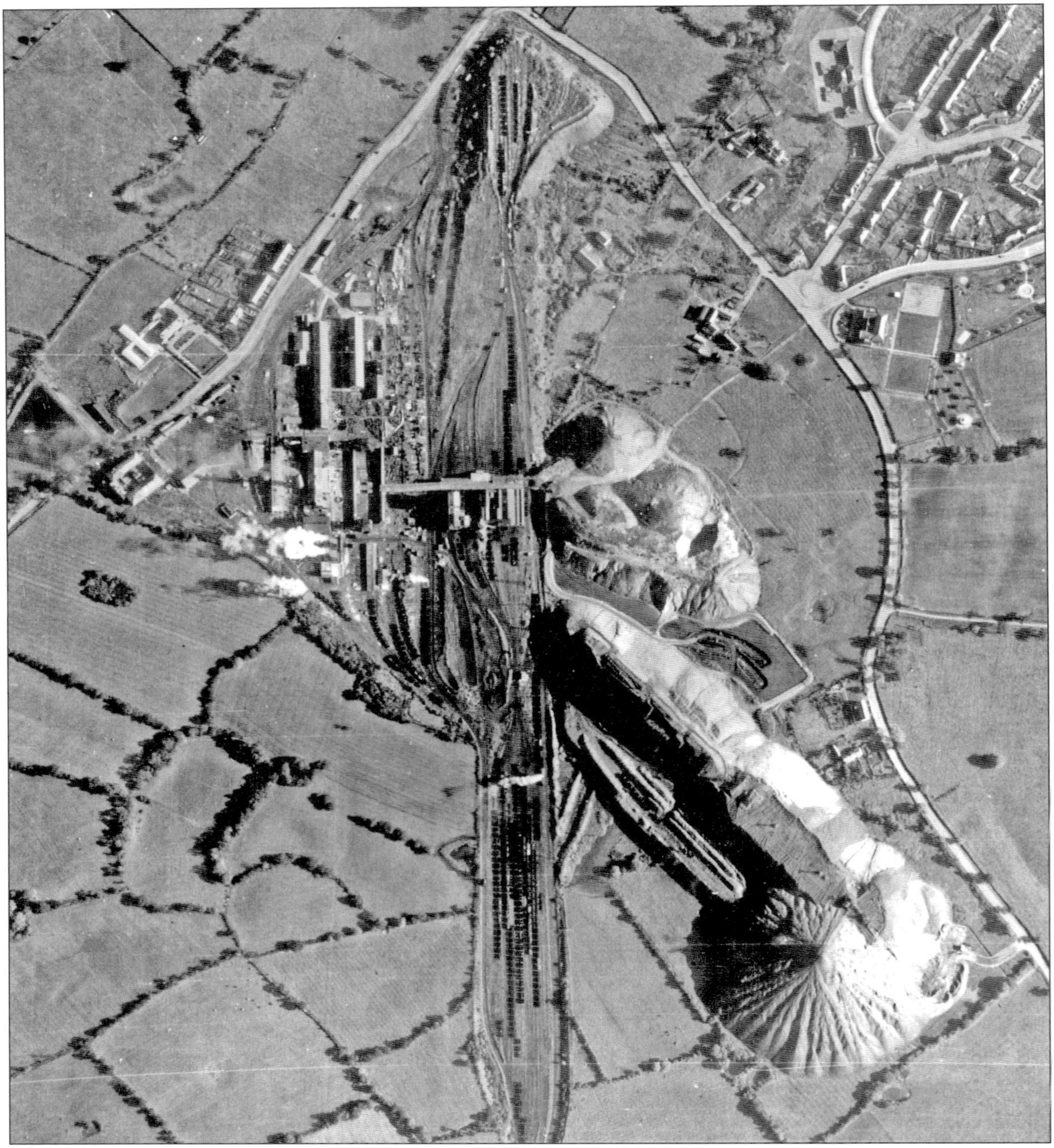

This aerial view of the colliery (c.1955) shows the site divided by the railway with lines of coal wagons ready for moving to the main line. A southerly wind blows smoke towards the colliery yard and the baths and offices (top left). Llay Green House is to the right of the railway (top) with Llay Green Farm just below. The Welfare and Recreation Ground is visible near the junction of First Avenue, New Road and the B5102 Llay Road on the edge of the model village of Llay. The lower right of the photograph is dominated by the colliery's waste tip and shows the conical form of the main dumping site, a major local landmark. [Llay Library]

One of the Christmas treats we used to look forward to in school was an outing to the Cinema where we were treated to a programme of cartoons. I thought this treat was over for me when I left school, but later on in life, Llay Main Colliery used to give me a day off from work, to allow me to prepare and show this children's performance at Christmas. The advent of television in the fifties ... led to the decline and final demise of the cinema in the early sixties.[25]

In January 1962, Lord Robens, Chairman of the NCB visited Llay Main Colliery. Alf Robens, a Labour politician, took up his appointment at the NCB in 1961 and was created a life peer as Baron Robens of Woldingham in Surrey on 28 June 1961. He became a controversial character, in particular when he delayed visiting the scene of the Aberfan disaster in October 1966 in order to attend his investiture as Chancellor of the University of Surrey on the same day as the tragedy. Of his visit to Llay in 1962, the manager said:

I found him to be a very courteous person with a pleasant personality who was interested not only in the condition and methods of work we were using but very keen to talk to as many people as possible including management, officials and workmen. He seemed to be very pleased with the interaction between myself , the officials and workmen and he was very keen to spend time with me rather than with the area officials.

There was discussion prior to his visit about possible closure of the colliery but he did not discuss that possibility with me during his visit. Overall he seemed to be satisfied with what he saw and heard and in my opinion the visit took the imminent closure of the colliery off the books.[26]

At long last the various reorganisations of mine workings, machinery and manpower seemed to be paying off and productivity began to improve. A declining workforce of 1,079 produced 294,733 tons in 1962.

When the Ruabon Yard seam was opened I seized the opportunity to change the system to a task system of payment rather than a piecework system. This led to an immediate increase in productivity and led to the contract workers at Llay Main being the most productive and highest paid contract workers in the coalfield. After 1962 mining operations at Llay were conducted solely in the Ruabon Yard seam.[27]

According to Ithel Kelly:

... as a result of the various reorganisation schemes productivity has increased as seen in the comparison of results of 1962 as follows:

A poor quality newspaper photograph of Lord Robens with Keith Folwell at Llay Main, January 1962.[28] [Coal News]

	1943	*1962*
output per man shift (face workers)	59.6 cwts	80.6 cwts
output (OMS) all persons employed	17.3 cwts	25.6 cwts

As to the future, … the prospects are good … the reserves of coals are ample … new reserves of coal beyond the Eastern fringes of the existing mining areas could be won from extension of the present workings or from new sinkings to the East.[29]

Despite Llay Main having achieved its highest OMS ever, the NCB intimated that the colliery's output was too low and the workforce was cut to allow for further mechanisation. Problems persisted.[30] Moy Jones recorded:

Things went from bad to worse at Llay Main – they were only working the Yard seam. Good quality coal but too low in depth to work it comfortably. Cheap ripping was introduced – instead of ripping the headroom – result – the roadways were caving in and becoming too low to transport materials - girders 12 foot long by rope along the top road for yards to get them near the face. Side and top pressure were causing the trouble. This was the beginning of the end of Llay Main Colliery as a profitable unit and a few months before the closure we were losing in the region of 98d per ton on every ton coming up the shaft.[31]

In 1962, the north Wales coalfield was producing 44,000 tons per week, but the demand was for nearly 80,000 tons. Based on this information, the Wrexham Trades Council asked the NCB to open another colliery. Unfortunately, this proposal was not helped by persistent absenteeism in the local pits.[32] While at Llay Main, Tom Ellis had been placed in charge of the absentee committee. In a story redolent of Jack Mary Ann, once a Llay miner and well-known rogue of earlier times, he wrote:

At Llay Main the committee met once a fortnight to interview half-a-dozen offenders at each meeting, trying through a mixture of appeals and threats to get them to attend their work regularly, but with little success I fear. The proverbial answer to the question 'Why do you work only on four days each week?' was 'Because I can't afford to work on three'. There were, however, moments of light relief. One man appearing before the committee for the umpteenth time gave as an excuse that he had a stomach ulcer and he clapped his hand to his side to emphasise the seriousness of the complaint. 'Look here,' I said to him, 'the last time you were here a month ago, the pain was on the other side'. 'Well, yes,' he replied, 'that's it you see. The doctors can't pin my ulcer down'.[33]

On 1 February 1964 Robert Norris took up the position of manager at Llay Main.[34]

Mr Norris soon saw the cause of the troubles at Llay Main – roadways and lack of ripping cenches. He started to put things right at once and had good high roadways and good roadway repairs going in no time, but the NCB were not tolerant of enough of Mr Norris and his attempts to put Llay Main back as a profitable unit because there was more dirt coming out of the pit than coal.[35]

Lord Robens again visited the colliery in 1964 and said that the 'shadow that had been hanging over north Wales on his last visit had now been lifted' and that successful introduction of

Llay Welfare FC, 1963. Back Row: Brian Jones, Malcolm Griffiths, Arnold Jones, Les Hughes, Malcolm Parry, Gren Parry. Front Row: Malcolm Davies, Clive Fisher, Gilbert Hughes, Cyril (Alec) Davies, Rob Taylor. [LLHSA]

mechanisation in the coalfield meant there was a bright future ahead.[36] The election of Harold Wilson's Labour government in October 1964 offered perhaps some hope for Llay Main but the national picture was bleak as the advent of cheap oil encouraged the government to move away from dependence on the coal industry. Jos Ellis, the North Wales NUM agent, warned that the increased use of oil was seriously undermining the local market for coal and called upon the local authorities to use more coal in their buildings. With regard to Llay Main, he said that the union was calling in their own engineer to monitor the situation because the management persisted with their claim that loss of profitability was going to cause the demise of the pit.[37] Ironically, the colliery's output figures were better – for 1963/4, 337,998 tons were raised from a workforce of 975 men. At 29.9 cwts per man shift, this was another record. Mechanisation appeared to be gaining ground.[38]

In 1965, the NCB adopted a classification system for collieries in its North West Division. Llay Main was placed in category C, 'uneconomic pits with a short life'. Closure was announced in November, but the NCB said that men would be needed in other collieries. They said, as a sweetener, that the future of Bersham and Gresford depended upon receiving men from Llay Main. The union accepted this argument and put up no resistance. Keith Saunders, the union engineer, provided the final verdict when he said that the colliery could only be maintained by incurring expenditure that would be considerably in excess of proceeds.[39] The Llay workforce had expected this outcome for some while and an atmosphere of quiet resignation pervaded the pit and the village.

In contrast, the first week in January 1966 began with the annual children's party for sons and daughters of colliery workers which was held at the colliery canteen. Tea was served to over 300 children by Jack Bray the canteen manager and his staff. 'Professor Humo', a local children's

Llay Main Under Officials annual cabaret dinner and dance at Llay Miners' Welfare Institute, c.1964. *Bob Adams (night overman), Peter Criddle (under manager), Bill Jones, Gwen Jones, Dorothy Criddle, Mollie Adams.* *[Michael Adams]*

entertainer[40] kept the audience enthralled with his magic tricks. In the same week, the Llay Main Under Officials held their last-ever social evening as over 120 miners and their wives sat down to a dinner and dance.[41]

On 19 January, a meeting was held between the NCB and the NUM. Will Paynter, the NUM national General Secretary, pleaded at the very least to keep the area workshops open at Llay. Robens however said that they would have to close and the Llay management stopped production immediately by pulling out of the 36s district.[42] Somewhat late in the day, the Llay Labour party protested to Labour headquarters about James Idwal Jones, the local member of parliament who had not been seen in the village when closure was announced.[43] Councillor Jack Owens of First Avenue, secretary of the Llay Labour Party, was said to be 'vociferous in attacking the MP and argued that a completely different response would have been forthcoming if a closure had been announced in the Rhos [Hafod Colliery].'[44]

By mid-February 1966, there were only about 450 men left at the pit when the NCB announced that its closure would take place on 11 March, followed by the closure of the area workshops a fortnight later.[45]

The headline in the *Wrexham Leader* of Friday, 11 March read 'Final pay-out for men at dead pit' and the front-page article went on to say that the last coal had been wound up a week earlier on 4 March. In the same piece Josiah Ellis, secretary of the North Wales Miners Union, was reported to have said that the union had done its utmost to save the pit, a statement that was far from accurate.[46] As it turned out, few men were to remain unemployed as a result of closure. The village had had time to prepare itself for this event, but nevertheless a great loss was felt. Two generations of miners had worked hard to provide coal for the nation. Eighty men had died in terrible circumstances. The 1967 annual conference of the North Wales NUM recorded its regret on the closure of Llay Main. Ironically the union had not put up a fight to save it.

No amount of mechanisation could alter the fact that the colliery had been built in the wrong place. Efforts to raise coal from deep and remote locations and from seams dipping at steep angles tipped the balance in favour of cost and against profit. In the last year of production 1965/6, 183,802 tons of coal were produced by a much reduced workforce of 607. After closure, the Llay

Miners after one of the last shifts at Llay Main, 1966. [LLHSA]

miners were transferred to local collieries or to other coalfields although around 80 were left unemployed. A few others were retained to deal with the removal of equipment:

> I stayed on with the salvage team to extract materials to the surface from the workings. Believe me when I say there are thousands upon thousands of pounds worth buried underground at Llay Main of machinery, cables, pipes, electrical equipment. I left Llay Main Colliery on 24 June 1966. I was on the NUM lodge committee for 20 years. I did have some experience of the hardships in the old pits locally, working hard for coppers in gassy, wet and dangerous conditions where man had to use his head and brain to earn a very poor living in dark, dusty and dangerous mines.[47]

The closure of Llay Main did not bring about a lasting benefit for other pits in the area. Hafod closed in 1968 but, unlike at Llay, the union campaigned to save it and, as Jack Owens had predicted, the local MP, a Rhos man, appealed to Harold Wilson for a postponement of the decision to close the colliery.[48] Ifton colliery closed in 1968, followed by Gresford in 1973, Bersham in 1986 and the last of the north Wales collieries, Point of Ayr, in 1996.

In 1968, the surface buildings at Llay were demolished

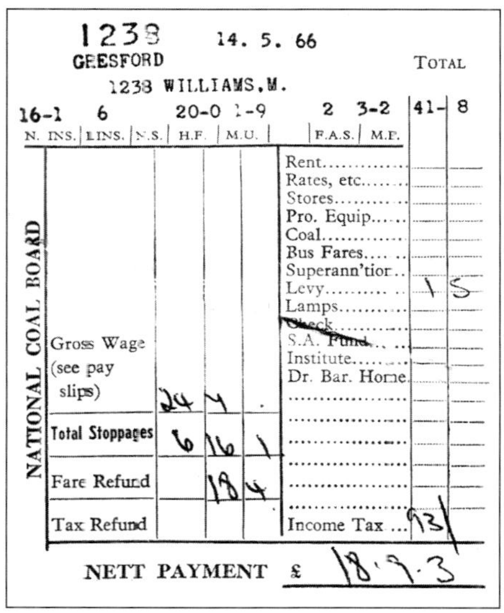

NATIONAL COAL BOARD

1238 14. 5. 66
GRESFORD
1238 WILLIAMS, M.

N. INS.	I. INS.	N.S.	H.F.	M.U.		F.A.S.	M.F.	TOTAL	
16-1	6		20-0	1-9		2	3-2	41-	8

				Rent		
				Rates, etc		
				Stores		
				Pro. Equip		
				Coal		
				Bus Fares		
				Superann'tion		
				Levy	1	5
				Lamps		
				Check		
				S.A. Fund		
				Institute		
Gross Wage (see pay slips)	24	4	.	Dr. Bar. Home		
Total Stoppages	6	16	1			
Fare Refund		18	4			
Tax Refund				Income Tax	93	

NETT PAYMENT £ 18.9.3

Transfer pay, 14 May 1966. The pay packet of Malcolm Williams on being transferred from Llay Main to Gresford Colliery. [Malcolm Williams]

Managers at Llay Main Colliery

Year	*Manager*
1913–15	Robert Oswald Gardner
1915–22	John Thaddeus de Seyfried
1922–24	George Beard Tristram
1924–26	Sidney L. Criddle
1926–28	E. A. Hughes
1928–45	Thomas W. Mottram
1945–48	Geoffrey Crowther
1948–52	Harry Bertram Lewis
1952–55	John Kerr
1955–57	David Holmes
1957–64	Keith Folwell
1964–66	Robert Norris

The last coal, 1966. Coal wagons are standing ready for weighing as all the buildings around them show signs of being dismantled. The colliery power house lasted a while longer as it continued to generate electricity for Gresford Colliery until 1968.[49] *[LLHSA]*

and the two shafts filled in with 36,000 tons of waste from the colliery tip. Having learned the lesson of the great depression of the 1930s, the Wrexham area had diversified its industrial base. Light industry became increasingly important for local employment and an industrial estate soon grew on the colliery site. In time, it would employ almost as many people as had worked at the colliery. What Llay had lost was work which had a common purpose and a workplace camaraderie in the 'happy pit' which was unsurpassed anywhere.

Llay Main

Grey day.
Shiny black rooftops.
The tall fat chimneys churn out leaden smoke
Onto the coal green holly in the fields.
Silver damp steam shoots out of the boilers
And disappears into the wet atmosphere.
Flattened Woodbine stumps in the gritty gutters
Lie neglected.
Miners, with the shift's dust mascara.
Around their red eyes,
Turn their bikes out of the sheds,
And pedal away from the great spidery winders
Whose spokes turn furiously,
Like skeletal Catherine wheels.
The cable dives back onto the drum
In the greasy green and red winding house,
Where Uncle Frank sits at his other chapel organ,
Pulling levers,
Reflected warmly in the brass.
And I walk through the little iron gate
To find only an echo in the ambulance room.
Then find the one I want
In the yellow warmth of the lamp room And say,
'Take me to the pithead, Dad'

Derek Crewe

The village of Llay will forever be associated with the colliery that caused it to be established. The colliery provided work for the villagers and funded the village schools and religious and social institutions. Its fortunes directly affected the villagers. From the tragedies and strikes of the 1920s and 30s a community was forged out of adversity and as a result both pit and village grew from strength to strength.

By the mid 1950s, it was becoming clear that a combination of dwindling coal markets and geological difficulties was pointing towards the end of coal production at Llay Main. The one-time largest and most technologically advanced colliery in Wales, and the deepest mine in Europe, met its premature closure only 45 years after the first shaft was sunk. The colliery closed in 1966 and an industrial estate was built on the site. The village has continued to expand with the addition of several private housing schemes, although its workforce is no longer focused on the single industry which created it.

The mining industry has mostly gone from this country. The burning of coal releases gases which add to global warming, but future technologies may be able to eliminate these harmful products. If such a time comes, there are still millions of tons of coal under Llay waiting to be exploited.

Happy drinkers at the Welfare, c.1966. Seated second from the right is Ziphorah Parry with Jane (Auntie Ginny Williams) to the left and R. T. Williams above. [LLHSA]

Llay Miners' Welfare Consultative Committee, 1965/6. Back row: E. H. (Ted) Evans, R. L. (Ron) Farrimond, J. R. (Jack) Davies, Eddie Gray, Joe Meacock, T. J. (Tom) Lewis (Trustee) , Herb Gaskin, K. Rowlands. Front Row: Peter Criddle (Trustee), T. J. (Tom) Jones (chairman), Raymond Jenkins (Secretary), M. G. (Moy) Jones (Treasurer). Ted Evans is thought to have been the last man up the pit.[50] [Herbert Gaskin]

Appendix

Llay servicemen killed in the two World Wars

1914 –18

Robert Oswald Gardner	of Home Farm. First manager of Llay Main Colliery. Died 8 May 1915. Aged 31. Captain, 'B' Coy, 3rd Bn Monmouthshire Regt. Buried near Ypres, Belgium.

1939– 45

William Derrick Astbury	son of William and Gwyneth Astbury. Died 23 June 1944. Aged 21. 93rd (6th Bn Argyll and Sutherland Highlanders) Anti-Tank Regt. Buried in Bari, Italy.
Emlyn Griffiths Baines	son of John David and Sarah Jane Beard. Died 21 May 1940. Aged 25. Lance Bombadier 61st (Denbighshire Yeomanry) Medium Regt, Royal Artillery. Buried near Lille, France.
William Lloyd Baker	son of Walter and Gertrude Lillian Baker. Died 16 June 1941. Aged 24. Royal Army Service Corps. Buried in Gresford.
Glyn Bannister	son of George Lawrence and Lily Bannister. Died 11 December 1942. Aged 18. Ordinary Seaman, HMS *Blean*. Name on Chatham Naval Memorial, Kent.
William Clifford Parsonage Davies	son of Thomas and Beatrice Davies. Died 21 August 1944. Aged 29. Steward, HMS *Kite*. Name on Plymouth Naval Memorial. Devon.
Reginald Edwards	son of William and Edith Edwards. Husband of Beryl Edwards. Died 2 August 1943. Aged 30. Lance Corporal, 12th Bomb Disposal Coy, Royal Engineers. Buried in Llay.
Alfred Ellis	son of Arthur and Jane Ellis. Died 17 July 1944. Aged 25. Fusilier, 4th Bn, Royal Welch Fusiliers. Buried near Caen, France.
Eryl Rowlands Hughes	son of Robert Thomas and Mary Ellen Hughes of Gresford. Died 3 January 1944. Sergeant, Flight Engineer, 57 Sqdn., RAFVR. Buried in Berlin War Cemetery.

Thomas William Hughes	Died 4 September 1944. Aged 26. Lance Corporal, 4th Bn, Royal Welch Fusiliers. Buried in Dunkirk, France.
Alfred William Jones	son of Mr and Mrs Alfred Jones. Died 17 July 1944. Aged 19. Fusilier, 6th Bn., Royal Welch Fusiliers. Name on the Bayeux Memorial, France.
Edward Thomas Curwen Roberts	son of Robert and Maria Roberts of Wrexham. Died 21 May 1941. Aged 26. Ordinary Seaman, HMS *Juno*. Name on Chatham Naval Memorial, Kent.
John Owen Roberts	son of Hughie and Florrie Roberts; husband of Doris Roberts. Died 19 December 1941. Aged 36. Musician, Royal Marines, HMS *Neptune*. Name on Porstmouth Naval Memorial, Hampshire.
George Rogerson	son of John and Emily Rogerson. Died 9 June 1940. Aged 19. Able Seaman, HMS *Glorious*. Name on Plymouth Naval Memorial, Devon.
Stanley Stratford	son of Stanley and Elizabeth Stratford. Died 4 August 1942. Aged 17. Marine, Royal Marines. Buried in Llay.
Hugh Thomas	son of Edward and Mary Thomas. Died 18 March 1943. Aged 23. Fusilier, 1st Bn, Royal Welch Fusiliers. Name on the Rangoon Memorial, Burma.
Raymond Tilston	son of Eli and Gertrude Tilston. Died 27 June 1945. Aged 25. Corporal, 4th Bn, Royal Welch Fusiliers. Buried in Gwersyllt.
James Wynne	son of David and Harriet Wynne, husband of Catherine Wynne of Perry Barr, Birmingham. Died 13 May 1944. Aged 29. Private, 1st Bn, West Yorkshire Regt. Name on the Rangoon Memorial, Burma.
Richard James Wynne	son of Thomas and Fanny Wynne; husband of Nancy Ellen Wynne of Southsea. Died 5 December 1944. Aged 25. Fusilier, 2nd Bn., Royal Welch Fusiliers. Buried in Digboi War Cemetery, Assam, India.

Notes

Abbreviations

DRO: Denbighshire Record Office.
FRO: Flintshire Record Office.
LLHSA: Llai Local History Society Archive.
NEIMME: North of England Institute of Mining and Mechanical Engineers.

1: The Great Enterprise (1906–17)

1. William Ashworth and Mark Pegg, *The History of the British Coal industry: the Nationalized Industry*, Oxford, 1986, p.131.
2. According to the censuses, it was occupied between 1871 and 1891 by the Griffiths family, grandparents of four Llay sisters, Gwen, Doris, Megan and Eirwen, the daughters of John William and Mary Elizabeth Jones (nee Griffiths), who lived at 61 Eighth Avenue.
3. DRO/QSD/SR/32/48/42, Denbighshire Quarter Sessions.
4. *Collieries of the United Kingdom at Work in 1880*, http://www.cmhrc.co.uk/static/list80.htm.
5. Ironbridge Gorge Museum and Archives, records of the Lilleshall Company. Bundle 93, ref. 1998.320 (DLIL/3) 683. 'NOTICE to terminate lease between Sir G. H. Lockwood and J. E. Horton and others , re: lands and mines at Hope, Flintshire, which are no longer profitable. 18.6.1880'.
6. Andrew Connolly, *Life in Victorian Brickyards of Flintshire and Denbighshire*, Llanrwst, 2003, p.198 'Llay Hall Colliery was only recently opened out by March 1845, when the landlord put it up for lease affording "a most eligible opportunity for investment of capital". One of the earliest shareholders was the father of the late owner, Mr E. S. Clark.'
7. G. C. Lerry, *The Collieries of Denbighshire*, 1946, 2nd edition (edited by Ifor Edwards) 1968, Wrexham, p.67.
8. FRO/D/B/2401, E. S. Clark family papers.
9. List of mines worked under the Coal Mines Regulation Act in Denbighshire during the year 1896.
10. Harriet Laura Bellis, 'A tribute to my mother, anecdotes from bygone times in Cefn-y-Bedd and Llay, *c.*1980', unpublished document p.1, LLHSA. Harriet's husband, Sam Platt, was firstly Edwin Stanley Clark's coachman, and later batman in the Royal Welch Fusiliers to Edward Stuart and Henry Denton Clark.
11. FRO/D/B/2401, E. S. Clark family papers.
12. ibid.
13. ibid /2399.
14. ibid /2398.
15. *Wrexham Advertiser*, Saturday, 25.8.1906 .
16. William Millington, Llay and Gresford before 1920, unpublished, *c.*1985, p.34, LLHSA.
17. This borehole came to be called the 'Llay Place borehole' by the colliery.
18. William Millington, *c.*1985.
19. FRO/D/DM/660/2204/34, Llay Main Colliery booklet 1923, p.2.
20. DRO/DD/LH/261, Memorandum of Association, Llay Main Collieries Ltd.
21. FRO/CB/15/1, Clark family leases – Indenture of 30.12.1911.
22. Bellis, p.8, 'up until then [1912] he [Edward] was single, living in the Grosvenor Hotel [Chester] but he married a Chester lady, Bessie Francis Royal. So they bought Llay Cottage'.
23. FRO/CB/13/1, National Coal Board Records, J. T. de Seyfried, 'A concise log which led to the constitution of the Llay Main Collieries Ltd, and of the history of this company since its formation', 1920.
24. www.shef.ac.uk/library/special/markham.html. 'Sir Arthur Basil Markham, Bart (1866–1916) was the son of Charles Markham who was part owner of the family mine, Markham Main Colliery in Chesterfield. On his mother's side he was the grandson of Sir Joseph Paxton, designer of the 1851 Great Exhibition's Crystal Palace. He was educated at Rugby School, and from 1900 served as Liberal MP for the Mansfield Division of Nottinghamshire, being created a baronet in 1911. Arthur Markham's technical skill, commercial insight and courage helped the development of considerable parts of the English and Welsh coalfields. He managed and owned a number of other coalmines, and there are many villages, businesses, streets and areas in Wales, Derbyshire and South Yorkshire bearing the name Markham. His brother was Charles Paxton Markham, owner of Markham & Co. Engineering of Chesterfield, and the firm was one of largest suppliers of coal mine winders. His brother was also director of Staveley Coal and Iron Company.'

25. One theory for the use of the term 'Main' as appended to colliery names is that it indicates those collieries that were exploiting the thickest or main coal seam. (see A. Hill. *The South Yorkshire Coalfield: A History and Development*. Stroud, 2002, p.7).
26. Examples of these are: Brodsworth Colliery and its model village of Woodlands near Doncaster and in North Derbyshire the collieries and villages at Markham, Hartington, Arkwright, Warsop Vale, Staveley, Barrow Hill, Speedwell and Poolsbrook. (information from *Woodlands – the birth of a dream 1905–2005*, booklet by Barry Hayes, Brodsworth Informer. www.lhi.org.uk/docs/woodlands and *North Derbyshire Collieries* by A. N. Bridgewater, 2009, p.111, http://myweb.tiscali.co.uk/colliery.
27. FRO/CB/13/1, H.G. Davies (NCB Area Surveyor) notes, 4.11.1955.
28. J. T. de Seyfried, (1920).
29. FRO/CB/13/1, National Coal Board Records. The bill for the winding engines was £12,400.
30. Information from Stefan Thatcher, Technical Historian, Friends of Pleasley Pit, e-mail to Vic Tyler-Jones, 22.3.2010.
31. FRO/CB/15/1, Clark family leases – indenture of 15.4.1914.
32. Celia Green, Customer Services Manager, Royal Welsh Museum, Brecon: '2nd lieutenant 1.5.1908, lieutenant 1.2.1910, rejoined as lieutenant 22.8.1914, captain 23.11.1914. His service before the First World War would appear to have been with the 4th Volunteer Battalion South Wales Borderers. We have his full dress uniform (*c*.1908) in our collection'.
33. W. H. B. Somerset, H. G. Tyler & L. D. Whitehead (eds), *On the Western Front. 1/3rd Monmouthshire Regiment*, Abergavenny, 1926, p.54: 'B Co dashed across the open to the front line. A dip in the ground, and the masking of the enemy's guns by the attack, favoured the advance and in consequence the casualties were few, but Capt. Gardner was shot through the heart as he entered the trench, a great loss. He was one of the finest looking and best soldiers in the Battalion. The line, which had given way elsewhere, held here, the enemy appeared to have had enough'.
34. Royal Welsh Museum, Brecon: Fact sheet No. B19: 'B Company of the 3rd Battalion earned special distinction by holding on in the front line, along with two companies of the 1st KOYLI, although quite isolated, the troops on both flanks having been driven back. Its stand has been picked out by the *Official History of the War* as 'among the historic episodes of the War'.
35. On Remembrance Sunday 2005, Christine Barron, grand-daughter of Captain Gardner, laid a wreath on the cenotaph at Llay Royal British Legion, her grandfather's name having been added to the list of the fallen.
36. *1933 Colliery Year Book and Coal Trades Directory*.
37. 1911 census.
38. *1933 Colliery Year Book and Coal Trades Directory*.
39. FRO/CB/13/1, National Coal Board Records.
40. *1933 Colliery Year Book and Coal Trades Directory*, 'J. T. de Seyfried, BSc, ME, Managing Director, Wigan Coal & Iron Co. Ltd, Managing Director of the Wigan Coal Corporation Ltd; Director of the following companies: The Lancashire Steel Corporation Ltd; Rylands Bros Ltd: Pearson & Knowles (Engineering) Co. Ltd; The Northern Employers' Mutual Indemnity Co. Ltd; Chairman, The Caucasian Manganese Syndicate Ltd. Formerly Agent, Engineer and Manager of Llay Main Collieries. Ltd, Gresford; Manager, Bullcroft Collieries, and Agent, Oxcroft Collieries and of Wyken & Craven Collieries, Warwickshire.'
41. FRO/CB/15/1, Clark family leases. Indenture of 13.4.1914 states: 'Whereas the colliery company are lessees (of Clark family lands) … and are about to sink a colliery to be called 'The Llay Main Colliery' … shall construct a line of railway sidings and other work … Marshalling and shunting to be by the colliery company.'
42. J. T. de Seyfried, (1920).
43. Paul Dally, BSc, MICE, e-mail to Vic Tyler-Jones, 22.3.2010.
44. FRO/CB/15/1. Clark family papers, leases – indenture of 1918 – extension of mining lease.
45. FRO/CB/15/1. Clark family leases – indenture of 15.4.1914, 'Indenture between (Denbighshire) County Council and Llay Main Collieries Company Ltd by Robert Oswald Gardner of the Home Farm, their manager and agent. '… the said colliery to carry a tramway line across the main road leading from Llay to Cefnybedd'. The sum of 10s every year was to be paid to the County Council.'
46. Quote from Mrs Mary May Jones, latterly of New House Farm in Llay (and known as Mrs Jones the Farm). Interviewed by Vic Tyler-Jones on 29.11.1996.
47. Bob Darvill, *Industrial Railway Society*, e-mail to Vic Tyler-Jones 26.2.2009, 'The loco was indeed built by Orenstein & Koppel and we are fairly certain it was works number 6915, a 20hp loco built in 1914 and delivered new to Llay Main Colliery to assist with the shaft sinking. Interestingly the OK records show the customer for the loco as Hickleton Main Colliery. Llay Main Colliery offered surplus plant for sale in 1926 and this included the OK loco. This is the last we ever heard of the loco.'
48. D. Fordham, *Bullcroft Colliery Carcroft & Skellow, Early Development*, 2009, p.11.
49. All the personal files relating to First World War internees held by the British Government were destroyed, probably by accident, during the 1970s. www.isle-of-man. com/manxnotebook/famhist/genealgy/intern.htm.
50. FRO/D/DM/660/34, Ithell Kelly papers.

51. Herbert William Hughes, FGS, ARSM, *A Text Book of Coal Mining*, Library of the University of California, from www.archive.org/stream/shaftsinkingind00riemgoog/ shaftsinkingind00riemgoog_djvu.txt.
52. FRO/D/DM/660/6, Ithell Kelly papers, notes on working collieries.
53. J. T. de Seyfried, (1920).
54. FRO/D/DM/660/2204/34, Llay Main Colliery booklet 1923, p.4.
55. FRO/CB/8/5, National Coal Board Records.
56. J. T. de Seyfried, (1920).
57. Records FRO/CB/8/5, National Coal Board 30.3.1917, letter from J. T. de Seyfried to Arthur D. Nicholson, HM Divisional Inspector for Mines. Suspension of operation – Llay Main 'On 12 April, the date given us by the Home Office for suspension of operation of no.1 shaft, we should have the work completed, and the sinkers can be released except perhaps for 2 or 3 days to remove the pumps. I believe the intention of the Home Office is for all men of military age to be released for the Army, unless they find employment of an essential nature, as for instance in a neighbouring colliery.' The letter continues, asking for a few men to be released to put up the headgear foundations – 'It is absolutely impossible to leave the place without someone in charge, and for a few men to maintain good order the valuable and expensive machinery which we have.'
58. 1933 *Colliery Year Book and Coal Trades Directory*
59. www.stuffynwood.com.
60. LLHSA – Deeds with map '10.5.1915. New House Farm – agreement between Llay Hall Colliery Company (owners) and Tom Wynne, 22 acres, two roods and thirty-five perches.'
61. Mary May Jones transcript of interview with Vic Tyler-Jones, 29.11.96.
62. FRO, Microfilm 843 – Gresford Parish Registers, baptisms.
63. William Millington, 'A Walk in the Past – Llay and Gresford before 1920', unpublished, 1980, p.11.
64. Bellis, p.9.
65. FRO census of churches and chapels 1851 (PRO/HO.129/362-3.459.610–13)
66. William Millington, 'A Walk in the Past – Llay and Gresford before 1920', unpublished, 1980, p.7.
67. 1911 census.
68. Bellis, p.12.

2: Model Colliery and Model Village (1919–26)

1. J. T. de Seyfried, (1920).
2. ibid.
3. ibid.
4. FRO CB/13/1, National Coal Board Records.
5. Interpretation of Fig. 27 by Keith Folwell, former manager at Llay Main Colliery, e-mail to Vic Tyler-Jones, 7.12.2010.
6. FRO CB/13/1, National Coal Board Records.
7. *Colliery Guardian*, 22.1.1922, provided by Dave Fordham.
8. Dave Fordham, *Bullcroft Colliery Carcroft & Skellow, Early Development*, , 2009, p.25.
9. Dave Fordham, *Brodsworth Colliery, Woodlands and Highfield, Early Development*, 2009, p.29.
10. From Barry Parker: www.wythit.com/Sites/wythit/Objects/Word_documents/BARRY_PARKER.doc.
11. DRO/QSD/CB/3/6 Licensing – Crown, Esclusham 'order for removal of this licence to Cross Roads Llay confirmed 25 March 1929.'
12. E. May, 'Coal, community, town planning and the management of labour South Wales, *c.*1900–1920', in *Planning Perspectives*, Vol 11, issue 2, April 1996, pp.145–66.
13. LLHSA, Alf Bannister, notes on his early years in Llay, unpublished, handwritten, 1999.
14. FRO D/DM/660/34, Llay Main Colliery booklet, 1923, p.6.
15. *The North Wales Chronicle*, 28.5.1921.
16. *Wrexham Leader*, 12.6.1920, p.2.
17. *Wrexham Leader*, 17.7.1920, p.2.
18. FRO/D/BC/2430, 30.7.1920. Agreement for sale of lands – Ed Stuart Clark and others to Llay Housing Association. By 1920, the Clark family had accumulated ownership or leases on over half of the total land area of the Llay township.
19. Alf Bannister (1999).
20. LLHSA, from a plan in a tenancy agreement of 5.3.1923 between Llay Housing Association and Llay Main Collieries Ltd. This shows houses already built at that time.
21. *Wrexham Leader*, 2.10.1920, p.3.

22. Dyfed Jones, letter of February 2003 to Vic Tyler-Jones.
23. LLHSA, Herbert Gaskin papers, catalogue page from Llay Housing Scheme.The cooking stoves were made by the Falkirk Iron Company.
24. Dyfed Jones, letter of February 2003 to Vic Tyler-Jones.
25. By 1931, the total population of Llay was 3,627. Of these, 633 were Welsh speaking and additionally there were 17 who could speak Welsh but not English (census 1931).
26. J. T. de Seyfried, (1920).
27. FRO CB/13/1.
28. *The North Wales Chronicle*, 28.5.1921.
29. FRO CB/13/1, NCB Area Services Office Report, January 1971.
30. ibid.
31. *Colliery Guardian*, 20.1.1922.
32. *Wrexham Leader*, 26.5.1922, p.5.
33. *Wrexham Evening Leader*, 6.3.1996, p.6.
34. *Wrexham Leader*, 5.5.1922, p.7.
35. *Wrexham Leader*, 11.8.1922, p.10.
36. *Wrexham Leader*, 1.9.1922, p.12.
37. LLHSA, Ena Randles, 'Llay – Rackery Treat 1917', unpublished, undated.
38. *Wrexham Leader*, 17.4.1922, p.2.
39. *Wrexham Leader*, 26.6.1922, p.5.
40. *Wrexham Leader*, 27.10.1922, p.12.
41. ibid.
42. Llay RBL Club Silver Jubilee programme, 1978.
43. *Wrexham Leader*, 2.1.1925, 'Llay Main Colliery Silver Band paraded through the streets (of Llay) on Christmas Day'.
44. *Wrexham Leader*, 3.7.1925.
45. *Wrexham Leader*, 25.8.1922, p.12.
46. *Wrexham Leader*, 23.9.1921, p.12.
47. *Wrexham Leader*, 27.10.1922. Scouts and the Boys' Brigade held meetings at Trinity.
48. FRO/D/DM/660/34. Llay Main Colliery booklet, 1923, p.6.
49. *Colliery Guardian*, 23.6.1922, provided by Dave Fordham.
50. Noel Ralphs, joiner, underground at Llay Main, interview 20.10.2010.
51. Roger Laidlaw (1996), notes for an exhibition to mark 30 years of the closure of Llay Main Colliery, held at Llay Park Junior School, March 1996.
52. *1923 Colliery Year Book and Coal Trades Directory*, published by The Louis Cassier Co. Ltd.
53. William Horsley Humble is the great-grandfather of the TV wildlife presenter, Kate Humble.
54. FRO/D/DM/660, Llay Main Colliery booklet, 1923.
55. Interpretation by Keith Folwell, e-mails to Vic Tyler-Jones, 10 & 12 December 2010.
56. From Stefan Thatcher, technical historian Friends of Pleasley Pit, Co. Durham, e-mail to Vic Tyler-Jones, 22.3.2010.
57. LLHSA, Llay (Infants) School Admission Register 1, 9.4.1923–20.3.1930.
58. FRO/D/DM/660, Llay Main Colliery booklet, 1923.
59. Geoff Bellis, a colliery secretary from 1924 to 1964. Interview transcript, Vic Tyler- Jones, 8.11.1995.
60. FRO/CB/15/1, Clark family leases, occupation of Llay Place, 13 June 1917.
61. Geoff Bellis, interview transcript, Vic Tyler- Jones, 8.11.1995.
62. *Wrexham Leader*, 9.6.1923, p.11.
63. V. Tyler-Jones (ed), *Llay at War*, Llai Local History Society, 2002, p.8.
64. *Wrexham Leader*, 17.4.1922, p.12.
65. Roger Laidlaw (1996).
66. *Colliery Guardian*, 24.8.1923.
67. *Wrexham Leader*, 16.2.1923, p.11.
68. *Colliery Guardian*, 21.3.1924, 'The Llay Housing Association have erected 400 out of the 1500 houses'.
69. The Oldham works closed in 2002.
70. FRO/D/DM/660, Llay Main Colliery booklet, 1923.
71. LLHSA, Herbert Gaskin papers, 'Specification of Works for the erection of cottages at Llay for the Industrial Housing Association Ltd', the Housing and Town Planning Trust Ltd.
72. LLHSA, Mel Jones papers, 1924 Register of Electors – Township of Llay.

73. DRO/ED/LB/79/1–3, Llay Council School Mixed Department log book, 1.9.1924.
74. ibid.
75. FRO/D/NM/732, NUM correspondence – Llay Main Colliery folder, 10.5.1924. Letter from E. A. Hughes (agent & manager) to Cyril O. Jones, solicitor. 'Dear Sir, as requested by Mr Hugh Hughes of the North Wales Miners' Association, we herewith enclose copy of notice that … all employees must be financial members of a registered Trade Union. We understand from Mr Hugh Hughes that you will accompany him to the colliery on Friday next the 16th inst to go into the question of membership of the Miners' Federation.'
76. G. C. Lerry (1968), p. 68.
77. FRO/D/NM/732, NUM correspondence – Llay Main Colliery folder, 6.5.1924.
78. LLHSA, John Cunnah papers, wage list 1924, from original time book.
79. Folwell, Keith, e-mail to Vic Tyler-Jones, 14.12.2010.
80. NEIMME, *Report on the causes of and circumstances attending the explosion which occurred at Llay Main colliery, Wrexham, Denbighshire, on the 5th December, 1924,* by Arthur D. Nicholson.
81. ibid.
82. ibid.
83. Geoff Bellis (1995).
84. *North Wales Guardian,* 5.12.1924, author's comment, 'In 2007, via a Welsh collieries website [www.welshcoalmines.co.uk], I found an offer of a Bible of the German family. Inside this was a silk commemorative bookmark dedicated to the memory of Edward Henry German. The items were then sent to me from Gateshead having been found in a car boot sale. In December 2007, at a meeting of Llai Local History Society, the Bible and bookmark were reunited with members of Edward German's family.
85. FRO/D/NM/73, Llay Main Colliery Disaster – Coroner's Inquiry, 22–4 December 1924.
86. ibid.
87. ibid.
88. Nicholson (1924).
89. LLHSA, St Martins Church Golden Jubilee Souvenir programme, 1975.
90. *The problems of the coal industry in the interwar years,* www.makingthemodernworld.org.uk.
91. *Wrexham Leader,* 5.6.1925, p.7.
92. *Wrexham Leader,* 29.5.1925, p.12.
93. *Wrexham Leader,* 5.6.1925, p.7.
94. *Wrexham Leader,* 12.6.1925, p.7 – leader column.
95. Nick Humble, grandson of William Humble, e-mail to Vic Tyler-Jones, 21.11.2010.
96. *Wrexham Leader,* 3.7.1925.
97. Llay Council School log book, 30.6.1925.
97. *Wrexham Leader,* 3.7.1925
99. ibid.
100. ibid.
101. *Wrexham Leader,* 10.7.1925 – leader column.
102. Keith Gildart, *Cooperation and Conflict: Episodess from the North Wales Coalfield, 1925–35,* in HSIR (Autumn 2001), p.44.
103. Llay Council School book, 28.7.1925.
104. *Wrexham Leader,* 7.8.1925.
105. Llay Council School log book, 11.9.1925.
106. *Wrexham Leader,* 18.9.1925.
107. Llay Council School log book,10.11.1925.
108. *Wrexham Leader* 30.10.1925, p. 7.
109. FRO, CB/8/5. Llay Main Colliery correspondence file.
110. Llay Council School log book, 9.2.1926.
111. *Colliery Guardian,* March and April 1926.
112. *Colliery Guardian,* March 1919.
113. LLHSA, Rod Challenor papers, transcript of the 1926 diary of Albert Jones, President of Llay Lodge of the North Wales Miners' Association.
114. Albert Jones (1926).
115. LLHSA, Herbert Gaskin papers, letter of 24 July 1974 from Revd Bransby Jones to Herbert Gaskin.
116. Albert Jones (1926).
117. ibid.

118. Keith Gildart, *North Wales Miners – a fragile unity, 1945–1966*, Cardiff, 2001, p.18, quoting *Wrexham Leader* of 13.8.1926.
119. Llay Council School log book, 2.6.1926.
120. Albert Jones (1926).
121. Geoff Bellis (1995).
122. *Wrexham Leader,* 9.7.1926.
123. Llay Council School log book, 29.7.1926.
124. Keith Gildart, p.18.
125. Information in the preceding four paragraphs from 1926 diary of Albert Jones.
126. Llay Council School log book, 3.9.1926.
127. *Wrexham Leader,* 19.6.1921. Subsequent reports seem to indicate that the land was gifted to the Education Authority.
128. R. D. Egerton, *Wrexham Leader*, 22.5.1925.
129. Albert Jones (1926).
130. ibid.
131. Llay Council School log book, 18.10.1926.
132. Llay Council School log book, 15.11.1926.
133. FRO, NUM records, D/NM/743 – Llay Main Colliery correspondence folder, letter from Carlton Main Colliery company Barnsley to E. A. Hughes Esq. (agent at Llay Main), 26.11.1926.
134. FRO/D/NM/743.
135. Keith Gildart (2001), p.18.
136. Albert Jones (1926).
137. *Past Forward,* Wigan & Dist Leisure & Culture Trust, issue 30, Spring 2002: www.wlct.org/culture/Heritage/pf30.pdf.
138. Geoff Bellis (1995).

3: Colliery and Community (1927–38)

1. Centre for Economic Policy Research (as above).
2. *Colliery Guardian,* 11.3.1927.
3. Gordon MacDonald, colliery joiner, 26.12.2009, V. Tyler-Jones notebook.
4. LLHSA, Llay Main Colliery price list for 1927.
5. *Colliery Guardian,* November 1928.
6. FRO/CB/8/5, letter from Leslie Crewe to T. W. Mottram, 6.5.1929.
7. *Colliery Guardian,* June 1929.
8. LLHSA, Church of St Martin Golden Jubilee booklet 1975, p.10.
9. Llay Council School log, 23.12.1929.
10. LLHSA, Graham Hughes papers, 'History of Llay Cinema', unpublished, 2007.
11. Laidlaw (1996).
12. ibid.
13. ibid.
14. Information from Peter Thompson of the Morgan Three-Wheeler Club.
15. http://www.rotherhamweb.co.uk/h/mining.htm.
16. LLHSA, *Llay Main Colliery Pithead Baths*, booklet produced for the opening ceremony, 9.8.1930, copy.
17. ibid.
18. Geoff Bellis (1995).
19. Norman Davies of Moss, interview transcript 1984, interviewed by Roger Laidlaw. Cassette c/1984/1 held at Wrexham County Borough Museum.
20. FRO/NCB Records, CB/15/4, Llay Main colliery re-organisation 1950, p.15.
21. ibid.
22. ibid.
23. LLHSA, items and information from Leri Morton.
24. Information from Gordon MacDonald, 26.7.2009, V. Tyler-Jones notebook.
25. Laidlaw (1996).
26. LLHSA, Conveyance of 7.1.1930 between The Hon. Mrs A.A. Madocks to T. H. Mottram and others. copy.
27. National Monuments Record for Wales, CADW, No. 19 list of Buildings of Special Architectural or Historic Interest, Wrexham Maelor, 7.8.1990.
28. From Llay Welfare Institute website http://llay-miners-welfare.co.uk/history.
29. Laidlaw (1996).

30. Notes attached to the photograph of the turf layers.
31. Llay Council School log as above, 29.8.1930.
32. Llay Main colliery re-organisation, 1950.
33. http://www.bbc.co.uk/wales/history.
34. Stanley Williamson, Gresford, *The anatomy of a Disaster*, Liverpool, 1999, p.177 and 179.
35. Geoff Bellis (1995).
36. LLHSA, Coal Mines Act 1911, 1925 and 1933 editions with Llay Main bye-laws, copies.
37. FRO CB/8/5, Llay Main Colliery, correspondence file.
38. Census 1911.
39. Laidlaw (1996).
40. Laidlaw interview, Norman Davies (1984).
41. Laidlaw (1996).
42. Most of this information has been obtained from the website www.cmhrc.co.uk, the Coalmining History Resource Centre/Mining Accidents Database (Raleys Solicitors). I have also used information from newspapers and record offices. Even so, I do not feel that these sources provide a definitive total and apologise for anyone omitted.
43. Llay Main Colliery Re-organisation, 1950.
44. FRO/CB/8/5, 13.8.29, letter from Mottram to Charlton.
45. Memo to J. Barnes, 17.9.1929.
46. FRO/CB/8/5, accident to Thomas Williams on 24.10.1929.
47. Letter from Mottram to Charlton, 5.12.1929.
48. FRO/CB/8/5, letter from Charlton to Mottram, 18.12.1929.
49. Laidlaw (1996).
50. *Wrexham Leader*, 21.10.1932.
51. *Colliery Guardian*, 25.8.1933.
52. *Colliery Year Book and Coal Trades Directory, 1933.*
53. *Colliery Guardian*, 29.6.1934.
54. LLHSA, *Wrexham Leader* special supplement, 12.2.1937, p.1, Sir Henry Walker's report (Chief Inspector of Mines).
55. Roger Laidlaw, *The Gresford Disaster in Popular Memory*, in Llafur Journal of WelshLabour History, Vol. 6, 1995, p.124.
56. Brian Robinson, mines rescue consultant, e-mail to Vic Tyler-Jones, 15.9.10.
57. *Wrexham Leader*, 5.10.1934, p.5.
58. LLHSA, Mel Jones papers, letter. Gresford was a national tragedy and like the other widows, Mrs E. Stratford received a letter of condolence from the local MP, Aled Owen Roberts, stating that 'the sympathy of the whole country is with you at this time'.
59. For one account, see Stanley Williamson, *Gresford: Anatomy of a Disaster*, Liverpool, 1999.
60. Sources: 1. Original handwritten report by Parry Davies, captain of the Llay N°. 2 rescue team. Provided by his grandson Philip Davies. 2. Handwritten note from J. C. Williams, captain of the Llay N°. 1 rescue team provided by his grandson Michael Adams. 3. Verbatim account of Graham Hughes, grandson of Daniel Hughes. 4. *Wrexham Leader* 28.9.1934. 5. The Special Supplement of *Wrexham Leader* of 12.2.1937. 6. Williamson (1999), pp. 4–7.
61. Parry Davies report.
62. According to the Williamson account, this was for a temporary mortuary.
63. Williamson (1999), pp. 4–7.
64. *Wrexham Leader* special supplement of 12.2.1937, p.7.
65. With our present knowledge, the exact make-up of the Llay No. 1 rescue team is uncertain. The quoted evidence given by J. C. Williams as on page 4 in the Special Supplement of *Wrexham Leader* of 12 February 1937 suggests that a five-man team was reduced to four before the team entered the 20s airway. The statement by Sir Henry Walker on page 7 of the same newspaper contradicts this and states 'during the course of a disastrous and ill-conceived exploration of 20s return, another four lives were lost … a rescue team of five men were sent in to this return.'
66. *Wrexham Leader* special supplement of 12.2.1937, p.7.
67. Handwritten note from J. C. Williams.
68. ibid.
69. Parry Davies report.
70. *Wrexham Leader* special supplement of 12.2.1937, p.7.
71. *North Wales Chronicle*, 28.9.1934, p.5.
72. Parry Davies report.
73. ibid.

74. LLHSA, Muriel Davies papers, photograph, Muriel is Parry Davies's daughter.
75. *Colliery Guardian*, 21.5.1935.
76. FRO/D/DM/316/5, 1936, report for the annual conference of the Institute of Fuel, p.12.
77. Laidlaw (1996) – except when otherwise indicated.
78. Llay Council School log book, 18.12.1926.
79. *Wrexham Leader*, 22.5.1925.
80. *Wrexham Leader*, 10.1.1936.
81. ibid.
82. ibid.
83. ibid.
84. Laidlaw (1996).
85. Geoff Bellis (1995).
86. LLHSA, Albert Jones, diary for 1931, donated by Rod Challenor.
87. LLHSA, agreement between Llay Main Colliery Medical and Hospital Fund and the Wrexham District Medical Association of 1.7.1924.
88. Information from Gordon MacDonald, 31.7.2005, V. Tyler-Jones notebook.
89. DRO/ED/LB/791, Llay Central School record book.
90. Llay Main colliery re-organisation, 1950.
91. LLHSA, Llay Council School Admissions Register 2, 15.9.1924–19.10.1937.
92. FRO/D/NM/763, reminiscences of M. G. (Moy) Jones.
93. H. O. Ball, *Wrexham Leader*, 17.12.1943.

4: Llay Main in the Second World War (1939–45)

1. LLHSA, Llay Junior School admissions register, admitted on 29.8.39 – Leslie Howard of 33 Bailey Street, Wallasey who came to live at 68 Pentre Lane.
2. John Jacques, *Llay Central School Magazine*, December 1939.
3. DRO, 'Wrexham RDC: A Record of the War Services of the District Council 1939–1945', Wrexham Rural District Council.
4. www.spartacus.schoolnet.co.uk/2WWbilleting.htm.
5. LLHSA, Beryl Jones.
6. From Graham Hughes, former underground electrician at Llay, 30.10.2010.
7. LLHSA, Doris Edwards, interview transcript, 12.11.1995.
8. LLHSA, Pat Williams.
9. *North Wales Chronicle*, 24.11.1945.
10. FRO/D/NM/370, air-raid precautions department, wartime lighting for collieries.
11. DRO, Llay Parish council minutes, 20.8.1940.
12. Laidlaw (1996).
13. Information from Gordon MacDonald, 14.11.2008, V. Tyler-Jones notebook.
14. T. H. Jones, *Fingers in the Sky – A Miner's Life Story*, Wembley, p.65.
15. LLHSA, Hilda Challinor.
16. LLHSA, Graham Hughes.
17. LLHSA, Beryl Jones.
18. LLHSA, Islwyn Evans.
19. LLHSA, Graham Crewe.
20. LLHSA, Beryl Jones.
21. LLHSA, Herbert Gaskin papers, 'Report on the houses of the Llay Housing Association', May 1941.
22. Dyfed Jones, letter to Vic Tyler-Jones, February 2003.
23. LLHSA, Graham Crewe.
24. LLHSA, Llay Infants and Junior School admissions registers.
25. LLHSA, Beryl Jones.
26. DRO, Llay Parish council minutes, 10.6.1941.
27. *Wrexham RDC: A Record of the War Services of the District Council.*
28. Llay Parish council minutes, 22.7.1941.
29. LLHSA, Graham Hughes.

30. *Wrexham Leader*, 7.2.1941, Llay News.
31. www.vam.ac.uk/moc/collections/toys/manufacturers/britain.
32. LLHSA, Graham Crewe.
33. Llewellyn T. Lister, *British Journal of Ophthalmology*, November 1925.
34. LLHSA, Cooper papers, letter from Dr E. Goss, Liverpool, 1.12.1942.
35. www.official-documents.gov.uk, Department for Work and Pensions Social Security Administration Act 1992, review, January 2007.
36. *Wrexham RDC: A Record of the War Services of the District Council*
37. LLHSA, Beryl Jones.
38. LLHSA, Graham Hughes.
39. Laidlaw (1996).
40. LLHSA, Graham Hughes.
41. From Harriet's niece, Sue Force, Llay school registers, Liverpool Blitz website.
42. LLHSA, Graham Hughes.
43. LLHSA, *Ace of clubs*, magazine of St Martin's Boys Club, June 1943.
44. *Wrexham Leader*, 12.12.1943.
45. LLHSA, Beryl Baigent, copy of 1944 radio broadcast programme.
46. www.culture24.org.uk/places+to+go/yorkshire/leeds/tra27580.
47. *Wrexham Leader*, 17.9.1943.
48. Haydn Macdonald, transcript of interview with V. Tyler-Jones 16.10.10.
49. ibid.
50. 32. *Wrexham Leader*, 28.1.1944.
51. BBC North East Wales website, Llay Main Colliery page, message from Clive Adams, 16.4.2008.
52. Laidlaw (1996).
53. LLHSA, Graham Crewe.
54. www.214squadron.org.uk.
55. LLHSA, Graham Crewe.
56. *Wrexham Leader*, 20.7.1945, p.1.
57. *Wrexham Leader*, 24.8.1945.
58. FRO/D/NM/763, reminiscences of M. G. (Moy) Jones.
59. H. O. Ball, *Wrexham Leader*, 17.12.1943.
60. List of mines in Great Britain and the Isle of Man, 1945.
61. Llay Main Colliery Re-organisation, 1950.
62. ibid.
63. LLHSA, Graham Crewe.
64. Llay Main Colliery Re-organisation, 1950.

5: Coal for the Nation (1946–54)

1. Ron Berry, transcript of interview with V. Tyler-Jones, 5.11.2010.
2. *Wrexham Leader*, Friday 18 1.1946, p.1.
3. ibid.
4. ibid, 10.5.1946, p.5.
5. From editions of the *Wrexham Leader*.
6. www.nationalarchives.gov.uk/catalogue.
7. *Colliery Guardian*, 1.1.1947.
8. www.num.org.uk/page/History-NumHistory-Nationalisation.
9. *Wrexham Leader*, 10.1.1947, p.8, Llay News.
10. *Wrexham Leader*, Friday 1.8.1947, p.1.
11. LLHSA, Graham Hughes papers, letter to Wrexham RDC, 5.11.1948.
12. *Wrexham Leader*, 23.4.1948.
13. LLHSA, Geoff Bellis, 'Random Thoughts', 1995.
14. FRO, 'Guide to British Coalfields, 1948 and 1949', published by The *Colliery Guardian*.
15. Geoff Bellis (1995).
16. Gildart (2001), p.51.

17. LLHSA, Herbert Gaskin papers, H. Gaskin's work notebook, 1947–49.
18. ibid.
19. *Wrexham Leader,* 13.8.1948, p.5.
20. Gildart (2001).
21. http://museums.leics.gov.uk/collections-on-line.
22. M. G. (Moy) Jones, c. 1975.
23. *Wrexham Leader,* 7.1.49, p.3.
24. Information from Gordon MacDonald, 23.4.09, V. Tyler-Jones notebook.
25. T. H. Jones, *Fingers in the Sky - A Miner's Life Story,* Wembley, p.71.
26. *Wrexham Leader,* 29.4.1949.
27. *Wrexham Leader,* 28.10.1949, p.9.
28. *Wrexham Leader,* 12.8.1949, p.5.
29. FRO/CB/15/4, from 'Llay Main Colliery Re-organisation' report by NCB North Western Division, submitted to NCB HQ, June 1950. This item includes the report of twenty pages and mine plans and correspondence.
30. Gresford Colliery booklet, NCB North Western Area, June 1971, p.4.
31. Llay Main Colliery Re-organisation, 1950.
32. ibid. The diminishing OMS per haulage hand between 1938 and 1945 was given as one of the main reasons for the gradual fall in overall OMS.
33. ibid.
34. ibid.
35. FRO/D/DM/660/6, Ithell Kelly papers.
36. Llay Main Colliery Re-organisation, 1950.
37. LLHSA, Beryl Jones.
38. LLHSA, Gwyn Hughes, electrician at Llay Main, reflections, 2000.
39. *Coal* Magazine, June 1951, p.15.
40. ibid.
41. *Coal* magazine, December 1953, p.11.
42. Clive Holt, electrician at Llay Main, note to Vic Tyler-Jones, 17.1.09.
43. www.thewi.org.uk.
44. Information from Tony Partington and John Parry, sons of the rescuers.
45. Drawing by Michael Adams from a diagram provided by Herbert Gaskin.
46. DRO/ED/LB/791, Llay Central School record book, transcribed by Vernon Crewe, 2.2.1999.
47. Gordon MacDonald, 14.11.2008, Vic Tyler-Jones notebook.
48. LLHSA, Herbert Gaskin papers, Llay Amateur Gardening Society, income and expenditure account, 5.11.1958.
49. Ron Berry, transcript of interview with V. Tyler-Jones, 5.11.2010.
50. ibid.
51. FRO/CB/13/1, NCB North Wales Services Office, 1971.
52. Greville Williams, transcript of interview with V. Tyler-Jones, 11.3.2010.
53. *Coal* magazine, December 1953, p.10.
54.Keith Folwell, notes, e-mail to Vic Tyler-Jones, 10.2.2011.
55. Clive Holt, 17.1.09.
56. Keith Folwell, notes, e-mail to Vic Tyler-Jones, 10.2.2011.
57. *Coal* magazine, December 1953, p.13.
58. Clive Holt, 17.1.09.
59. Keith Folwell, notes, e-mail to Vic Tyler-Jones, 13.2.2011.
60. Brian German, *A History of the Parish of St Francis of Assisi, Llay with Christ the King, Rossett 1914 to 2000,* Lancaster, 2001.
61. Llay Main Colliery Re-organisation, 1950.
62. Gildart (2001), p.52.
63. www.num.org.uk/page/History-NumHistory-Nationalisation.
64. Tom Ellis, *After the Dust has settled,* autobiography, Wrexham, 2004, p.91.

6: The Last Miners of Llay Main (1955–66)

1. Tom Ellis, p.86.
2. Clive Holt, 17.1.09.

3. *Wrexham Leader*, 19.8.1955.
4. *Wrexham Leader*, 30.9.1955.
5. *Denbighshire Historical Transactions 1998*, pp.147–72.
6. ibid.
7. Information from Stefan Thatcher, 21.10.2010.
8. Ellis (2004), p.86.
9. FRO/D/NM/763, reminiscences of M. G. (Moy) Jones, p.15.
10. Noel Ralphs, underground joiner, transcript of interview with V. Tyler-Jones, 27.10.2010.
11. NCB North Western Area Public Relations Department, April 1979.
12. Keith Folwell, notes, e-mails to V.Tyler-Jones, 14.11.2010 and 13.2.2011.
13. ibid.
14. *Wrexham Leader*, 5.6.1956.
15. Gildart (2001), p.56.
16. FRO/D/NM/1433, notes from R.J. Roberts (Area Industry Relations Officer) dated 3.12.1959 to Mr J. Williams Secretary, Bersham Lodge NUM.
17. LLHSA, NCB Colliery Record Sheet (historical) (1987) and NCB Public Relations Western Area Colliery Profile Llay Main, April 1979.
18. LLHSA, St Martin's Boys' Club Management Committee, meetings minute book 1961–67.
19. LLHSA, Graham Hughes, 'Memories of Llay Cinema, 2007.
20. Gordon MacDonald, colliery joiner, 14.11.2008, V. Tyler-Jones notebook.
21. ibid.
22. LLHSA, Graham Hughes, 'Memories of Llay Cinema', 2007.
23. ibid.
24. Rubber-soled shoes, usually for sports e.g. gym, tennis.
25. LLHSA, Graham Hughes, 'Memories of Llay Cinema, 2007.
26. Keith Folwell, e-mail to V. Tyler-Jones, 15.11.2010.
27. Keith Folwell, e-mail to V. Tyler-Jones, 14.11.2010.
28. Photograph from *Coal News*, January 1962.
29. FRO/D/DM/660/6, Ithel Kelly papers.
30. Gildart (2001), p. 88.
31. FRO/D/NM/763, reminiscences of M. G. (Moy) Jones, pp.16–17.
32. Gildart (2001), p.75.
33. Ellis (2004), p .96.
34. LLHSA, copy of letter to R. Norris, 7.1.1964, donated by his daughter, Joan Hutton.
35. M. G. (Moy) Jones, c.1975, p.17.
36. Gildart (2001), p.75.
37. Gildart (2001), p.82.
38. NCB Public Relations Western Area Colliery Profile Llay Main, April 1979.
39. Gildart (2001), p.88.
40. www.professorhumo.co.uk. The current Professor Humo is the son of this performer.
41. *Wrexham Leader*, 4.1.1966 p.3.
42. Gildart (2001), p. 90, notes of a meeting between the NCB and NUM, 19.1.1966.
43. *Wrexham Leader*, 28.1.1966, p.1.
44. Gildart (2001), p.83.
45. *Wrexham Leader*, 15.2.1966, p.1.
46. Gildart (2001), p.90.
47. M. G. (Moy) Jones, c.1975, p.20.
48. Gildart (2001), p.90.
49. NCB Public Relations Western Area Colliery Profile Llay Main, April 1979.
50. e-mail from David Evans to V. Tyler-Jones, 23.12.2010, 'Dad was the last Deputy to leave Llay Main. The cage/winding gear could not have been used without a deputy in attendance. Therefore by logic, on his departure the pit would have been formally closed to operations below ground.'

Index

Heavy type indicates image

People